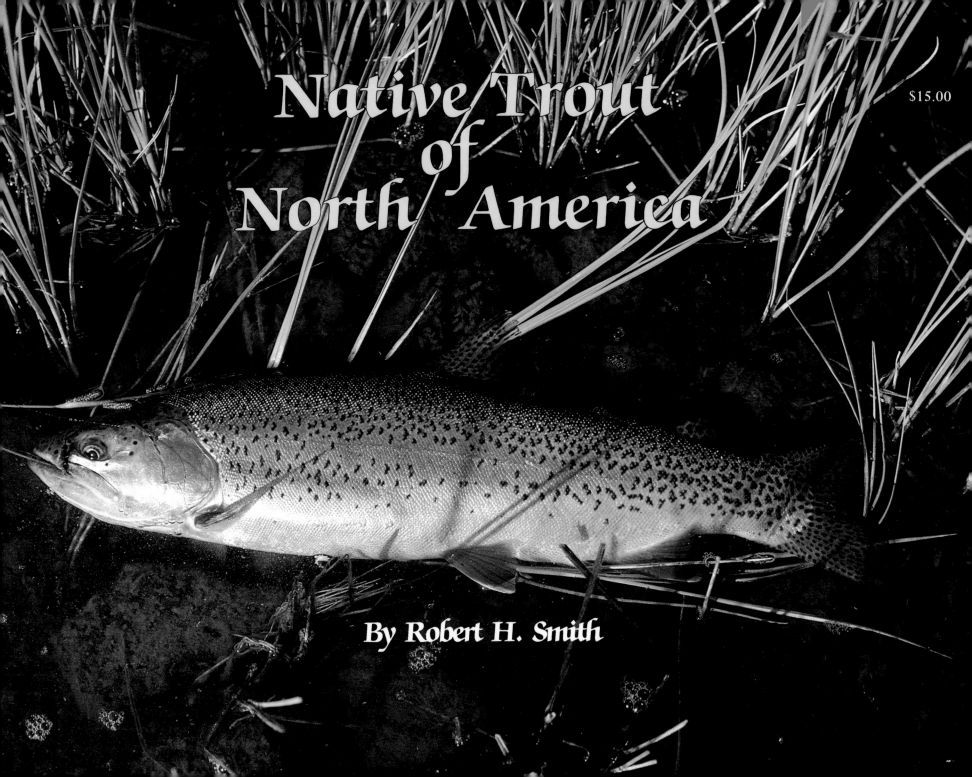

Native Trout
of
North America

$15.00

By Robert H. Smith

Native Trout of North America

By Robert H. Smith

Cover Photo by Bill McMillan
Illustrations by Howard G. Hughes

Frank Amato Publications   Box 02112, Portland, Oregon 97202

Dedicated to
the preservation
and enhancement of
wild trout streams and the
jewel-like trout they nourish.

Graphic Design: Kathy Johnson — Graphic Production: Joyce Herbst

Table of Contents

FOREWORD 6
ACKNOWLEDGEMENTS 7
INTRODUCTION 8
PROLOGUE: Geology and Trout 9
CHAPTER 1: Beginnings 15
CHAPTER 2: Evolution of an Angler 18
CHAPTER 3: Coastal Cutthroats 21
CHAPTER 4: Westslope and Mountain Cutthroats 25
CHAPTER 5: Yellowstone and Fine-Spotted Snake River Cutthroats 32
CHAPTER 6: Native Trout of the Lahontan Basin 37
CHAPTER 7: Trout of the Bonneville Basin 44
CHAPTER 8: Native Trout of the Alvord Basin 48
CHAPTER 9: Native Trout of the Central and Southern Rocky Mountains 52
CHAPTER 10: Rio Grande Cutthroats - 1 58
CHAPTER 11: Rio Grande Cutthroats - 2 63
CHAPTER 12: Redband Trout 68
CHAPTER 13: Golden Trout of the High Sierras 72
             Identification of Color Plates 80
             Color Plates 81
CHAPTER 14: Native Trout of the Lower Colorado System 103
CHAPTER 15: Rainbow Trout - 1 108
CHAPTER 16: Rainbow Trout - 2 111
CHAPTER 17: Rainbow Trout - 3 114
CHAPTER 18: Trout of the Sierra Madre Occidental 118
CHAPTER 19: Atlantic Salmon 125
CHAPTER 20: Lake Trout 128
CHAPTER 21: Arctic Charr 132
CHAPTER 22: Dolly Varden Charr and the Bull Trout 135
CHAPTER 23: Eastern Brook Trout 140
CHAPTER 24: Mending the Cast 143

Foreword

THE NATIVE TROUT of the continental United States exist today largely as isolated, remnant populations in tiny rivulets beyond the reach of hatchery trucks. Except for Alaska, current fish populations in most primary trout streams are a mixture of exotics and exotic/native hybrids that out-compete and ultimately replace the original, genetically pure endemic strains. To meet the insatiable public demand for more fish in the creel, state fish and game departments feel pressured to continue the policy of stocking trout waters with hatchery-produced trout of questionable lineage — many of "catchable" size. In my home state of California, for example, in 1979 the Department of Fish and Game planted a total of 12,302,838 catchable trout. Bob Smith, the author of this book, is outraged by the artificiality of casting flies to these pellet-fed "rubber trout" that are now offered to the non-discriminating public in lieu of trout fishing. These essays constitute his revolt.

The conversion of native trout populations to assorted exotics has occurred largely in the past half-century. I personally learned to cast a fly to the beautiful cutthroats that evolved in the clear streams of Northern New Mexico. In the early 1920s my father used to take the family each spring for a week's camping trip on the Pecos River near the old Pecos ruins of an earlier culture. I still remember my first trout, taken on a Royal Coachman and dragged unceremoniously out of the stream and up on the bank. I pounced on the 10-inch beauty and sat in the grass, admiring its bright colors and heavily spotted tail. From that moment on I considered myself a fly fisherman.

In subsequent summers I was invited by my uncle, Jack Kenney, to accompany him and my cousins on a camping trip to the Brazos River near Tierra Amarilla. Uncle Jack was a lawyer and he and the other lawyers and judges from Santa Fe camped together during the annual session of court in Tierra Amarilla, the county seat of Rio Arriba County. The court was always scheduled during early summer (prime trout season), and after each day's session the litigants would all go fishing. A local man, Sam Gallegos, ran the camp, tending to the woodcutting, cooking and cleanup details. Sam had an enormous frying pan that each morning he filled with several lovely cutthroats. When the fish were cooked on one side he flipped the whole batch in the air and they came down in orderly fashion, all in the pan (as I recall). There was never any shortage of fat trout for that pan. Even I contributed a few. Such are my recollections of the cutthroat fishing on the Brazos a little over 50 years ago.

As early as the late 1930s, when I was in college, I returned to fish the Pecos and the Brazos and found rainbows in place of the red-throated cutts of earlier times. I recall my puzzlement at the rapid conversion. Clearly the hatchery trucks had been busy. If there are any native trout left in either the Pecos or the Brazos, they must be far up some obscure branch, above a waterfall that precludes genetic miscegenation by the aggressive rainbow.

On a few recent occasions, I have caught pure native trout in wilderness settings. One of the most remarkable was a horseback-packing trip into the Sierra Madre along the Chihuahua/Sonora border in 1948. The Rio Gavilan at that time was still flowing clear, but the sawmills and accompanying Mexican homesteaders were moving into the headwaters, and the river was doomed. But what fascinating trout we caught then — unlike any I had ever seen. I brought home a few in preservative, which stimulated Paul Needham and Dick Gard to return for an adequate sample. A few years later Bob Smith and I returned there for a wild turkey hunt in winter, but we did not sample the trout. I know, however, that there are trout in other branches of the Rio Yaqui — some I am sure new to science and as yet undescribed. There remain a few wild spots to explore for truly native fish.

I am enough of a realist to accept things as they are. By avoiding streams stocked with catchables, I can fish for wild trout, acclimated to their foster homes. Rainbows, browns and brook trout are all fine fish, and I seek them eagerly with a dry fly. Bob Smith is not so easily satisfied with a changed world. His pleasure results from stalking the remnants of endemic trout to their ultimate retreats in isolated brooks and springholes. I greatly admire his ideals and obvious appreciation for the beautiful little natives and the wilderness settings in which they reside.

Remnant populations of native trout almost invariably occur in wild places, far from highways or navigable waterways. That, of course, is precisely why the trout are native — they have not been bastardized by the hatchery truck. In following Bob Smith's travels to distant brooks and hard-to-reach headwaters, I have come to realize that wilderness settings enhance the quest for endemic trout. In his lifetime Bob has been exceptionally fortunate in knowing most of the truly wild areas in North America.

The lakes of the voyageurs, the Arctic prairies, the wild coast of British Columbia, the Cascades, isolated ranges of the Rockies, and even the southern swamps have been his playgrounds. Little wonder that he has developed a taste for pristine places and the native wildlife found there. What better way to exercise this predilection than to combine wilderness travel with the search for native trout.

But more importantly, with regard to science and conservation, Bob is contributing knowledge of where trout remnants are found as well as serving as an impetus to their preservation. Some creeks supporting unique fishes are now being declared ecologic sanctuaries with the intent to preserve pure genetic strains which may ultimately restock waters of origin. The goal thus goes far beyond pleasuring in the wilderness. Bob Smith knows that his crusade for the perpetuation of native trout has purpose and value. In *Native Trout of North America* he recounts his experiences with a warmth and fervor that is contagious.

A. Starker Leopold
University of California, Berkeley
May 18, 1983

Acknowledgements

THIS BOOK COULD NOT have been written without recourse to the printed word on many subjects: ichthyology, geology, botany, hydrology and ecology, and thus I am grateful for the research of numerous investigators.

I am particularly indebted to Dr. Robert J. Behnke, of Colorado State University, for furnishing numerous unpublished manuscripts and for critical reading and advice on the manuscript; to Bob Wethern for initiating the project in the first place and for careful editing; to the many state fish and game biologists who assisted me in locating rare trout in remote areas; to Art and Betty Hawkins and to Margaret Alley for advice, encouragement and critiques of the manuscript, and for a certain amount of pushing and shoving to get me going and to maintain my momentum; finally, to Jack K. James, a long-time companion of many steep and tortuous trails whose patience and forebearance I must have sorely taxed.

All photographs are by the author except where credit is indicated.

Introduction

THIS IS A BOOK ABOUT native trout and charr — what they look like, where they live, what has happened to them, and my experiences in fishing for them. There is nothing here of instruction on the mysteries of reading the water, the tying of blood knots or the proper presentation of a fly to a trout in its lie. I have assumed that you already know these things; if not, booksellers' shelves groan under the weight of "how-to" and "where and when" books.

Neither is this a technical book, and technical terminology has been avoided except where there just isn't a common name for certain parts of a trout.

I had thought originally to include a table showing structural differences between the various species and subspecies of trout as an aid in identification; for example, the number of scales in the lateral series, the number of gillrakers, pyloric caeca and vertebrae, all referred to in technical descriptions. After preparing this, however, I was struck by the amount of similarity and overlap of the various characteristics. I concluded that to a layman it would be more confusing than helpful. Even ichthyologists must rely on *mean* values of these traits, for a trout having structural characteristics toward the extremes cannot be identified by these alone. We must, therefore, rely on what can be seen of the trout in hand — its colors, the sizes and shapes of its spots and the distribution of these features on the body; the presence or absence of slash marks, parr marks and other apparent differences. For these differences, in the final analysis, are the criteria that separate many subspecies of trout from each other.

In the scientific nomenclature used here for the various races of trout, I have followed the lead of Dr. Robert J. Behnke, as set forth in his *Monograph of the Native Trouts of the Genus* Salmo *of Western North America* and *A Systematic Review of the Genus* Salvelinus, representing the latest and most advanced research on the subject. Consequently, some of the names are different from those which have been in common usage during the past.

The photographs are representative of each particular species or subspecies, although slight variations may occur between watersheds, and color intensities may vary seasonally as well as between sexes. I think, however, that the photos are real aids in identification.

Through narratives of my excursions in seeking and catching native trout I have tried to convey a feeling for the country — its fauna and flora — and to point out some of the geological features which lend distinctive flavor to each area. Finally, I have attempted to create a better understanding of how native trout came to be where we find them today.

Prologue:

Geology and Trout

WE TEND TO THINK OF the landscape around us, our visible world, as permanent and indestructible – the "eternal hills" of the poets, so to speak. Actually, what we see are transient landforms, everchanging over eons on a scale unimaginable. Ever since the earth's crust hardened there have been periods of cataclysmic convulsions: shearings, thrustings, foldings and tiltings, with upwellings of magma spouting forth as volcanoes or passive fissure flows, forcing segments of crust along zones of weakness and stress to manifest as mountain ranges, valleys or awesome trenches under the sea.

No sooner had the continental crust been elevated into domes and ridges than the forces of destruction took over. Rain, running water, frost and wind began the slow transport of the detritus to lower levels, the valleys and the sea. Once the crust was base leveled, the sea encroached upon the lowlands and vast deposits of sediment accumulated, finally becoming sedimentary rocks, their tremendous weight triggering further adjustments of the crust and starting the process all over again – the new building on the stumps of the old.

These planetary paroxysms appear to occur in ordered sequence, the slow "rhythm of geological time," separated by a quarter billion years with intervening periods of minor uplifts, each followed by a glacial period. There have been at least four of these major mountain forming epochs and we live near the close of the last one, when the uplands are still high, carved into jagged crests and peaks by glacial ice. In fact, the last glaciation is still manifest; there is enough water locked up in present land ice to raise the sea level two hundred feet or more, should it all melt.

Moreover, the crust is still shifting about as molten magma deep within the earth upwells in convection currents, jostling tectonic plates against each other, causing earth tremors and vulcanism. In the Cascade Mountain Range in Washington State, the eruption in 1980 of Mount St. Helens blew 1300 feet off her peak in response to such internal pressures, scattering volcanic debris far and wide in a cataclysmic explosion that devastated forest lands, obliterated lakes and laid waste over 150 miles of prime trout and salmon streams. St. Helens has done this several times in the past, her last previous eruption occurring in 1842. Yet after each holocaust the surrounding streams purged themselves of ash and mud flows and the trout and salmon populations re-established themselves.

There are hundreds of other volcanoes in the "ring of fire" girdling the Pacific, some believed to be "extinct," others quite active and still smoldering, biding time until pressures build up to force eruptions. Those of us who live in the Pacific Northwest dwell in their shadows as witnesses to what has happened in the past and predictors of what is likely to occur in the future.

Even though our time coincides with the close of the last great epoch of uplift and distortion, there are still adjustments being made as continental blocks seek to attain equilibrium with surrounding masses and the upwelling of molten magma from the depths continues to drag the tectonic plates around like pans of shifting pack ice in the Arctic Sea.

If it were not for the mountains extending high up into the heavens, the planetary winds would circle the globe unobstructed and the weather would not be worthy of discussion. The climate would be uniform, monotonous, varying only with latitude and whether oceanic or continental. But the mountain barriers have changed all that, diverting the even flow of air, causing eddies and cross currents, forcing it upward, cooling it and causing condensation of water vapor to fall as rain or snow. Thus we owe our present diversification of climates to the past convulsions of the earth's crust, which has made possible the multitude of micro-climates and ecological niches found in mountainous regions; where we may find a rain forest on one side of a range and a desert on the other.

The aggregate impact of these past events has shaped the destinies of all living things. Some, unable to adapt to the vast changes, became extinct. Others, more suited to survive the changes in their environment, prospered and evolved into new genera and species. The process continues. Since these slow changes do not seem to account for the mass extinctions such as befell the dinousaurs and mammoths, it is theorized that other cataclysmic events as yet undetermined must have occurred.

Of all evolving living creatures, the fishes of the sea were the least affected by the geological events that were altering the face of the globe. The oceans respond more slowly and to a lesser degree to climatic changes wrought by crustal upheavals and provide a much more equitable environment for marine life than the often harsh conditions the continents offered to land-based creatures. Consequently, evolutionary changes in sea creatures have been slower and less drastic than in land animals and as a result there are still many primitive types of fish in existence today. One such fish, a "living fossil," was hauled up off the African coast in 1938 and christened *Latimeria*, a member of the Coelacanths which were thought to have been extinct since the Cretaceous Period 60 to 100 million years ago, a time when dinosaurs still trod upon the earth.

The salmonids are also a primitive type of fish in form and structure with the earliest known fossil records going back 40 to 60 million years ago to the Eocene Epoch. As cold water adapted fish, trout and salmon probably evolved in the Arctic, possibly 10 million years ago, when the climate of that region resembled that of our temperate zone today. Shortly thereafter the ancestors of the European brown trout and Atlantic salmon may have become isolated from the ancestors of the trout and salmon of the North Pacific region. It is thought that North America was the place of origin of these western trout and salmon and that they became established in Eastern Asia by way of the Bering Land Bridge which appeared at intervals during the last glacial epoch.

Before vulcanism built up the Cascade Range and well before the last glaciation, a giant saber-toothed salmon and a trout called *Rhabdofario* found a home in what are now the desert basins of Eastern Oregon, leaving their fossils buried in sediment. Although *Rhabdofario* became the common trout of Western North America during the Pliocene Epoch immediately preceding the last glacial period, it is not known exactly when or from what ancestors our modern trout evolved.

Probably the first of the present races of trout to become established on the Pacific Slope was the Mexican golden trout, the probable progenitor of the Apache and the Gila trout. The Mexican golden trout may also have been a remote ancestor of the redbands and the rainbows which later displaced it except in a few headwaters draining out of the Sierra Madre.

The first modern trout to invade the waters of the Pacific Northwest, however, was the cutthroat, and it became established in waters denied latecomers by the formation of impassable barriers. Next on the scene in the Northwest were the redbands, which displaced the cutthroats of interior drainages below the barriers in most places. Finally the rainbows appeared and displaced the redbands where they came in contact.

Thus the geological upheavals of the past built vast mountain ranges, leveled the plains, re-arranged the drainage patterns and altered the climate which in turn was responsible for the glaciation that sculptured the high country and accelerated the tearing down processes. All of these actions and interactions have merged to create the myriad ecological niches that now exist, each with its own distinctive plant and animal communities. These are particularly abundant and varied in Western North America, resulting in the richest trout fauna in the world. Here they occur throughout five separate life zones — from upper Sonoran to Arctic-Alpine. There are at least five and possibly six recognized species of trout and twenty subspecies, as well as five species of charr each evolved to its present state of adaptation by responses to particular environmental pressures.

What remains today as a legacy to that once abundant and widespread pristine world of trout — particularly in interior drainages — are scattered remnants hanging on precariously in a few remote headwater streams. In roughly 100 years man has practically destroyed that which took natural processes millions of years to create. The degradation of the waters by poor forestry practices, overgrazing, channel blocking dams, water diversion and pollution have all contributed to the decimation of native trout populations, but the crowning indignity, the coup de grace, was the introduction of non-native trout resulting in the displacement of natives either through competition or hybridization. It is now a common experience to fish a beautiful mountain stream and catch almost every kind of trout under the sun — except a native! Some anglers and fisheries officials do not seem concerned about this, as long as there are plenty of trout to be caught . . . any kind of trout. It is for those of us who do care, who value quality over quantity and hope for the return of the "native" that I have written this book.

Spawning Habits

THE SPAWNING BEHAVIOR of all of our native trout of the genus *Salmo* is so similar that a generalized description will apply equally to all species. All are spring spawners, excepting the fall spawning Atlantic salmon and its subspecies. Spawning time depends upon water temperature which varies with altitude and latitude. All spawn in streams, selecting gravel of suitable size in fairly shallow water with a moderate flow, often in the tailout of a pool just above a riffle. Once the pair have selected a site the female turns on her side and moving slowly upstream flaps vigorously with her tail and body against the bottom, pushing gravel to either side. She does this repeatedly until the redd is completed, usually a somewhat oval depression about the length of her body and of a depth equal to hers. At this point the male, who has taken no part in digging the redd, begins courting his mate, nudging her with his snout and rubbing his body against her sides. At the proper moment both glide into the redd and side by side, their vents in close proximity, eggs and milt are extruded simultaneously, the eggs settling to the bottom immersed in a white cloud of milt. Immediately after spawning the female covers the fertilized eggs by pushing gravel in from the sides.

In a short time another redd is begun, a little upstream and almost in line with the first so that gravel displaced and washed down by the current will settle in and over the first redd. Redd construction and spawning are repeated until the female has released all of her eggs, whereupon both parents go their own ways, leaving the redds unguarded. The female, of course, is completely spent, but the male may mate with other females until he, too, is spent.

The time of hatching depends upon water temperature but is usually about thirty days. After the eggs hatch the fry remain in the gravel until the yolk sac is absorbed, whereupon they struggle to the surface to face life on their own.

Native charr, in contrast to native *Salmo*, are fall spawners but due to cold water temperatures over winter the eggs do not hatch until spring. The Dolly Varden, bull trout and Arctic charr dig redds in stream gravel and the latter spawns in lake gravel beds as well. Otherwise, their redd digging and courting activities are similar to the *Salmo*.

Lake trout, however, do not dig redds but spawn over rocky lake bottoms or reefs, the fertilized eggs settling down in the cracks and crevices. There is some site preparation, however, the males arriving at the beds first and cleaning the rocks of sediment and algae by rubbing against them with their bodies. The same spawning sites are used each year and it is thought that the scent of previous spawning activity attracts them there. It is also thought that the males, by rubbing against the rocks, mark them with an odor, a chemical signal or pheromone, which attracts the female to the site. Spawning takes place during stormy nights when surface waters are rough and agitated and possibly the resulting turbulence helps settle the eggs into cracks and crevices of the rocks. After spawning, both sexes disperse, the eggs hatching the following spring.

Classification and Identification

WE ANGLERS ARE OFTEN nonplused when confronted with the seemingly unpronounceable scientific names of the trout we seek. We may throw up our hands and say, "that's Greek to me," and so it is — Greek and Latin or Latinized names, for the early naturalists turned to the classical languages to transcend linguistic barriers between countries.

In the beginning, of course, only one name was used for a species and then as more and more closely related forms were discovered, one name was found to be inadequate. That problem was solved by Linnaeus, a Swedish botanist, who in 1758 brought forth his *Systema Naturae*, a work describing his method of bi-nomial nomenclature — a double name (genus and species) and it is still the basis of scientific classification. Since then, as more races of individual species were recognized, a third name was added — subspecies. Thus, for the Rio Grande cutthroat for example, we have *Salmo clarki virginalis* (*Salmo*, the genus of the trout; *clarki*, the species of cutthroat; and *virginalis*, the subspecies of cutthroat native to the Rio Grande basin). This name is precise. It means but one particular race of cutthroat trout and its meaning is the same world-wide . . . a sort of pedigree. Contrast this with the multiplicity of common names which vary with locality and language.

At first classification was used primarily as an inventory, a cataloging of the Earth's living things; then, with increasing knowledge of comparative anatomy, classification became based on structure and form and finally, after the Darwinian concept of the role of genetics in heredity, classification became based on kinship, the relatedness of one group to another.

During the early days of exploration and settlement of this continent a veritable gold mine of new species and races of plants and animals was unearthed. Many of those collecting specimens were not trained in taxonomy or even in fundamental biology and so sent their preserved specimens to others who were, back East or in Europe. Consequently, during this bonanza new species were formally described and named right and left with little regard to what others were doing in the same field and in the process many of like kind received a number of different names. David Starr Jordan, the patriarch of American ichthyologists, estimated that every species of fish in North America was named at least twice and some, of course, had enough aliases to cause a con man to blush.

Now much of this confusion has been resolved for the international rules on scientific nomenclature require that the name first used has precedence and so many synonyms have been deleted, but not all. Problems are still found, particularly within the redband-rainbow complex and the group of Arctic charr. I would like to believe that all is neat and tidy and that the names used in this book are the last word, but I doubt that such is the case. As new research is accomplished and more sophisticated techniques employed, there probably will be some changes made again and this may go on for as long as there are trout to study and men to study them. Anyway, the names used herein are the latest in current use or proposed for such.

Western trout of the genus *Salmo* are not "good biological species." There are no sterility barriers so that all species of this genus are capable of hybridizing and the hybrid offspring are fertile. Under natural conditions when a new species or subspecies invades the domain of another, several things can happen: 1) the invader is either repelled by or replaces the original occupant; 2) the invader finds an ecological niche where it can co-exist with the original occupant without competition (called sympatry); 3) the two species or races introgress to become a new and different race.

All of the above events have occurred and were probably most frequent during the unstable and shifting drainage patterns following the melting and withdrawal of the last ice sheet. Since that time the various species and races of trout became fairly well stabilized in their own environments but that was a slow process requiring thousands of years.

If the situation just described were true today, it would be a simple matter to identify trout. All we would need to know would be the natural range of the fish and what streams and watershed we were fishing in. At the present, however, all we know is what trout we *ought* to find but our actual catch would probably be any trout except a native, for the delicate balance between species went to pot following the massive introduction of hatchery fish. But there are still a few streams in the lower forty-eight where native trout occur, some of which are remarkably good fisheries and are managed for the native species. The upper Yellowstone comes to mind in this respect and then, of course, there are many remote headwater tributaries beyond the reach of the hatchery trucks.

As there are few places left to us where native trout occur in their ancestral waters, what other means can we rely upon for identification? The classical taxonomists, those ichthyologists who are the only experts in the field, rely on those characters that they consider inherited (meristic), such as numbers of gillrakers, vertebrae, pyloric caeca, scales in the lateral series, fin rays and the presence or absence of certain teeth. None of these values are fixed, however, for even within a single population the numbers vary somewhat and so the mean or average numbers are what count. All of the foregoing characters are of little help to the fisherman for their determination requires expertise and special equipment that few of us have. Consequently, we must rely on what can be seen of the fish in hand, its colors and the size, shape and distribution of its spots.

Color is an extremely variable character in many species of fish. Some of the groupers can change their colors to suit their mood; some flounders can alter their color pattern to match the background they happen to be resting on and in some fish the sexes are of completely different hues. Fortunately for us, trout are not so well endowed but even so their colors vary with age, with the light intensity of their habitat and with the season (especially at spawning times). Some races of trout are genetically programmed to develop high coloration while others are not; for example, contrast the colorful golden trout of the High Sierras with their near neighbor, the dull-hued Lanontan cutthroat. Within a given race the intensity of color may vary somewhat among individuals but the basic hues and their pattern on the body of the trout are quite constant and are important clues in identification.

The other visual clues of a trout's identity that are readily apparent and can be evaluated are the spots, for the trout, like the leopard, can't change them at will. These are permanent markings of each individual fish and no two of the same race are exactly alike. They grow in size as the fish grows, like scales, but their shape, relative size and pattern of distribution over the body remain constant. As extreme examples of spotting, examine the plate of the Rio Grande cutthroat of the Pecos and contrast this with the fine-spotted Snake River cutthroat; in the former there are huge round spots concentrated posteriorly and in the latter there are fine, irregular-shaped speckles well distributed over the body. These contrasts are not so marked between most races of trout but there are differences and these differences are a considerable aid in identification.

Parr marks are sometimes confused with the permanent black spots in trout of the genus *Salmo*. In most races of trout parr marks are ephemeral and disappear with maturity and greater size but in some, as in the golden and Paiute, parr marks persist throughout life. Perhaps these two species are like those of us who fish for them; we never really grew up, just got bigger.

Parr marks are large, round or oval, dark-colored splotches distributed laterally from gillcover to tail, straddling the lateral line in numbers varying from seven to twelve. In some races, particularly redbands, there are smaller, round, auxiliary parr marks distributed above, below and sometimes between the larger markings.

The rainbow redband clan and the cutthroats are aptly named for their distinctive markings; the red or pink "rainbow" stripe in the former and the red or orange "slash marks" on the lower jaw of the latter. But like all "rules" regarding trout there are exceptions so that these characters by themselves are not necessarily definitive. To be sure, all redbands and coastal rainbows have the rainbow stripe at some time during their lives but cutthroats may have them, too, as do the Gila and the Mexican golden trout. Although I have never seen a cutthroat without slash marks, most redbands have them to a greater or lesser degree as do some Alaskan rainbows and the Mexican golden trout. Furthermore, in salt water and in some lake dwelling populations, these markings, if present, are generally muted but come on strong in adult fish during the spawning season.

Most ichthyologists consider color and spotting to be environmentally produced (phenological) and therefore of much less importance in delineating species and subspecies than meristic characters. Even so, they are genetic and are passed on from generation to generation and are distinguishing characters of every individual race of trout. After all, every evolutionary change in the long chain of life was the result of environmental pressures and if this were not so, our remote ancestors would never have taken that fateful flop from the water onto the primordial mud of some ancient swamp. And finally, in many instances, taxonomists themselves resort to differences in color and spotting to distinguish between certain subspecies.

Gillrakers

The short projections of the inside of each gill arch.

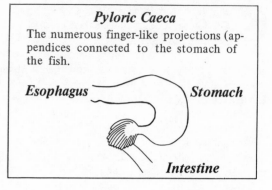

Gillrakers

Red gill filaments

The number of scales in the lateral series are usually counted four rows above the lateral line between the edge of the opercle and the caudal fin — the length of the body of the fish. This then becomes a numerical expression of the relative size of the scales.

Basibranchial or hyoid teeth found in cutthroats are located on the extreme rear of the tongue and can usually be detected with a finger tip.

Pyloric Caeca

The numerous finger-like projections (appendices connected to the stomach of the fish.

Esophagus   *Stomach*

Intestine

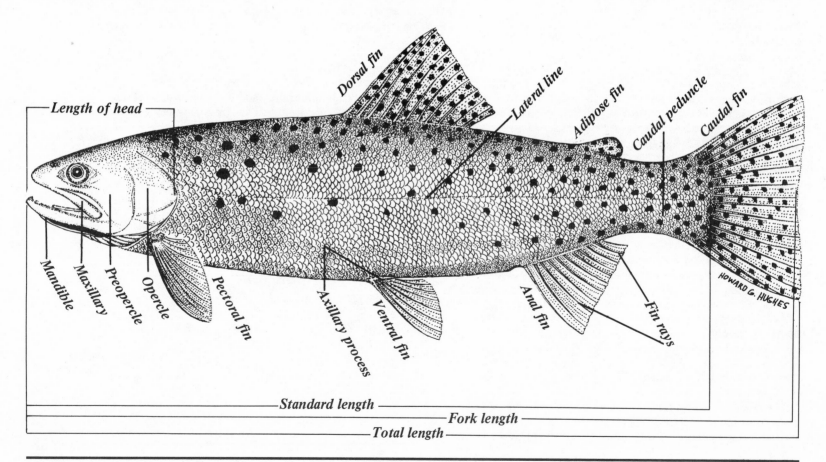

Dorsal fin

Lateral line

Adipose fin

Caudal peduncle

Caudal fin

Length of head

Mandible

Maxillary

Preopercle

Opercle

Pectoral fin

Axillary process

Ventral fin

Anal fin

Fin rays

HOWARD G. HUGHES

Standard length
Fork length
Total length

14

CHAPTER 1

Beginnings

WHO COULD HAVE guessed that my first forays for trout over a half century ago in New Hampshire and Vermont would have striking parallels today in the remote, high places of the West? Now, as then, each mini-stream presents stalking challenges before yielding its sparkling native trout treasures. Each has a different, dramatic background. This is all *any* boy-man angler could hope for. The end result for me — finding and photographing beautiful and rare native trout — is infinitely more satisfying than frying them.

I surfaced in Mason City, a small town in North Central Iowa, in 1908. As with all small towns of that era, the "country" began almost at our doorstep and I soon developed a rapport with the natural scene and all things wild. My mother fostered this natural bent by feeding me a rich menu of children's nature books, probably grateful that I had a predilection for the lesser of the evils that might occupy a small boy's mind.

My family had a summer cottage on nearby Clear Lake, ten miles west of town. Father was a keen fisherman and introduced my sister and me to angling as soon as we could navigate. She fished only under duress, but I took to the gentle art and Father and I became real pals.

My first tackle was not so gentle, however. The long cane pole had heavy braided line tied to the tip. Tied directly to the other end was a black japanned hook; also a sinker and a bobber, and, of course, a worm.

There were yellow perch, sunfish and bullheads in Clear Lake and I spent countless hours on our dock with the community's other small fry, watching our bobbers for a bite. We spoke only in whispers so as not to scare the fish.

After a few summers of apprenticeship with the cane pole I acquired a bait casting outfit — a Bristol tubular steel rod, a Shakespeare reel, and an assortment of spoons, spinners and plugs. When I could fling out a lure without a backlash, Father would take me on expeditions to Lime Creek, ten miles north of Clear Lake, where we fished for smallmouth bass.

We also made frequent excursions to tiny little creeks to fish for bait. With minute hooks tied to strong thread we caught shiners, chubs and dace. Such bait fishing was as much fun as angling for gamefish, and gave me an early appreciation of wee "cricks."

Every August at this stage of my life the family would load up the old touring car. What wouldn't fit inside was secured, along with the luggage, to a rack on the running board. Away we would go to the North Woods, to Lake Vermillion in Northern Minnesota. There were few tourists in those days, and lots of fish. We fished mostly walleyes and northern pike, plus a few bass and, in the deeper lakes nearby, lake trout. I think I fished every day that the weather was calm enough to take out a boat.

At age twelve I was allowed to have a gun, a single-shot .410 gauge shotgun, and became a hunter of ducks, coots and rabbits. As an aspiring trapper I haunted the creeks, marshes and woodlands for mink, muskrat and skunk. I became so engrossed with all outdoor activities, in fact, that my scholastic accomplishments just about went by the board.

In desperation, my family packed me off to boarding school for at least a modicum of book learning. This worked to a slight degree and, as a consequence, I was eventually admitted to Dartmouth College. There I learned, somewhat incidentally, something about zoology, botany and geology. More importantly,

I found out how to fly fish for trout and learned also about woodcock, grouse and whitetailed deer.

But the best learning experiences during those college years occurred with a small group of classmates during annual summer forays into the Quetico-Superior Wilderness. That country, straddling the international boundary between Minnesota and Ontario, has since become famous through the paintings of Francis Lee Jaques and the writings of Sig Olson.

In that pre-Jaques/Olson era we traveled by canoe and we cruised light and fast. We considered it normal to paddle 20 to 30 miles daily, portaging our canoes and gear over five to ten "carries." What we lacked in brains we made up for in energy, but we learned a lot in the process.

We saw few, if any, humans but lots of moose, deer and loons. Sometimes the days were hectic with the wind and waves on the lakes, the steep, lung-bursting portages and the mad rapids of the rivers. The nights, though, were still and serene, the quiet broken only by the wild calls of the loons and the sloshing of moose feeding in the lily pads.

The fishing was superb. The walleyes and northers were abundant and big by any standards.

As I look back on those youthful ventures into that pristine wilderness I wish that we had traveled more slowly, had looked and listened more, and had fished at every opportunity. Youth and maturity operate on different sets of criteria, however; by the time we are old enough to know it's too late.

Shortly after graduating from Dartmouth in 1932 I got a job with the old Biological Survey, later to become the U. S. Fish and Wildlife Service, and was sent off to the White River Refuge in Arkansas with the title of Junior Biologist. Salary: $2,000 annually!

My work there was in waterfowl research, but there were lots of fishing opportunities and I used them all. A transfer to the Sabine Refuge in Louisiana three years later exposed me to more bass and to saltwater fishing. In just months, however, I was transferred to Washington, D. C. There I survived for three years, keeping my sanity through frequent fishing excursions to Chesapeake Bay for sea trout, striped bass and croakers.

Fish and Wildlife wanted me to stay in Washington, but I finally kicked over the traces again and went to Winona, Minnesota, as the Mississippi flyway biologist. For seven years I traveled up and down the flyways from the Arctic Coast and the prairie provinces of Canada to the Gulf states and into Mexico. In between trips I made the most of the fact that my home base was part of the original range of the Eastern brook trout.

By then I had acquired a Phillipson split cane rod of 8½ feet, the first really good rod I had ever owned. The streams near Winona were small — "cricks," really — and the trout mostly were browns. But a few native brookies survived in the headwaters and there I put that rod to good use.

As it became obvious that the airplane was the key to scouting remote areas of waterfowl populations, common sense dictated I learn to fly. That led to aerial surveys of nesting waterfowl in the Canadian Arctic and into Mexico for counts of wintering concentrations. My first plane was a Stinson L-5, a small, single-engine land plane and not very suitable for the total job. The next was a Grumman Widgeon, a medium-sized, twin-engine amphibian — better, but still short on range. Finally I had a Grumman Goose, a large, twin-engine amphib with range to take me all over the Arctic, including the Arctic Islands.

Transferring to the West Coast as Pacific flyway biologist, I headquartered first at Klamath Falls and later at Medford, continuing to fly the migration routes. After 20 summers in the Arctic and 21 winters in Mexico and Central America I had been with the same outfit for 32 years. By then, 1967, I had logged over a million miles — mostly at tree top level.

"I've probably used up all my luck," I thought. So I turned in my suit.

Looking back, those early years in the Arctic and sub-Arctic were fantastic. The only people in the country were in small settlements around Great Slave Lake, along the MacKenzie to the Arctic Sea and east along the coast. The universal transportation was by water, so the settlements were where the boats could get to. What flying was done followed the same routes, down the river and along the coast, with a few routes cross-country from Yellowknife on Great Slave Lake to places on the Arctic coast — Coppermine, Bathurst Inlet and Cambridge Bay.

Our bird survey routes took us into the big middle of the wilderness, hundreds of miles from the nearest settlements and off the beaten track. There weren't even any Indians or Eskimos. Not a sign of man. Not a mark.

In those days, the maps were mostly blank — a few dotted lines for rivers and a few lakes drawn in — but in the wrong places. All bore the same warning: "Unsurveyed." Any elevations the cartographers were bold enough to add were followed by the sign ± (plus or minus)!

We flew by time and bearing, and if we didn't exactly know where we were it didn't make any difference as long as we could find our way back to the gas cache. After all, we were well bracketed: the Arctic Ocean on the north, Hudson's Bay on the east, the tree line to the south and the crest of the Rocky Mountains at the west!

CHAPTER 2

Evolution of an Angler

MY REBELLION WITH THE "rubber trout" planting programs began gradually enough, but grew as more and more of the poor things were dumped into our streams. The final straw snapped a decade ago on Oregon's North Umpqua River.

I was fishing for steelhead, but had caught only trout. Rubber trout! I had just pulled in one of the poor creatures, about a foot long, fin-clipped and otherwise mutilated.

It lay there in the shallows on its side, leering at me in a lipless grin. Its maxillary was gone.

"My God," I thought, "is this the reward for a day on the stream? Is this what my license money supports?"

Fishing should be an experience in beauty. Beautiful waters. Beautiful settings. Beautiful sounds and smells. And, yes, beautiful fish.

The mutilated monstrosity at my feet settled it. I returned him to his pitiful freedom and began the search for mine. Today I find it in waters too small and too remote to stock with rubber hatchery trout. The little wild natives matching the beauty of their ancestral habitat have become the ultimate criteria for me.

Precious few fishermen begin at that point, and certainly not me, as confessions of my Midwestern boyhood have revealed. No, the evolution of an angler generally involves much time, many facets and varied experiences. As tackle and methods become refined, one's philosophy also undergoes a metamorphosis. If all has gone well, the angler ultimately prefers a limited or "no kill" catch, quality fishery, rather than great quantities of hatchery products dumped for immediate harvest.

My exposure to trout and fly fishing began over a half century ago on the brooks and streams of New Hampshire and Vermont. As a Midwesterner I knew nothing of trout except what they looked like, having seen their pictures resplendent in colors on the covers of sporting magazines and tackle catalogs.

I still have my first trout rod — a three-piece 9-footer of about six ounces, bearing the name "Armax" on the reel seat. It cost at least ten dollars. The reel, a simple, single-action, had a hard rubber frame and spool that held a level line of unknown weight. Attached to the line was a six-foot gut leader with three snelled wet flies, sizes 8 or 10.

The usual fly patterns of the period adorned my flybook — Reuben Wood, Queen of the Waters, March Brown, White Miller, Black Gnat, Scarlet Ibis, Grizzly King, Yellow Sally, Alexandria, Montreal and Parmachene Belle.

Those eye-stoppers had lots of appeal for the fisherman if not the trout. Old-timers had assured me I needed bright flies on bright days and dark flies for dull days. Especially I needed a Parmachene Belle for Eastern brook trout. The native squaretail was the creme de la creme, preferred over the exotic rainbows and browns.

To cast properly I was advised to think of a dictionary clasped between my elbow and ribs, moving only my wrist. "Let the rod do the work," they said. Naturally I couldn't cast very far, even without the dictionary. Long casts were unnecessary — impossible, in fact, on the small waters affording little room for backcasts.

My first assaults on the brooks were dismal failures, of course, and I learned more about the flora along the banks that somehow became attached to my flies than of the trout in the waters. Eventually, I caught my first unsuspecting squaretail, just over six inches of pure, sparkling beauty. Since then it is I who have been hooked!

New scenery dictated new equipment when I came to Oregon

in 1948. A two-piece Winston by Lew Stoner was just the ticket. That 9-footer was used for years on West Coast steelhead and Arctic grayling, Arctic charr and lake trout in the Far North.

The pattern of my northern surveys exposed me to the fish in lakes and streams never seen by other men. Arctic grayling and lake trout were everywhere for the taking and they were eager. Arctic charr abounded along the coast. Hooking fish was possible until the casting arm tired and interest waned. And all native fish — no hatchery products there!

Even for lake trout a fly was fished exclusively. The northern waters were so cold the lakers were always near the surface. My largest lake trout, taken on a red-and-white bucktail pattern, was 25 pounds at least. The scales wouldn't read any higher!

In more recent years I have used an Orvis Battenkill on everything from the smallest rills to broad steelhead waters. A 7½-foot stick with 3-7/8-ounce medium action, it throws a No. 6 line and can be fished comfortably all day. By comparison, the big Winston feels like a hoe handle.

Granted, the Orvis is a little light for steelhead — but adequate. Once on the Cooper River, a tributary of the Skeena, it accounted for a 16-pound steelhead. The fish took a No. 6 Thor on a day when no one was doing *anything*, on lures or whatever. Being the only fly fisherman on the river and having taken the only fish, I was about as popular as a bastard at a family reunion.

Today's pressures for "instant everything" have infected the philosophies and practices of many state fish and game departments and some of the federal fisheries services. The practice of rearing and stocking "catchable" trout for "instant fishing" is prevalent and widespread.

Beyond angler license dollar pressure, new hatcheries are provided also as mitigation to compensate for dam-building losses of habitat and spawning areas. Millions upon millions of domesticated trout, bred selectively for life in a concrete tank rather than stream environment, are dumped into our rivers annually.

The consequences, as the rubber trout replace our stocks of wild, native trout, are appalling. Consider the example of streams in Utah's Great Basin. During pioneer days the Utah cutthroat was the only trout present, yet abundant enough to provide a commercial fishery. Massive introductions of non-natives have hybridized most Utah cutthroat out of existence. Only a few relict populations of this trout now exist in tiny headwater streams. This, with few exceptions, is the same dreary story throughout the West.

It was this dismal situation, including my revulsion in being forced to fish for factory trout, that made a final change in my personal ground rules for fishing. Henceforth I would angle only for wild, native trout in their ancestral habitat. I would use fly only and would take only those specimens necessary for photographs in natural color.

My new tack presented immediate difficulties. Where *were* all the relict populations of native trout? How would I get to them? Could I identify a pure native once I found one?

Literature available to me was of limited help. Even so, I soon dog-eared my copies of *American Food and Game Fishes* by Jordan and Evermann, revised and published in 1923, and *Check List of the Fishes and Fishlike Vertebrates of North and Middle America North of the Northern Boundary of Venezuela and Colombia* by Jordan, Evermann and Clark, published in 1930. These were detailed but badly out of date — many of the species and subspecies described were no longer considered valid. Recent, more popular works tend to lump all cutthroat races and all rainbow species with a brief statement that there are geographical races involved that vary somewhat — and leave it at that.

More clues were winnowed from the pamphlets and periodicals of state fish and game departments. I talked with state and federal fisheries biologists and with ichthyologists at colleges and universities and got still more leads. Some kindly gave me reprints of papers published in scientific journals. I began to see light at the end of the tunnel.

One fact above all stood out from my contacts with various fisheries experts: All of them considered Robert J. Behnke at Colorado State University the ultimate authority on native trout. I just had to meet him.

Shortly, a meeting was arranged at Sun Valley where Dr. Behnke was attending the annual conclave of the American Fisheries Society. For two days I picked his brains, and it was productive picking. In addition, he furnished me with voluminous copies of technical papers and unpublished manuscripts dealing with native trout.

At last the way was clear! The where and the how were known. I hastened to set out for the high country — to the alpine meadows where tiny streams purl among the sedges and wildflowers or tumble down rocky slopes bordered by lodgepoles and spruces.

Still, as with any expedition, much planning and many preparations lay ahead; especially so for what were to be unusual forays into unique corners of the high and the wild. In many places I would be treading the same ground as the mountain men of 150 years ago — Bridger, Carson, Sublette and old Bill Williams.

Those men had only the crudest maps, if any. A limited variety were available to me, some of them only in the minds of the men who would take me to places where native trout populations had been pinpointed by Behnke.

Most trips would be beyond trailhead, involving a long hike or a longer packstring transport. It would be vital to keep gear to essentials. The utilitarian Orvis rod would have to suffice for catching specimens. Two heavier cameras were set aside in favor of two single lens reflex 35-mm cameras.

I could hardly wait to get going on what would develop into nearly a full-time quest for native trout in Western North America and in Spain and North Africa. Each exploration would be unique; each stream different. On some of them I would not see any sign of man except my own tracks.

CHAPTER 3

Coastal Cutthroats

WHAT BEGAN AS A WILD GOOSE chase of a caribou count ended as my first exposure to the coastal cutthroat, a most roundabout way to meet the grandsire of all existing cutthroat races. A reported sighting of caribou on Graham Island, one of the Queen Charlotte Islands off the coast of British Columbia, had excited Canadian Wildlife Service (CWS) officials, as that race of caribou was thought to be extinct or nearly so.

The race of caribou in question was described by Ernest Thompson Seton in 1900 as *Rangifer dawsoni*, and in his words, ". . . it is a runt, the last remnant of a worn-out, dying race." Apparently never abundant, at least in historical times, they last had been reported in 1908 when two bulls and a cow were taken by hunters on Graham Island. (Quotation from *Lives of Game Animals,* Vol. III, Part 1, Pg. 146, by Ernest Thompson Seton; published in 1929 by Doubleday, Doran & Co.)

The CWS asked me to check out the sighting through an aerial survey whenever I was nearby.

The opportunity came as I was returning home from an Arctic waterfowl survey. I had stopped off at the airport at Annette Island, just off Ketchikan, in a venerable Grumman Goose, an amphibious aircraft affectionately dubbed the "iron duck" by those who flew her. At Annette I was as near the Queen Charlottes as I would ever be, about 125 miles across the Dixon Entrance to Sandspit.

The weather was marginal or somewhat less, about a 200-foot ceiling and a quarter-mile visibility — "Alaska VFR." But Sandspit was reporting only broken clouds and expected it to remain that way throughout the day. Assured that Annette weather wouldn't improve, I took off, flying under the overcast. Soon the "underneath" gave out and wisps of clouds mingled with the spray of foaming waves. I have spent thousands of hours flying at a hundred feet — plus or minus fifty — doing waterfowl surveys over Arctic tundra and sub-Arctic forests, but this was a bit hairy. I could go back to Annette or climb through the overcast and proceed to my destination on top. I chose the latter and bored up through the cloud deck to bright sunshine and visibility to the far horizons.

Below was a cottony white blanket of overcast. Solid. Not a break that I could see, and it looked solid all the way to Kamchatka. Sandspit reassured me by radio that they were still broken and I pressed on, foolishly perhaps, but brimming with faith and hope and leaning on the bush pilot's crutch — "Trust in God and Pratt & Whitney" — for all it was worth. An hour later I saw a break dead ahead, and straight down under that hole was Sandspit Airport, a beautiful sight!

I found no caribou on the Queen Charlottes, but I did find a beautiful little creek. If it had a name I have forgotten it, but I shall never forget the sea-run cutthroats I found there. The airport manager at Sandspit, an avid fly fisherman, took me in over a narrow, rutted trail in an ancient pickup truck that matched the condition of the road. When we reached the end of navigation we walked through a lush meadow to the upper edge of a salt marsh. At a tongue of timber thrusting into the marsh at the upper end was a wee estuary where the mouth of the creek entered the salt.

We entered a different world in that timber, the cool, dark, mossy world of a rain forest. Scattered shafts of sunlight barely filtered through the dense canopy of huge old cedars and Sitka spruce. There were mosses everywhere. They mixed with fine, delicate ferns, covering the boles of the trees, the branches, even the prostrate tree trunks mouldering on the forest floor, almost hidden by the rank fronds of sword ferns. Old-man's-beard swayed gently from every twig, like Spanish moss draped on cypress along a Louisiana bayou.

The creek flowed gently through the center of this lush wonderland. Its murmurs muted over shallow, graveled riffles and thrust silently against tangles of matted roots exposed on cutbanks and swirled in the foam-flecked eddies in quiet pools. The water was stained slightly from bogs and peat, showing a tea-colored cast in the shallows, and darkening the deeps to inky blackness.

My host advised bright flies, preferably with a silver body. Rummaging through my fly book I found a bedraggled Alaska Mary Ann that originator Frank Dufresne had given me. A bit large, I thought, inspecting the No. 8, but I knotted it on my leader.

"Save a few of the larger ones for supper," my friend admonished as he started downstream toward the estuary.

I worked up, fishing the deep runs and holes with a natural drift, but the few trout flashing at the fly didn't take. A few more shows with no takes and I retired to a downed log, thickly upholstered with gray-green moss, to light my pipe and think on the situation. I had been told that sea-run cutthroats were predaceous creatures and yet I had been fishing a flashy minnow imitation upstream without imparting action to the fly. When the truth dawned I cut back from the creek and walked up, keeping well back from the water and avoiding thickets of devil's club and prickly salmonberries, intercepting the stream again at a sharp bend a half-mile above.

There I began fishing down and quartering across the deeper runs and shadowy pools, twitching the fly during the swing and retrieve. Shortly I had a solid take, followed by deep surges and a splashy jump. From gravelled shallows I carefully lifted out a foot-long fish, my first sea-run cutthroat. Its primitive appearance — long, lean and big-jawed — was impressive. The basic ground color of silver, from the salt, was tinged with brass. Irregular black speckles covered the back and sides. The cutthroat slash marks were faint orange and the abdominal fins were yellowish. The fish blended perfectly with the dim shadow world of the primeval rain forest and the dark somber waters of the stream. Mindful of the promised fish fry, I made a bed of wetted sword ferns in my creel for the fish.

Downstream I found numerous trout in the deeper, slower stretches, a few of the larger ones joining the first in my creel. All seemed mirror images of each other, the slight variations in basic brassy tinge indicating the length of time the fish had been in the

amber waters of the creek. I tried patterns other than the Alaska Mary Ann and the trout took them all.

Fishing that tranquil little stream through the lush verdure and under the towering mass of moss-encrusted forest was a lovely experience, a new dimension in sensations. There, capsulized, was the life/death experience — the sheer exuberance of growing things intertwined with mouldering decay matter being recycled into nutrients for new growth. It was a dim, shadowy world, but the somberness was broken here and there by splashes of brightness, the endpoints of scattered shafts of sunlight briefly highlighting a mossy trunk, a patch of fern fronds or a tuft of old-man's-beard. It was a realm of quiet as well, the only sounds the muffled gurgles of the creek and an occasional birdcall, low, muted and seldom heard. All animal life seemed concealed as if in waiting for the intruder to pass. I saw a tiny winter wren dart, mouselike, into a thicket and a fox sparrow scurry furtively into a tangle of upturned roots. Both were a deep chocolate shade; small wonder that they were so dark, spending their lives as they did in half light and shadow. I felt like an alien in this environment, as if I had stepped back in time into the dark, gloomy fern forests of the Cretaceous Period. Even the trout from the amber waters of the creek had a primordial look about them.

When I reached the point of our beginning, I met my host returning from the head of the estuary and he, too, had saved a few fish. We gutted and gilled our catch on a mossy log and wiped their body cavities with dry moss and ferns. All were pink-fleshed and in prime condition and all but one had fish remains in their stomachs. We ate them that night for supper — pan-fried, moist and flaky, absolutely delicious.

The shadowy beginnings of the coastal cutthroat may go back ten million years to the Miocene Epoch, when it was thought that the western salmonids separated from a common ancestor with the Atlantic salmon and the brown trout. Whatever the sequence of events and the changes that must have occurred, *Salmo clarki clarki* is still considered to be a "primitive" type fish, retaining many primordial characteristics, although the ancient form surely differed from the present trout we know as sea-runs, bluebacks and harvest trout.

Coastal cutthroats presently occupy an enormous range, extending from Northern California to the apex of the big bend of the Alaskan coast beyond the panhandle, essentially the same area they inhabited before the advent of Europeans in North America. For the most part they are anadromous, ascending every suitable stream, although there are non-migratory or land-locked populations throughout this vast stretch of the Pacific Northwest. Sea-run cutthroat are more stay-at-home than steelhead and Pacific salmon, seldom venturing far from their home estuary, drifting in and out of brackish waters with the tides. Because of this, they are more available to anglers over a greater period of time and provide an extremely valuable fishing resource.

Many coast slope steelheaders are surprised and delighted with sea-runs as an incidental catch, as was I shortly after my Queen Charlottes experience. They turned up practically in my backyard in the upper Rogue River, over 100 miles from the sea, where I was fishing for summer steelhead. There the river ceases its mad plunge through the Cascades and flattens out on the valley floor, winding through pastures, meadows and scattered woodlands of oak, madrona and yellow pine. The water was low and clear, ideal for steelheading; yet, though August was almost gone, the steelhead were scarce or maybe just dour. I had touched several and one had broken me off, but as evening wore on it became evident the steelhead would not come to life this night. As crickets tuned up for their nightly chorus in the approaching dusk I fished slower, deeper runs not ordinarily considered prime steelhead fly water. Hard by a great pile of drift a solid strike was followed by short, powerful runs toward the snag pile, but I held firmly with side pressure, gradually coaxing the fish away from the tangle and into a pool below.

While the struggle had lacked the speed and explosiveness of one with a steelhead, it had been a bulldog stubborn contest from a cutthroat of about 17 inches too colorful to be mint-fresh from the sea. Its slash marks were brilliant red, the back was greenish, shading to yellow on the lower sides and belly. Large, rose-colored blotches daubed the lateral line, the lower fins being quite orange. Small black specklings, the hallmark of the coastal cutthroat, were liberally distributed over the back and sides, clearly branding the fish as a *clarki*. I hooked two more of similar proportions before dark that evening that I also judged to be sea-run fish. Non-migratory cutthroats seldom attain that size in upper Rogue waters. My largest coastal cutthroat in the upper Rogue was just over 20 inches and weighed 2½ pounds, which included an eight-inch rainbow in its belly.

Most upper Rogue tributaries contain coastal cutthroats — those without barriers have both migratory and resident populations, while those with obstructing falls have only non-migratory fish, most of which have been severely hybridized with hatchery rainbow stocks. The natives must have invaded the upper watershed quite recently, geologically speaking, for it has been only 6,000 years since Mount Mazama ejected pumice and other volcanic detritus in prodigious quantities, burying the entire countryside before the cone finally collapsed to form Crater Lake. Following that cataclysmic event the area comprising the entire upper Rogue watershed must have been uninhabitable for any life for a considerable period of time.

Coastal cutthroat waters most familiar to anglers, and the areas that sustain most angling pressure, are the riverine tidewaters of the Pacific Northwest, from the Central Oregon Coast to Southern British Columbia. These waters traditionally have been the domain of trollers, chugging up and down in midstream, dragging a string of flashers and bait, "ford fenders" and worms. This is an effective way to catch cutthroats, if not very sporting, but the participants are primarily after tasty meat, not sport. Surprisingly, there are more fly fishermen turning to the fishery and there is no question that it opens entirely new horizons in our world of steadily shrinking fly fishing opportunities.

Fly fishermen Stan Stanton and Terry Coleman of Eugene, Oregon, initiated Robin Thorp and me to this specialized type of tidewater fly fishing. We had discussed the feasibility while steelheading on the lower Rogue, and had arranged to meet in a fortnight at the boat ramp at Mapleton, a small village near head of tide on Oregon's Siuslaw River. Gathering at the appointed place and hour in the half-light of a misty September morn, we launched driftboats trailered from Eugene by Stan and Terry. It had rained all night and the moisture-laden air was heavy with the fragrance of wet leaves, tidewater and the resiny pungence of freshly-sawn lumber and sawdust of a nearby mill. We slid the boats into the dark, still river with tide at high slack, just ahead of its slow, inexorable ebb to the sea. Stan searched his flies and presented me with an orange and white bucktail with a silver body wrapped on a No. 8 hook.

"Just the thing," he said. "They like lots of color."

The Siuslaw is a small river, a short river heading on the west slope of the Coast Range and meeting the sea just below the town of Florence. We fished it where the stream emerged from the mountains and flowed slowly across the flats of the coastal plain, bordered by pastureland and meadow. The current was two-way, depending on the tide — out on the ebb and in on the flood. If there were any pools or deep runs, they were not apparent and the water appeared uniform, more canal-like than river. The banks

were steep, almost vertical cutbanks for the most part, crowned
with tangled mats of alders, blackberries and vine maple, their
branches drooping in the water at high tide. The water was deep
right to the bank and Stan said that was where the trout were, close
in under the branches and alongside old half-rotted pilings.

The casting demanded accuracy and in the half-light I managed
to find more than my share of twigs and branches. We could hear
the trout slosh now and then under the brushy canopy, but none
came to my fly so I manned the oars to let Stan demonstrate the
technique. He did, beautifully, shooting the fly through small
holes in the brush, laying it close alongside half-submerged
branches, stripping line and twitching the rod tip on the retrieve.
But still the trout ignored us. In this way, alternately rowing and
casting, we worked our fishless way up to the very head of tide
where the river spilled over a shadow riffle. Behind a ledge below
the riffle I hooked a trout. It was a beautiful bright fish of 15
inches, bluish on the back and silvery along the sides with a profusion of small cross-hatched or crescent-shaped spots. The slash
marks were a faint orange and there were sea lice firmly attached
alongside the anal fin. It was fresh out of the salt.

The water level fell as the tide ebbed, making it easier to cast
under the branches, and we hooked a few more fish. The trollers
showed up with the sun, chugging slowly up and down in midstream, dragging their ford fenders and worms close to the bottom.
The few fish they caught were unceremoniously hauled in with
heavy tackle and scooped into the boats. I was surprised, though,
at the number of fly fishermen; there were actually quite a few
— more than I had expected to see.

We met Terry and Robin about noon and pulled in for a streamside lunch of bread, cheese and salami, washed down with beer.
Their luck had been about the same as ours and as we started out
again we changed partners, fishing through the warm, sunny afternoon with little change in luck. While a far cry from wilderness
fishing, it had its own charm, heightened by the hazy Indian summer day. The coastal foliage was in full color, the big-leaf maple
a burning yellow, the smaller vine maple a deep crimson — providing sharp contrast with the dark spruce and fir on the far hills.

We were completely caught up by the lazy day and a leisurely
way to fish, watching the yellowed leaves drift along on the slow
current and not really caring if a fish took or not. We were fishing, in our chosen way, for native trout in their ancestral waters.
Fish in the bag were a lot less important than those fish in their
home waters.

CHAPTER 4

Westslope and Mountain Cutthroats

TRACKING DOWN *ALL* DISTINCTIVE members of the first race of interior cutthroats thought to have diverged from the sea-run's ancestral form is a self-imposed assignment I'm glad isn't yet finished. We are wedded by wanderlust, the westslope trout, *Salmo clarki lewisi*, and I, just like its namesake explorers.

The westslope, also known as the Montana black spotted trout, has irregular black spots similar to its coastal ancestor, but differently arranged. Somewhere in its travels and establishment of a new home range, the westslope also developed a genetic tendency toward brighter coloration.

That home range first was considerable, the westslope colonizing the upper Columbia systems and crossing the Continental Divide in at least two places. It became established in the headwaters of the South Saskatchewan and the upper Missouri, and also penetrated into some of the middle tributaries of the Snake, the Salmon and the Clearwater.

Introduction of hatchery rainbows and Yellowstone cutthroats severely hybridized the westslope, but a few pure or nearly pure populations remain in some headwater streams. When Bob Behnke furnished some unpublished manuscripts concerning this distinctive race, I knew where to look.

I had company when I first tried, in the headwaters of Montana's Jocko River, a Flathead River tributary heading up under the serrated peaks of the Mission Range. Once Art Hawkins completed his nesting study of redhead ducks in the Flathead Valley, I joined him and his wife, Betty, at Allentown, Montana, early one June.

We obtained Flathead Tribal Reservation permits and drove into the threshold of the Missions on the north fork of the Jocko. The lower Jocko held only rainbows and browns, but the headwaters were reputed to have "native black spotted trout" — the fish we were after. The Jocko was a beautiful little creek flowing clear and cold through a forest of fir, pine and spruce, the towering Missions looming large in the background.

Art caught one that appeared to be a good *lewisi* type, but the others we caught were hybrids, various mixes of rainbow and Yellowstone cutthroats with native stock, and by afternoon we gave up hopes of finding better fish to photograph.

We regrouped in Allentown, examined our maps again and decided to look into possibilities on the Continental Divide's east side the next day. By skirting the mountain barrier to the east, following the Blackfoot to cross the Divide at Rogers Pass, then heading north again, we ended up at Choteau, almost directly opposite from our start — not far across, but a long way around.

Locals in Choteau put us onto Dupuyer Creek, and we set out again, across the prairie on a graded gravel road, heading due west toward the sheer scarp of the Front Range. We were crossing the western limits of the high plains and the short grass prairie was just beginning to green up, brilliant blues and yellows of spring flowers splashed throughout. Meadowlarks sang from fenceposts and longspurs fluttered from the shoulders of the road. Once we passed the last of the few lanes leading off to ranch buildings, our highway became a dirt road and finally fanned out in a network of tracks across prairie sod. Selecting one that seemed headed in the right direction, we straddled its deep ruts and dodged its big rocks.

The landscape became broken with coulees, benches and occasional clumps of aspen and dwarfed limber pine as we approached the mountains. Fording a tiny stream, we climbed a long ridge above a series of beaver ponds and then dropped into a narrow valley out onto a bluff above the south fork of Dupuyer

Creek. Before us lay the portals of the Rockies, the stream emerging through a narrow gap in the near vertical rock face, tumbling down through a series of short pools and cascades and on through the broken lands to the broad prairies. Dupuyer was small — 10 to 12 feet wide at most — clear as crystal, with all the earmarks of first class trout water.

Art started exploring the upper reaches while I crossed the creek at the old ford and followed down along the edge of a bench through aspen groves and limber pine, cutting back to the stream when the water began to flatten out. In a deep glide just above a riffle I hooked two little westslope type cutthroats, releasing them as immature and "unphotogenic." At the head of a pool under a cascade I hooked a good fish for the water's size — a brilliantly-colored male of 12 inches. Its lower sides and gill-covers were reddish orange, the upper sides and back were greenish with a silvery cast. The spots were small, irregular and profuse, except under an arc beginning at the anal fin and extending forward slightly above the lateral line and curving down to the pectoral fins — a typical *lewisi* spotting pattern and trademark of the race. In another pool I took a 13-inch female, less colorful than the male but with an identical spotting pattern, and I added her image to that of the male on my roll of film. Other trout hooked were not as large as that pair but all were beautiful and added to the impression of completeness in a setting of primitive splendor, the abrupt transition of the mountain massif to the high plains abutting against the ancient overthrust fault at the foot of the range.

We found our way back to Dupuyer's north fork the next day over a much easier route which led us to the junction of the two forks, a trail crossing the streambed there and heading up the northerly fork. What had once been a ford was a desolate expanse of water-worn boulders; if there was any water at all, it had to be underground. Crossing there, we picked up the track on the far side, following it until it gave out and then continued on foot. Sloping meadows with thickets of Saskatoon berries, aspen and spruce eventually led to the "gate" — a wedge-shaped gash in the sheer mountain front which the stream had cut out in ages past. There we found water, intermittent pools at first, then a steady flow. Art wanted to explore the upper reaches but I couldn't resist the siren call of the tumbling water and so I slipped and slid in a shower of gravel and dirt to the bottom of the canyon.

Shallow pools produced nothing until, further into the canyon, the current circled a huge boulder and formed a deep pool. I dropped a No. 10 caddis nymph in the flow, letting it drift around the boulder. I saw my line tighten and, raising the rod tip, was fast to a solid, heavy fish. The fish had nowhere to go, but it thrashed around on the surface until the hook came free. The trout had looked to be about 15 inches, a mighty big fish for a stream I could jump across.

Upstream was another bigger, deeper pool, a submerged boulder barely visible in the center of its depths — a likely hidy-hole for a big trout. Flattening against a rock face in the shadows I inched along to a position where a short cast dropped the fly by the sunken boulder. Instantly a trout of 18 inches or more swirled up at the fly and dropped back. Changing patterns to rest the fish and my racing heart, I laid out another cast and again the fish showed without taking. Another rest, another pattern change and another try. This time a smaller fish rushed out, gulped the fly and churned up such a commotion that the big fish went down, and I moved on. The canyon opened onto a meadow with a few suitable pools and smaller trout so I returned to the deep pool where the big one sulked, but it wouldn't come again. As I back-tracked to rendezvous with the Hawkins, I pondered the presence of such a big fish in such a tiny stream. While the stream had little fishing pressure, the potential of *lewisi* in fisheries management still seemed obvious.

Almost exactly a year later we returned to Choteau after Art finished his duck studies in the Flathead Valley, hoping to get into Dupuyer Creek again. Dupuyer was running high and dirty from heavy snowpack melt in the high country, however, and the weather was in a tantrum of driving rain and soggy snow. We only managed to explore a bit of the Teton River and make arrangements with Chuck Blixrud of the Seven Lazy P Ranch to get packed into the Bob Marshall Wilderness later in the summer.

We convened again in mid-August and camped in the forest near the Teton River, handy to the corrals of the Seven Lazy P. Our party now numbered five, for Art and Betty had brought their two daughters, Ellen and Amy. It took us a day of sorting and high grading our gear, packing and balancing the grub supply in pack boxes. Early the next morning, all in readiness, we presented ourselves at the dude ranch's loading dock. Chuck and his packer, Gene Sentz, surveyed the pile of gear, hefted each piece, and roped all into a half-dozen tarp-covered bundles to be mantied onto the pack mules. They loaded the mules and saddle horses into a truck and we rumbled off toward trailhead. The weather, which had been bright and clear, turned sour and a fine rain was falling from low, gray clouds. The Hawkins' initiation to pack string travel was to be a soggy one.

At trailhead, stock unloaded and saddled, the serious business of packing the mules began, and had to be done just so. A sort of ritual was involved — each item picked up and joggled to heft the weight and decide which goes where; the heaviest went low on the sides with the lighter, bulkier pieces on top and in the middle. So Chuck and Gene joggled and hefted and re-hefted to be sure. Then the pack boxes were slung to the Decker saddles, low on the sides, the rest distributed according to weight and bulk with tarps covering each load. Finally, the packs were secured with lash ropes, cinched tight with diamond hitches and our "Rocky Mountain Freight Train" was ready to roll.

Gene headed out, leading the three pack mules, followed by Amy, Ellen, Art and Betty. I brought up the rear. The trail led up the west fork of the Teton, along the flank of a ridge, through a clearcut area and then into a forest of ponderosa, Douglas fir, spruce and groves of aspen. We angled up the ridge's slope, skirting alpine meadows where flowers bowed their heads in the rain — blue gentians, geraniums, harebells, purple fireweed, orange paintbrush and yellow cinquefoils. When we reached Teton Pass, topping the Continental Divide, we were at the threshold of the Bob Marshall Wilderness and we dismouted to stretch our legs and check the packs for security. It was still raining and the forest smelled of wet duff and aromatic spruce, for we were still below timberline.

The trail steepened into descent, crossing numerous rills tumbling down to form Bowl Creek, a headwater of the middle fork of the Flathead/Columbia River drainage. The horses picked their way carefully through the many boggy places, lunging and slipping in the soft mud and ooze. When we came to the junction of Basin Creek, Bowl Creek had become a fair stream and, about fourteen miles from trailhead, on the edge of a long, narrow meadow, we set up camp under sheltering spruces and lodgepoles and still close by the creek. The rain relented while we put up tents and arranged gear and we were pretty well settled in before the downpour resumed.

The next morning, when Gene left us to trail the stock back to trailhead, it was still raining.

"Be back in ten days," he said, adding, "Sure hope it quits raining."

We hoped so, too, but the rain continued steadily out of a low, gray overcast that obscured the peaks and even the lower ridges.

We rigged a wickiup with poles and ponchos over the fireplace so that food could be prepared in relative shelter, felled a couple of dead lodgepoles for a wood supply and then I went fishing, reasoning I couldn't get any wetter standing in the creek than around camp. I fished down the meadow reaches and caught several cutthroats to eight inches. Each one I examined appeared to be a good representative of the westslope race.

Art had explored upstream and had also found numerous small westslopes as well as a big bull trout that refused all offers. We knew that big Dollys came into the small tributaries from the Flathead on their fall spawning run, and we hoped to entice a few with a fly. That one bull trout, however, was the only one seen on the entire trip.

Our camp remained wet and soggy during our ten days at Bowl Creek, but everyone seemed in high spirits, probably because of the delicious cooking aromas that steamed out of the pots under Betty's watchful eyes. Once, during a thunderstorm, a bolt of lightning shattered a spruce within 200 yards of camp with a blast that shook the ground.

Normally the last half of August provides perfect weather in the Rockies — bright, warm days and crisp, cool nights, but multiple frontal systems continued to foul up the pattern. We managed to accomplish the things we came to do, nonetheless. Art and family explored the trails, climbed mountains and sampled trout in nearby creeks while I fished the canyon waters of Bowl Creek below the meadow. Possibly because of weather we saw little game — mule deer in the meadows, a few families of blue grouse, moose tracks in swampy swales fringing the creek, and those of a grizzly bear that had walked the trail not a quarter-mile from camp.

Canyon fishing in Bowl Creek was superb. Apparently the itinerant fishing pressure was restricted to meadow reaches of easy access and good campsites. All signs of man vanished in the canyon — not even a track. The water was perfect for fly fishing, trout were plentiful and larger than those in the meadow waters — up to 13 inches — reflecting the lessened fishing pressure. All but one I hooked appeared to be good *lewisi* type, the odd one having a typical Yellowstone coloration and spotting pattern. It was surprising to find the *lewisi* genotype so prevalent as literally tons of non-native trout have been stocked in the Flathead over the years and there were no barriers between the main river and Bowl Creek, as evidenced by the spawning migration of the bull trout.

The morning of our departure was beautiful, sunny and bright, the pack boxes as light as our hearts, as we were about out of grub. The ride out was an experience in sheer beauty — alpine grandeur on every side that had been shrouded in low clouds and rain on our way in and made our arrival back in civilization a let down. The amenities of hot water and dry shelter were appreciated, but the solitude of the high country and the pristine waters of Bowl Creek already were sorely missed.

The Hawkins left immediately for Minnesota but I stayed on, drying out camping gear and browsing through manuscripts to see where other populations of westslope cutthroats might be found. Spotted Bear River and Upper Twin Creek, both tributaries of the Flathead's south fork, promised populations of *lewisi* judged "essentially pure." As a crow flies they were only twenty miles from our Bowl Creek campsite, but to get to them by road would involve closer to 200 miles, around the other side of the ranges and up the south fork — three sides of a giant rectangle. Securing loose gear in the camper, I hooked in to The VW Beetle's tow bar and started out.

The morning was beautiful there on the great plains — tawny grasslands and great golden wheat fields where combines were gathering the harvest. The Front Range to the west stood out sharp and clear, like ramparts, sheer and bold. Cumulus clouds already were pushing up castellated turrets over the mountain mass and I wondered if rain was falling again at Bowl Creek. Through the Blackfoot Indian Reservation we rolled, turning west to cross the Continental Divide at Marias Pass, which may have been one of the access routes of the westslope cutthroat to the upper Missouri system. Prior to building the Great Northern Railway, Summit Lake at the top of the pass drained both ways, providing a direct water connection between the Columbia and the Missouri.

Down the road from West Glacier I found a campground and set off from there in The Beetle to learn what I could about roads, trails and cutthroats. I talked with a nearby packer, with rangers at Hungry Horse Ranger Station and Spotted Bear Ranger Station, and even some folks at a dude ranch. The facts emerging were that I could get to upper Twin Creek with a two-mile hike over an easy trail and that I could find access to the lower reaches of the Spotted Bear from the road. My informants thought it odd, I'm sure, that I was interested in small streams having small trout when the nearby Hungry Horse Reservoir was full of big, fat hatchery fish.

Twin Creek was first. From trailhead on was easy with no steep grades, as advertised, but with numerous bogs and soft spots where horse traffic had cut it up badly. Although only twenty miles straight across from Bowl Creek, and roughly 2,000 feet lower in elevation, the difference in the character of the forest was striking. Many tree species were the same, but more dense and luxuriant, and there also were western larch and red cedars. The undergrowth was solid thimbleberries, dressed in golden autumn colors with a few mushy berries still hanging on. This part of the range obviously received greater rainfall than the eastern slope. Nearing the stream I could hear rushing water and soon could see the sunlit pools and riffles through the trees. The water was low and clear, with deep pools under and around logjams — definitely trouty-looking and mostly free of brush for easy casting.

I strung my rod, knotted on a No. 12 nymph, cached my rod case under a spruce and started upstream. The pools swarmed with small trout so eager that I replaced the nymph with one on which the barb was mashed down. All were beautiful — typical westslope specimens — and I saved two of about nine inches for photographs.

At a bend in the creek I sat in the shade of a spruce to have a smoke and a rest. It was hot in the sun, with only a few little popcorn cumulus clouds floating about. My vantage point view up the narrow valley was a vista better than any watercolor or oil on canvas. The soft light of late afternoon accentuated the shadows, bringing out the folds and creases of the mountains and near slopes, the deep green spires of fir, spruce and larch extending in unbroken runs to the uppermost ridges. The valley floor was not over 200 yards wide, open meadows lighted with purple asters and fireweed and the yellow blooms of cone flowers and goldenrod. Dense thickets of willows and red-stemmed dogwood choked the low swales, and there were small clumps of conifers. A dim trail followed the course of the stream, crossing and recrossing the creek as it meandered through the lush bottom, much more traveled by elk and deer than man.

The stream itself was the agent that had set the stage for all this; the valley was of its making and it was still cutting — slowly, inexorably, down to base level. Now it was in a youthful stage with falls and barriers at its lower end, insuring the genetic purity of its stock of westslope cutthroats. The ancient race had ascended the stream before there were any falls, probably before the last great crustal heavings of the earth's rind, and they must have found a refuge here during the periods when the surrounding mountain mass was covered with ice. They were still here, and in abundance, thanks to the barrier falls.

A raven sailed across the valley, its croaks unusually loud in the clear, windless air, and I got up and started back. I had exercised enough small trout for one day and had two on film for the record. As I climbed the ridge on the forest trail, a snowshoe hare drifted on silent feet into a thicket, and as I skirted a wet, boggy swale, a family of blue grouse scurried from the trail into the thimble-berries. At trailhead, I was tired and glad to see The Beetle. It had been a good day.

Spotted Bear River was thought to have an essentially pure stock of westslope cutthroats so I followed it up from its conflu-ence with the south fork of the Flathead for several miles. From the road it looked to be a good trout stream, but I failed to see how trout in the lower reaches could be genetically pure, as there was no barrier between the south fork of the Flathead and Hungry Horse Reservoir. The barrier, Dean Falls, was ten miles upstream from road's end. Some said there were fish above the falls, but an equal number said no, so I decided to try the lower stretch.

I found only whitefish until, at a sharp bend where the flow formed a deep hole bordered by a slowly gyrating eddy, I hooked a trout of about 13 inches. It charged around at a great rate, making a circuit or two of the eddy before I slid it onto the bar and got a picture. The size and shape of its spots and their ar-rangement over the body were typical of the westslope race, but it lacked the bright red and orange tints I had found in other populations of *lewisi*. The subspecies has genetic potential to de-velop such colors, but that production depends upon the water and available foods. A smaller fish I hooked under a logjam furth-er upstream was the only other trout I saw.

There is a strain of westslope cutthroats that are lake dwellers or big stream fish that drop back to the big water after spawning, and this could have been the situation I encountered at Spotted Bear. I wanted to try again, earlier in the season, when the spawners are still in the tributaries.

In 1932 the Canadian ichthyologist, J. R. Dymond, described a race of cutthroats from tributary headwaters of the upper Columbia in British Columbia which he named *Salmo clarki alpestris*, the mountain cutthroat. Whether or not this is a valid race seems a moot question among other ichthyologists, but the fact remains that there was a cutthroat trout in the mid-Columbia basin thought to have been replaced by later invading redband trout, so that the only populations of these cutthroats to survive

were assumed to be relicts above barriers where the redbands couldn't reach.

Paul Doe took Jack James and me into just such an isolated headwater of the John Day River, a mid-Columbia tributary rising high in the Greenhorn Mountains of northeastern Oregon. Paul had fished this tiny stream for over forty years and as far as he knew he was the only one to fish it.

The Greenhorns, like the Wallowas, the Elkhorns and the Strawberries, are western outriders of the Rocky Mountains, al-most, but not quite, engulfed by the flood of lava that, during the Miocene, covered the region at various times to depths of thousands of feet, burying the entire countryside except for the highest parts. Those islands in a vast sea of congealed lava later were sculptured by glacial ice into their present alpine grandeur.

Being the highest ranges in the Blue Mountain system, they annually collect a heavy snowpack, which sustains the excellent trout streams draining their slopes.

We went in by pickup truck, winding by a series of switch-backs to the top of the Greenhorns on a narrow, rutted track through stands of yellow pine, Douglas fir, western larch and lodgepoles to open benches and alpine meadows near the crest. Though mid-July, clear and hot, it was still spring on top with spring flowers adding color to the gray-green benches and parks. There were lupines, Indian paintbrush and numerous others unknown to me.

From the pickup, parked on the divide between north and middle forks of the John Day, we hiked down the north side along an old cart track, past remnant snowbanks with beds of purple violets peeping out of the wet duff along the borders. Elk tracks pocked the wet ground where the trail crossed a couple of tiny rills that would join to form the stream we were to fish. After several miles we branched off on a game trail, plunging down the slope through dense timber. At the bottom a meadow nestled between the steep slopes and vertical rock cliffs, a tiny basin carved out by the ice during glacial times, a minia-ture hanging valley above a series of barriers. Undoubtedly this had been a lake during the ice melt, for its floor was covered with silt and peat, wet and boggy underfoot.

Paul sent me out on this unlikely looking morass with the ad-monition to keep low and tread easy while he went below the barriers at the meadow's far end. The meandering creek had carved a series of tiny potholes in the silt and peat, deep and steep-sided with undercut banks and connected to each other by underground seeps and flows. I saw a trout rise in the first, a pothole of no more than five feet in width, but the fly I flipped out put it down. I approached the next pothole more carefully, crawling close through the mire on hands and knees. There was no sign of a trout until I dropped a fly on the surface, whereupon four or five small fish dashed out, nudged and bunted the fly, then retired to their hidy-holes. I rested the pool a few minutes while changing fly patterns and when I tried again a trout raced out and seized the new offering.

Soon a beautiful little cutthroat of about 10 inches was flopping in the grass. Its colors were vivid, olive green on the back, shading to orange-yellow on the sides, rose tints along the lateral line and an immaculate white belly highlighting the orange-red slash marks and gillcovers. The fish somewhat resembled the westslope cutthroat, *lewisi*, but the spots were larger and more rounded, I noted as I photographed my catch from all angles.

Other pothole fish were hard to come by, spooky and suspicious of my offerings, but I hooked a few, saving four specimens which were later put up in formalin and sent to Bob Behnke for examination. Bob later wrote that they appeared to be an aberrant form of the westslope with the possibility of some ancient mixing with Yellowstone (*lewisi* x *bouvieri*), since the ancestors of both races passed through this area during their initial invasion. He also stated that the subspecies named *alpestris* is probably of the same origin, making it synonymous with *lewisi*. Behnke also indicated that more specimens from different localities were needed to verify his conjecture.

That left me with a mandate to seek out other relict populations in the middle Columbia Basin, a prospect I relished.

Two years passed before the lure of the Greenhorn and the Strawberries brought me back, as they must have lured the Hudson Bay trappers working out of Fort Vancouver and Fort Nez Perce. The British were later to enjoy a virtual monopoly of the fur harvest of the region but in the winter of 1811-12 it was up for grabs when competition appeared in the form of the "Overland Astorians," a party of American trappers led by Wilson Price Hunt bound for the mouth of the Columbia. Two of their number, John Day and a companion named Crooks, fell ill and lagged behind. Upon reaching the Columbia at the mouth of a southern tributary, they were plundered by hostile Indians, who stripped and robbed them of all their gear. Henceforth this Columbia tributary was called John Day River and today its drainage basin is known as the John Day Country.

Half a century or so later gold was discovered in Canyon Creek, a John Day tributary, and the area boomed for awhile, leaving a number of ghost towns and tumbled-down headframes in the mountains as mute reminders of the boom and bust days. But the streams are still there and they nurture native trout, even though their lower reaches have been diverted to irrigate pastures and hay meadows in the John Day valley.

I again sought out Paul Doe and parked my camper in the backyard of his ranch home overlooking the valley. Together we pored over forest maps, checking access to the many streams draining into the upper basin of the John Day. Although Paul had spent his early life in the general area, there were many streams he had never fished and he was as eager as I to go exploring.

We decided to try Indian Creek first, for a few museum specimens of cutthroats had been collected there years ago. Paul called George Ray, a rancher through whose land Indian Creek flowed, and George volunteered to meet us the next morning and act as our guide.

When we crossed Indian Creek on the highway there was barely enough water to wet the streambed gravel. Farther up, at another crossing, the stream hardly flowed but when we arrived at the Ray Ranch it looked like a real creek.

George joined us in the pickup and we went on up the road, out of the meadows and into the forest. Finally the road angled off and we followed a track down to the creek. George said the best cutthroat water was higher up so up we went, hiking past trouty-looking water — deep pools, slick runs and dancing riffles, the creek being about twenty feet wide and the brush not too bad.

Usually I can resist everything but temptation, and this beautiful water was too much. I dropped down to the creek and popped a fly into a slick glide, hooking a redband of about 10 inches. A little further up I took a cutthroat of about the same size. There were numerous fish and I hooked many — redbands and cutthroats in about equal numbers — saving a few to be preserved in formaldehyde for later inspection by Bob Behnke. All of the cutthroats except one looked like good pure stock, as did the redbands. The odd one appeared to be a hybrid, later confirmed by Behnke. The cutthroats were replicas of those taken two years before from Lost Creek, a tributary of the north fork of the John Day. The overall resemblance to the westslope race, *lewisi*, in spotting pattern and coloration was striking, though the spots were larger and rounder.

George had lived by the side of Indian Creek since he was a small boy and had fished its trout for over sixty years. He knew every pool, glide and riffle and the changes that had occurred over the years. He said the stream had never been stocked, that the redbands and cutthroats had always been there, and that steelhead ascended the stream in their late winter spawning runs. Farther up than we fished, George reported there were only cutthroats — no redbands, and that before irrigation diversions warmed the lower waters the cutthroats had occurred further downstream. Altogether it was a real pleasure to have George as guide and mentor, for we learned far more about the fish and the water than we would have had we blundered in there by ourselves.

We explored and fished seven creeks in as many days and found cutthroats in all but one. A few specimens were saved and preserved from each creek and later sent to Bob Behnke for diagnosis, and all proved to be pure with the exception of the one hybrid from Indian Creek. The redbands, Bob said, resembled those from middle Snake drainages, the Salmon and the Clearwater.

In addition to finding good populations of mid-Columbia cutthroats, previously thought to be extremely rare, the fact that resident redbands and cutthroats were found living happily together in the same water with no physical barrier between them has never before been recorded, for it was thought that redbands replaced cutthroats throughout the mid-Columbia Basin.

The two species seem to have partitioned the water between them; as a rule of thumb, the cutthroats occupying the upper waters with the redbands lower down but there is a zone of overlap. Where overlap occurs the cutthroats tend to be found in the deeper, slower water with the redbands in the shallower, faster sections. Sharing the same streams are also bull trout and in some cases, anadromous redbands — steelhead.

Behnke has posed the question, "What is different about the John Day?"

There are many things unique about the John Day Country, whether or not they relate to the unusual relationship between the cutthroats and the redbands. Like a verdant alpine island, the Blue Mountains are surrounded by aridity — the most westerly extension of the Rocky Mountain system in the "lower 48," with the typical Rocky Mountain fauna and flora. The highest parts protrude above one of the largest lava plateaus in the world, as ships riding a sea of basalt. And native trout abound — wonder enough in this day and age of hatchery trucks.

One other saving grace of the John Day Country: Grant County, the heart of it, has more cows than people!

CHAPTER 5

Yellowstone and Fine-Spotted Snake River Cutthroats

WIND SURGED DOWN THE VALLEY, invisible but hard and forceful, wrenching and tearing at everything in its way. The stronger gusts whipped sheets of spray from the riffles and wavelets of the river. Clouds racing overhead were tattered and torn by the gale's force. The air had the feel and smell of snow; it had snowed, in fact. There were still thin patches under the lodgepoles, and when I passed along the furrowed waters of Yellowstone Lake on the way in, the flanks of the Absarokas below the clouds were powdered white.

I had stopped at Fishing Bridge at the outlet, where the main river made up, to watch the big cutthroats mill around. They were hard to see through the roughened surface, but I did spot a few gliding about in the lea of the bridge piers — big, wild native Yellowstone cutthroats! It was trout such as these that I hoped to find and photograph.

This trout was formerly classified with the westslope cutthroat, *lewisi*, even though a few ichthyologists recognized that there were differences. Now Behnke has resolved the problem by naming the Yellowstone trout *Salmo clarki bouvieri* after Bendire, who described the type specimen from Waha Lake, Idaho, in 1882.

A few hardy souls were lined up as deep as they could wade through a long slick glide downriver when I looked for a place to fish. I sought more seclusion in less favored stretches, being one who feels that solitude is a necessary ingredient of a day astream. A few miles down, a turnoff led to the river at a picnic area, forsaken now except for a chipmunk who promptly whisked out of sight, leaving me in sole possession. Once I had donned waders and strung up my rod, I walked to the water's edge to assess the probabilities. Directly in front, the river made a slight bend, cutting into the far bank in a broad sweep, then turning back over a riffle, forming an eddy just above. At the apex of the eddy a trout was showing.

When I waded out to cast to the fish, the wind took the line in a great belly, dragging my small floating fly like a windblown leaf. A decent cast was almost impossible and when I did manage a passable throw, the fly was all but blown off the water. Enough of this, I thought, stumbling back to the bank and hunkering down in the lea of a clump of lodgepoles. It was warmer there, and quieter. After all, what was the hurry? I had all day and maybe later on the wind would drop.

From my small perch I contemplated the Yellowstone Plateau — an interesting place geologically, apart from all geothermal phenomena. Completely covered with ice at least three times, the valley became a huge lake to below the Great Falls when the last ice sheet melted back. The old lake bottom, where I sat, once had been covered by 150 feet of water. The old lake then drained southwest to the Snake and on to the Columbia. Later a small creek to the north cut back in headward erosion through the volcanic rhyolite, weakened by solfataras and fumaroles. Once it tapped the lake the outlet to the Snake was left high and dry, changing the drainage from the Pacific to the Atlantic. In the process it cut the great canyon of the Yellowstone, leaving present Yellowstone Lake as a remnant of its former self.

Whether the cutthroats first entered the Yellowstone from the direct connection with the Snake at the time the lake drained southwest, or came later by way of Pacific Creek and into Atlantic Creek, still a direct water route, is open to question. Evidence favors the latter; on August 9, 1837, Osborne Russell, a trapper of Bridger's party, while enroute from Rendevous on Horse Creek to the Yellowstone, camped at or near Two Ocean Pass. He recorded in his journal that "Here a trout of twelve inches in length may cross the mountains in safety." (*Journal of a Trapper, 1834-1843, Osborne Russell,* edited by Aubrey L. Haines, University of Nebraska Press, 1965.) Nearly a half century later, the ichthyologist Evermann actually observed this phenomenon. But they did get there and are still here, probably the greatest pure native cutthroat fishery left in the West. Originally they worked downstream as far as the Tongue River, but now the cutthroats below the falls lead a precarious existence due to hybridization and competition with introduced non-native trout. They are still the native trout in the upper Snake system above Shoshone Falls, except for a section of the upper river between Jackson Lake and Salt River where the fine spotted cutthroat, an undescribed race, is prevalent.

Ancestors of the Yellowstone trout spread far and wide during the post-glacial or interglacial periods, invading both Lahontan and Bonneville basins. By headwater transfers they entered such diverse drainages as the Colorado, South Platte, Arkansas and the Rio Grande, creating possibly eleven other races of cutthroats, two of which probably are extinct. They may also have contributed to a small degree in the heredity of the mid-Columbia cutthroat regarded now as an isolated form of the westslope. Thus all interior races of cutthroats but one, the westslope race, were evolved in whole or in part from one parent stock, after it in turn had been separated from the coastal type. Quite an imposing record for this trout of the mighty Yellowstone.

My daydreams of such past events were interrupted by a coyote trotting up the far bank, the wind rippling his fur in waves. He paused occasionally to nose and sniff about under down logs and clumps of brush. He spied me, stopping only momentarily to stare, before continuing his quest for mice and whatever he might turn up. If a coyote can hunt in the wind, surely I should be able to fish, I thought, so I struggled to my feet and examined my fly and tippet. The wind still roared down the valley, whipping by an occasional yellow leaf stripped from the nearly naked clumps of aspen. Dry flies were impossible. I chose a nymph with more density and less fluff; if the wind bellied my line, the drag on the fly would be less evident — to me, at least, if not to the trout.

I waded down through the shallow riffle to a glide of broken water with deeper pockets. The wind now was at my back. A cast straight across allowed a forty-five-degree downstream drift that I could control by holding my rod low. The nymph swam through an arc on a tight line, as if I were fishing for steelhead, and the method worked. I hooked a good fish, a beautiful specimen of the Yellowstone cutthroat of at least a pound, and probably a female. Its back was burnished brass, becoming yellowish on the sides and flanks, with large, rounded spots well distributed over the body. The bright reds and oranges of its close neighbors, the westslope race, were lacking except for the deep orange slash marks and a slight tinge of carmine on the cheeks. The light was too dull for good color photography. I twitched the fly from the trout's jaw, held it upright in the current and in a few seconds it glided quickly into the depths.

The wind did not abate as I fished on, hooking and releasing a few more handsome fish, and the cold was working through my innards. I waded out of the river and stiffly made my way back to the car. One thing you can bank on in the high country is the uncertainty of the weather.

When I returned to the Yellowstone country a few years later it was earlier in the season and summer still lingered over the high plateau. I had been in Jackson Hole, fishing the Snake, and there fisheries biologist Jon Erikson of the Wyoming Fish and Game Department had told me of a unique cutthroat found only in Sedge Creek, a tiny tributary to Yellowstone Lake. Their uniqueness arose from complete isolation, Sedge Creek being blocked in its lower course by Turbid Lake, a warm, sulfurous, evil-smelling body of water lethal to any aquatic life and an effective barrier to fish from any other waters.

Ron Jones, fisheries biologist at park headquarters on the lake, took me in to have a look. We drove east along Yellowstone's shore from Fishing Bridge, cut off on a side road for a few miles, then left the pickup and started out on foot, across open meadows and through scattered stands of lodgepole and spruce. We broke out on a bluff above Turbid Lake, startling a band of Canadian geese that had been loafing and preening on the mud flats. The lake was no jewel, even though set in beautiful surroundings. Brown and murky waters burped up foul-smelling gases. Turbid Lake looked to be, and was, absolutely sterile, Ron advising that water samples showed no trace of oxygen. In contrast, Sedge Creek flowed, clear as glass, into the lake from the north, a tiny stream two or three feet wide. Near Turbid the gradient of Sedge Creek was fairly steep as it cut down through the bluff, but above there it was a meadow stream, meandering through the narrow valley in slow, deep runs with undercut banks and occasional small pools in the bends.

We began fishing the lower stretch and I took a small trout in a pool hard against a rock ledge, a beautiful little fish of eight or nine inches. The bronze cast typical of the Yellowstone was very slight, more gray-green than yellowish. The spotting pattern really set it apart — no spots forward of the dorsal fin — like the original *bouvieri* that Bendire described from Waha Lake in Idaho over a hundred years ago. There was more color, too, the gillcovers being reddish, and there were a few rosy blotches along the lateral line. Bob Behnke considers the Sedge Creek trout to be an aberrant form of Yellowstone cutthroat, probably evolved in relatively recent times, the difference in spotting pattern having been fostered by their isolation from the parent stock.

Farther up, at a sharp bend, the current had cut a deep hole against a high bank on the far side. The bank literally bristled with exposed roots and other hazards to fly and tippet. I crossed the creek below and crawled close enough on the high bank to see without being seen by a fish in the pool. I shortened my line to only a few feet of leader and, working the rod with leader dangling through the branches, I dapped the fly at the head of the pool. As the current sucked it under, I was fast to a good fish. Pressure kept it out of the roots and as it flopped and splashed at the surface I passed the rod from hand to hand to get around the trees and branches. Finally, working it to the tail of the riffle above, I scrambled down to inspect my prize.

It was a big fish for this water, between 11 or 12 inches, and probably as large as could be found in such a small creek. This fish was a mirror image of the first, except for size, and after a couple of quick shots with the camera I released it, watching as it swam slowly back to hide under the roots.

I then was at the threshold of the meadow, a lush green basin bordered by a rolling upland of open benches and patches of timber. I saw not a living thing, but it was comforting to know that practically all forms of wildlife that had lived here in historic times were still around — buffalo, moose, elk, deer, black bear and grizzlies, cougar, coyotes and bobcats. Only the big wolves were gone, along with roving bands of Indians who had hassled the Mountain Men in their quest for beaver. In fact, not far from this place a party of trappers lost five of their number to the Blackfeet in 1839.

Slowly up the meadow I walked, watching the water for signs of trout. There were shallow, gravelly stretches interspersed with narrow, deep runs with undercut banks and occasional pools at the bends. Just around a timbered nose of upland jutting into the meadow I saw Ron crouched a few feet back from the creek, rod extended and intent upon the water. Suddenly, he raised his rod. It bent into a bow, then straightened as the line went slack. He looked around, grinning.

"That was a big one," he said, "felt solid and heavy."

We fished upstream, taking a few smallish trout, but the creek was getting smaller and more difficult to fish. In places it was not over a foot wide, with bordering sedges forming a canopy over the water — impossible to put a fly even close to a fish.

The meadow was hot under the full sun. We found shade on a terrace at the end of the flat and dug out our lunch. As we chewed our bread and cheese Ron told me about the fisheries management plan for the park and how they had electrofished this stream, moving a few hundred fish by helicopter to streams draining into the south end of Yellowstone Lake in an attempt to establish a resident population that would stay put. The trout from the lake only entered these streams to spawn, then dropped back, leaving them barren for most of the year. Ron was gratified to learn that Sedge Creek was maintaining a viable population of trout, for if the experiment proved successful, more fish might be moved in the future.

We had worked the little stream for most of its fishable length and had caught a few trout — enough to see what they looked like — and I had taken a number of pictures. We headed back along the ridge, paralleling the meadow on a well-worn buffalo trail. It had been a beautiful day, fishing in an unspoiled country for pure native trout — unique and native only to Sedge Creek.

Another race of cutthroat in the upper Snake System is an as yet undescribed subspecies, though it has been there since before the Mountain Men. It is the fine-spotted cutthroat, occurring in a seventy-mile stretch of river between Jackson Lake and Palisades Reservoir. Not only is it unique in spotting pattern and coloration, its range is completely circumscribed by the Yellowstone cutthroat which is found in the Snake both above and below. In pre-dam days there were no physical barriers between the two, yet each race has retained its own characteristics with no apparent mixing. The unmixed distribution of the two forms has completely baffled ichthyologists, since the two races are recognized as being distinct from each other, yet no one has come up with an adequate explanation. Whatever the reasons, we are fortunate in having another distinctive cutthroat, a beautiful trout and a superb gamefish, as a part of our faunal heritage.

The fine-spotted's natural range embraces one of the most

spectacular alpine valleys in North America, Jackson Hole, where the Snake traverses the basin between the Tetons, the Gros Ventre and the Shoshones. Besides being a place of scenic grandeur, the basin is a historical site of the early days of the fur trade, a focal point of the Mountain Men, named for its discoverer, David E. Jackson, a partner of the renowned Jedediah Smith and William Sublette. If that famous trio ever fished the Snake in Davey Jackson's Hole in those early days, the fine-spotted cutthroat were the trout they caught.

I had floated the Snake in the Jackson Hole country off and on for over a period of years. I had also fished it from the bank in various places, but the Snake is too big a river to wade effectively. The best waters always seem to be out of reach. A rubber raft or any craft that can be handled in fast water is practically a must, making accessible miles of water that otherwise could only be viewed from a distance. Regardless of whether I was floating or floundering along the bank I was awed, almost overwhelmed, by the near presence of the majestic Tetons in their many moods — whether standing bold and clear in the bright sun or with their peaks shrouded in shifting veils of mist, exposing different views of the sheer fault scarp like a peep show. I admit to many rises of good trout missed as I stared, mesmerized, at the peaks instead of watching my Humpy pattern bouncing jauntily through good holding water.

My first float on the Snake occurred many years ago when fishermen were fewer and the trout more numerous and larger. I had launched my rubber dinghy in the river about eight miles above the village of Moose early on a beautiful, bright September morn and had the whole day to make my drift. Conditions were ideal; the river was low and clear and there was not a breath of wind. The view across the water almost overpowered me. The first rays of the sun highlighted the snow fields tucked into defiles amongst the rocky crags of the Tetons, rearing up over the gray-green benches of the river terraces. Every draw leading to the river flaunted patches of yellow-leaved aspen, contrasting with somber spires of spruce, while the cottonwood and willows along the river bank were still in their summery greenery. It was too much sheer beauty for one to absorb in a single gulp — it needed to be sipped slowly, like fine old wine.

The spell finally broken, I got my gear together and pushed off, gathering speed in the fast flow. The Snake is a broad river with numerous bars, low islands and multiple channels. I soon found I had to plan ahead, to assess the water downstream and decide where I wanted to pull out and fish. Otherwise I would be swept by and there would be no going back. The confluence of two channels just below islands or bars seemed the most productive, along with pockets and pools below logjams and other hard-to-get-at places. I hooked numerous trout of good size, a few approaching 20 inches. They were beautiful fish and distinctively marked — silvery with yellow tints on the body with bright orange lower fins and slash marks. Their bodies were profusely spotted overall with very small, irregular pepper-like marks. They looked almost like colorful versions of the coastal cutthroats.

My best trout of the day, and the last one, I caught just above Moose almost at dusk. I had beached my dinghy a short way above the mouth of a small tributary that spilled out into the river over a gravel sill, forming a dropoff into deep, slower water. Approaching this along the main bank I saw a trout swirl close to the shelf — a good fish by the size of the boil. Crouching low I eased up within casting range and dropped a nymph into the tributary, letting the current wash the fly into the dropoff. Almost immediately I was fast to a strong, heavy fish. It surged around the pool, then tried desperately for the heavy current, but I managed to turn it and keep it in the slower water, eventually sliding its broad, speckled sides into the shallows — all 20 inches of it. I let the pool rest a bit and tried again, hooking another but briefly. It felt as big and powerful as the one I had landed, but on its first mad dash the fly came loose, leaving me slack line and a sagging jaw.

In the deepening dusk I walked back to my dinghy, pushed off and rowed the short distance down to the boat landing at Moose and hauled out, awaiting my pre-arranged transportation back to my car several miles upstream. It had been a day to remember — a good day, of which the fish and the fishing had been only a part.

I fished the Snake again in more recent years and found that conditions had changed considerably, but not for the better. The fishing pressure was much greater, the fish fewer and smaller. And the river traffic was unbelievable — at times a constant procession of huge rubber rafts, "baloney boats" stuffed full of tourists floating down through the length of Davey Jackson's Hole. It seemed as though everybody wanted to float the Snake, and did. Although a lot more people now enjoyed an old experience, the total impact on the solitude I had experienced before was devastating.

I sought to catch a wild, native fine-spotted cutthroat of sufficient bulk and girth to photograph and this, I found, no longer was an easy task. I fished a number of tributaries, the Gros Ventre, the Hoback and Grey's River, but I caught only factory fish and a few small wild trout. Then I tried the main Snake above Moose, walking the river bank and fishing the few spots available to a bank fisherman. I was upstream a mile from my car back at the end of a track where boats were sometimes launched or hauled out, and had caught nothing worthy of a photograph. Further upstream a sandspit curved out from the bank and hooked around into a point, forming a great gyrating eddy, brushed by the main current at its lower end. There were fish showing in the gyre and I sneaked up close, stripping off a few coils of line. Glancing over my shoulder to check for back cast obstructions I saw a moose at the edge of a willow patch, a magnificent bull, no more than one hundred yards away. We watched each other closely, somewhat apprehensively. I had experienced previous encounters with bull moose, one in particular not far from Jackson Hole, when one on the prod invaded our camp high in the Wind River Mountains, roaring and grunting, running off our horses and putting my partner up a tree.

This moose, though, showed neither aggressiveness nor fear — just interest — so I laid out a cast. As the Humpy circled the eddy I had a take and soon had a whitefish splashing at my feet. I glanced at the moose hurriedly — he hadn't moved — then twitched the hook free of the tough snout and sent the fish back. Drying the fly on my shirt I checked the moose again. He hadn't batted an eye as far as I could tell, so I laid out another cast, then another, and yet another, glancing quickly at the moose between each one. A "baloney boat" drifted by, the human cargo pointing, shouting and snapping pictures. The bull, however, never moved a muscle. Completely ignoring the boat, he continued to stare fixedly at me. Whatever his thoughts, they seemed benign.

As the Humpy drifted along the fast water's edge, I hooked a good fish. It dashed into the heavy water, jumped once and then, under pressure, came back into the eddy where it circled the gyre, thrashed on the surface, and was finally coaxed into the shallows. This was the one I had been looking for! I laid the 14-incher, resplendent in burnished silver, orange fins and profuse fine black specklings, on my canvas creel. In between quick glances at the moose I took several pictures. I had my fish and the pictures and the bull had kept his peace, though I was still edgy and watchful. I remembered all too vividly his counterpart high in the Wind Rivers, red-eyed and on the warpath, storming through our camp. Back country guides had told me they would rather have a confrontation with a grizzly than with a bellicose moose and I could do without either, particularly when armed with only a fly rod.

I left the lord of the meadows and willow swamps, surveying his domain undisputed, with a breathtaking view of the river, the high benches beyond and the crowning mass of the Tetons in the background — all of that and the "baloney boats," too. Taking a short cut back to the car I cut through a neck of timber and a boggy swale, chopped up with the fresh tracks of several moose. Apparently, the Old Boy had not been alone.

CHAPTER 6

Native Trout of the Lahontan Basin

THE BOY'S FACE FELL WHEN I mentioned the beaver pond and the big trout. His cowboy dad didn't notice as he sipped the coffee we were sharing. Neither did his mother or the brood of small-fry brothers and sisters bounding around their spike camp on Gance Creek, northwest of Elko, Nevada.

But I had observed the lad's ears prick up when fishing was introduced into the conversation of mostly weather and politics, and his crestfallen look now surely meant his chief interest all summer was to be catching *that* very fish.

It mattered not to him the trout was a special subspecies offshoot of the Lahontan cutthroat, and I decided it didn't matter that much to me, either. Coffee and conversation finished, I left their camp of tents and rope corral holding a remuda of several horses.

After all, I'd had *my* chance at that same fish the year before.

While heading back down the road to Elko, I marvelled at the surrounding hostile environment of the undescribed trout and his more prominent Lahontan relative — *Salmo clarki henshawi* of Pyramid Lake. Since time immemorial, harshness and instability have been hallmarks of the Lahontan Basin where today glacial Lake Lahontan is no more, a phantom that left its traces 530 feet above Pyramid Lake in etched shorelines and deposits of algal tufa.

Once glacial Lake Lahontan occupied over 8,000 square miles of Western Nevada and Northeastern California, almost one-half the size of pluvial Lake Bonneville with which it was contemporaneous. A product of glacial melt waters from the Sierras on the west to the East Humboldt and Rubies on the east, Lahontan's levels fluctuated drastically until, finally, only Pyramid and Walker lakes remain.

During periods of dessication and low lake levels, the climate in the Great Basin was much as now — arid — and the two races of trout evolving from a Yellowstone-like ancestor became "survivors" in the starkly real sense of that word. They had been exposed to monumental changes there even before glacial Lake Lahontan, probably arriving through a water connection to the Columbia during the greatest ice advance, the Illinoian stage. Low water periods forced them into the lowest sumps and especially into the headwaters of the four main tributaries: the Truckee, the Carson, the Walker and the Humboldt.

The harsh ecological environment of the Humboldt's north fork system seemed an unlikely place for the undescribed Lahontan, but Bob Behnke had put me on to Gance Creek, a sometime tributary, where I set out to find them. The year before, Gance had been as dry as the proverbial covered bridge when I first crossed its streambed on the highway north of Elko. Cow tracks were molded in the crust of mud caking the creekbed. It looked as though water seldom flowed there except in flood.

Still, the survivors here were in harmony with their environment, hostile though it was, as they were with the first people who roamed the land — primitive hunters, seed gatherers and root diggers. The hardy trout were dispossessed in the lower reaches only when white settlers staked out holdings along the watercourses, diverting them to irrigate hayfields and pastures. Still they continued to survive in headwaters when less adapted hatchery fish were introduced in massive plants ". . . to improve the depleted fishery."

But where, exactly, were they? The east face of the Independence Mountains a short distance to the west showed the green of trees, in contrast to surrounding sagebrush flats and table-topped arid benches. That meant water, and turning in that direction I found it at a ranch surrounded by lush green meadows veined by creek bank willows. Beyond the ranch the road became a track and entered a canyon where water-nourished willows formed a veritable magpie heaven in the valley floor, the track hanging precariously above on the side of a bench.

The creek forked, as the ranch foreman had said it would, and the track dipped to ford it near the junction. I parked The Beetle in a grove of old, gray-barked aspen to fish up the tiny south fork, as directed by the foreman. The few little trout I found in diminutive pools and pockets were unquestionably adults, but retained juvenile markings and were not what I sought for photographs. In color and spotting pattern they resembled the trout of Willow and Whitehorse creeks in Oregon and well they should, having a probable common ancestor and evolving in a similar environment.

I ran out of creek altogether in about half a mile, so went back to try water below the forks. The stream had twice the volume, though not much wider, winding through the narrow bottom in a trench cut through silt of the valley floor. The only trails through the nearly impenetrable willow thickets were cow trails, made by and for cows, not a man packing a fly rod. It was all I could do to worm my way through, let alone fish, but near the forks I came upon a beaver dam with a pond above. I crawled close to watch and had not waited long before a trout stuck his neb up and rolled back down — a big one, maybe 12 inches! He came up again in the same place, too far away to dap for and impossible to cast to. The rod I couldn't raise or wave conventionally I flexed as a bow, holding it low and at right angles, and shot the nymph and leader under dead willows to the fish. Though not a delicate presentation, the fish took. When I tried to tighten, the rod hit a branch and I only turned it over. We went through the same routine again in a few minutes and then the fish was down for good.

I still wonder if the young cowboy finally managed the big trout.

Downstream, in more open water, I engineered a short flip, hooked and hoisted out an eight-incher. Though far smaller than the monster above, I spread it out, got a photo, and shortly took another from the same place. They were long-headed little fellows, yellowish bronze, with prominent elliptical parr marks and a profusion of small, round, auxiliary parr marks. The spotting pattern was similar to the Lahontan cutthroat, and the general ap-

pearance and dull coloring were typical of Great Basin trout, but they were beautiful fish in harmony with their somber surroundings.

I worked out a consolation alternative to the Gance Creek monster back at Elko with Pat Coffin, a fisheries biologist with the Nevada Fish and Game Department. He said Frazier Creek's native stocks were considered absolutely pure, a nearby BLM office provided maps, and at daylight the next morning I skirted Gance Creek and the south end of the Independence Range. Across Independence Valley and the desert beyond lay Midas, a ghost town in the midst of an ocean of sage. Had I been seeking horned toads and rattlesnakes, this real desert would have been the right spot. Rolling sagebrush plains and greasewood flats, dissected here and there by dry, gravelly washes, made for a most untrout-like looking place. An occasional jackrabbit loped into view and once a badger bustled across in front. I saw no other life nor met any other travelers; there was nobody out there and no place to go but on.

Near Midas, in sight of distant ranch buildings, a trail I hoped led to Frazier Creek ended at an abandoned mineshaft and headframe. Desperation drove me into the ranch for directions to the creek's turnoff; I had passed it without recognizing it. The map and its symbols and surrounding country seemed entirely unrelated. Backtracking as directed, I found the turnoff, crossed a dry wash which proved to be Frazier's sometime creekbed and followed it to the end of the track on the brink of a low rim.

Directly below, the creek flowed through lush greenery and I scrambled down to look and to fish. I could jump across the tiny stream, but the little pools and riffles were full of baby fish, an inch or more in length, swarming like schools of minnows. Receding water below must have forced them upstream for I was near the lower limit of the flowing water. Further up, the baby trout disappeared.

Carefully I sought the parents of those numerous smallfry, and in a long, narrow pool above I found, hooked and lost one — a nice trout of 10 or 11 inches. The little valley upstream became a narrow rimrock canyon, so brushy that numerous detours over the rim were necessary. Fishy-looking places were so brushy most had to be passed up, but I managed to hook a number of six- or seven-inch trout and had another good one pull free.

In a beautiful shaded glen, alongside a big pool hard against a sheer rock face, I lunched on a slab of bread and a hunk of cheddar and made plans to try for the bigger trout I had marked on the way up. At the reststop pool, however, once lovely and deep but now silted and quite shallow, I caught a trout and scared another. Further exploration upstream was abandoned in the face of a line of big, black thunderheads shouldering up out of the southwest. The storm kept moving in, blotting out the sun and herding me downstream amidst rumbles of thunder. But between me and the car was a pool I simply couldn't resist.

Circling around, I knelt at the lower end and cast under the lip, the deepest part where the water boiled under a tiny cascade. As the fly hit the water, a big trout had it in a splashing rise, and I almost had the fish on the bank when the fly pulled loose. In the pressure of hurrying I had horsed it too much. The trout raced from the pool's head to its tail, stirring up a muddy cloud opposite me. As the mud drifted and settled I could see the trout plainly — close enough to touch! The fish was excited, its gills pumping madly, but it hadn't seen me and didn't know what had happened. Ever so slowly I stripped in all but two feet of leader, grasped the rod in the middle, and dapped the nymph about a foot ahead of its nose. The trout paid no heed to the first two drifts.

The sky was getting darker and the thunder louder. I had to do something, and soon, as I wanted that trout badly. It was the best one I had seen all day — just under a foot long and a dark brick red in color, so I kept trying. Finally, annoyed at the nymph drifting by, it made a sudden spurt to midpool and I thought I had spooked it. Apparently not, for it almost immediately drifted back to the former position. As I sat quietly watching, the fish's breathing slowed and it turned slightly for a drifting morsel. I dapped the nymph again. The trout turned for it; I raised my rod and the contest was on for the second time. The fish was all over the pool and the air above it until I slid it onto a gravel flat, pounced on it, laid it out and dug out the camera. By opening the lens aperture to its widest stop I got enough fast-fading light to get the trout on film. It was a beautiful fish, more colorful than the Gance Creek trout, perhaps a manifestation of age or size.

I hurried back to The Beetle amid claps of thunder and gusts of wind, hastily stowed my gear and got going. I wanted to get off those greasewood flats and back to the gravel road before the rain hit. The wind already was raising clouds of yellow dust and a line squall was bearing down on me, the roll cloud blue-black and ominous. The race to the gravel road ended in a dead heat with the line squall; we arrived there together amid sheets of rain hurled

along by the gale. A lightning bolt ignited sagebrush about a quarter mile away, sending up billowing clouds of black smoke. The deluge doused the fire shortly just as the desert's blackness quickly masked the lightning flashes. In a few minutes the line squall's violence had passed, things quieted down and I again could see through The Beetle's windshield. But it was raining steadily, and I was happy to be inside and on a hard road, not back in Frazier Creek canyon, seeking scant shelter in the lee of a rock.

My seeming preoccupation with such small trout doesn't mean that big fish hold no interest for me. I would have loved to have fished for the monstrous, pure Lahontan cutthroats of Pyramid Lake, but I entered the scene long after they were gone. Water diversions from the lake's only tributary, the Truckee, dwindled the flow until, finally, there was not enough water for spawning. The last spawning run in 1938 produced fish that averaged 20 pounds, and a 41-pound leviathan is considered to be the record, although fish over 60 pounds were reportedly taken in Indian net fishing.

Pyramid Lake has been stocked heavily with Lahontan cutthroats derived from other sources in recent years. Unfortunately, the stocked fish, even though taxonomically identical, lack the unique genetic background to produce the really big fish of the original Pyramid Lake strain. Since all the lake's present stock is of hatchery origin, some even with a hybrid rainbow taint, I have found it difficult to generate enough enthusiasm to give it a try, particularly since a big lake is not one of my favorite places to angle.

I have fished for pure Lahontan cutthroats only once, in fact, and then very briefly when pausing in a volunteer role with the California Department of Fish and Game's project involving a close relative, the Paiute trout, *Salmo clarki seleniris*. The stream was only five miles away from camp, according to the map, rising high against the Sierra Nevada Divide, but involved a twenty-six-mile round-trip horseback ride because a rugged mountain ridge had to be skirted to reach it. Getting there and returning before dark meant lots of hard riding and too few hours fishing, so I was saddled and ready when the mid-September sun topped the ridge. The grass was dew-soaked, not frosty, but the aspens were beginning to show yellow.

The blaze-faced roan I rode was a good, fast walker and easy enough to get along with, though not noted for an easy gait, and was possessed of an active imagination. He shied at every stump and rock, almost jumping out from under me every time a chipmunk scurried across the trail. I couldn't be sure if he was really spooky or just trying to establish the fact he hadn't gone to sleep.

Our route down Silver King Creek Valley dropped us through a series of long, narrow meadows separated from each other by sharp declivities and ragged patches of timber. As we dropped down, Jeffrey's pines appeared among the lodgepoles and spruce, and it became warmer for both me and the roan. I could smell him sweating under his saddle blanket, so I pulled up for a breather and shed my jacket in the bargain. We splashed across the creek and began our climb through Poison Flat, startling a family of coyotes still foraging for breakfast in the mostly open country of scrubby grass and sagebrush. Three pups, nearly three-quarters grown, raced for cover, but the mother, further across the meadow, sat down, dog-like, and watched us pass.

The trail climbed again at the far end of the flat until we broke out to the deep chasm of the East Carson, an awesome gap breaching the granite-ribbed Sierra. I was glad to have the roan to get me back up the trail we now angled down in a series of switchbacks, past grotesque rock formations and salt-encrusted seeps. At the bottom, on the edge of a narrow meadow, the trail joined another that followed the course of the valley. I rode past Soda Springs forestry cabin, forded the river and found a spot to tie the roan without him tangling in brush and downed timber. I hoped the bear and cougar that had made fresh tracks in the powdery trail dust a short distance back were far away now. My chipmunk-skittish mount would really throw a fit if either showed up, and I would be afoot.

Hurriedly I strung my rod for it had taken half a day just getting to this home of pure Lahontan cutthroats. In knotting on a small nymph I mashed down the barb with pliers, for these were rare trout and I had no desire to kill any. Though the water was low and clear, the streambed had been ravaged by recent floods, leaving wide, scoured gravel bars, silt deposits in backwaters and evidence of severe cutting on the high banks. Though still called a river, here at its headwaters it was actually a medium-sized creek, maybe twenty feet across. The water, flat and shallow where I stood, slowed above and deepened into a glassy smooth glide. In the glide along a log a trout was rising. Wading across and sneaking within casting distance, I kneeled at water's edge and watched. The trout was a good one — 12 or 13 inches — coming up for just what I couldn't tell; there was no visible sign of a hatch. It came to look at my nymph, but that was all; thereafter it showed no interest

whatsoever. I could now see other trout, also big ones, holding in the glass smooth flow, and I cast to each one but with the same results — a cautious inspection of the offering but no takes. I broke off the nymph and tied on the smallest floater I had, a No. 18, but still no takes — only mild interest at first, then nothing.

I was getting desperate. There was no time to experiment further, so I left the picky trout for a pool against a cutbank, behind a half submerged snag. No trout were showing so I knotted on a smaller nymph and a trout took, but I only turned it over. More casts produced nothing and I abandoned that pool for a bigger one with an eddy on the far side. The first cast produced the solid strike of a heavy trout and I soon had it splashing in the shallows — where it also came loose.

I was too anxious; I had horsed that fish. "Take it easy," I counseled myself, "*relax*!"

I propped my rod against a branch, dug out my pipe and stuffed the bowl full. I lit it slowly and carefully, making sure the crown glowed evenly all around, then sat on a rock and puffed, watching the smoke drift downstream. The water's chuckle reminded me of a day on the Rogue when I had hooked steelhead all afternoon, but never got a fish to the beach. This was equally frustrating but desperately different. I might never again be here in this pure Lahontan land. Just *one* fish to see and to photograph! Then I would release it.

I knocked the ash from my pipe, checked tippet and nymph and laid out a cast. As the nymph circled the eddy I saw my line stop, then move forward slightly. I raised the rod tip.

"Oops! Turned that one over, too. Whatthehell!"

Reeling in, I detoured around a tree leaning over the water at a crazy angle and came into the pool almost at its head. There, kneeling, I cast under the lip, letting the nymph drift down naturally. Several casts later my line stopped again. Carefully I raised the rod — and the hook sank! Treating the fish most gently — just enough pressure to hold it out of roots and snags — I led it into the quiet water by my knees. As it lay exhausted, gills pumping, I slipped my hand under the fish's side, raised it gently to the beach and got a quick shot with the camera.

Then I lowered the fish back into the water, admiring its beautifully streamlined form of about 11 inches, the parr marks still showing faintly. Large, perfectly round spots covered the back and sides against a lemon yellow to olive background. Its belly was white, immaculate, and there were many small, auxiliary parr marks. There were slight orange margins to the gillcovers and the slash marks were brilliant orange. I held the fish upright in the current until its breathing settled down. Shortly, with a flip of its tail, the trout was back home in the pool.

I breathed deeply myself and felt better. The pressure was off. I had what I came for and was satisfied. But there was no time to luxuriate; daylight was running out fast and I had to get moving. Still, walking back I couldn't resist another cast or two at the better looking holes. I landed a trout that looked to be a littermate of the one just taken. Quickly twitching the barbless nymph from its lip, I tried still another cast, hooked a fish and lost it. I hurried on, pausing briefly to cast to the reluctant fish in the smooth glide, but they were just as snooty as before and I forged on. I wallowed through an old beaver meadow. Grass reaching my belly concealed downed aspen logs and old canals, some of which I tripped over or fell into. Finally I found the grove where the roan was tied, cased my rod, adjusted the saddle, slipped the bridle on and we were off — up out of the canyon. I pulled up to let the roan get his wind and looked back into that awesome hole. There were some fine trout down there, far bigger than I had caught and apparently much smarter. I had fished two hours, caught two, lost two and turned two over.

"Could have done worse," I consoled myself, "could have lost them all."

The ride back was uneventful but painful. My leg joints stiffened and hurt and I had saddle sores where they counted most. As we broke out into the last meadow, just below our Paiute project camp, another coyote appeared, running as if the devil were hard on its tail. The animal looked back to be sure there was nothing in hot pursuit, then melted into the shadow of the timbers. When I rode into camp the sun had just set, but there was still light.

I had left those snooty Lahontan trout too soon. I could have fished another thirty minutes!

Our project camp on Silver King Creek was right in the middle of Paiute trout country, another offshoot of the Lahontan, the only place on earth where they occur naturally. Theirs is a minuscule world — upper Silver King Creek — a headwater of the East Carson, and a few tiny tributaries. They have had a precarious existence as a distinct race. With inadvertent introduction of nonnative trout, the main population in Silver King Creek has become hybridized more than once, and just as often has been eradicated by rotenone, the population then being re-established with pure Paiute trout from tributaries above barriers. Paiute trout have al-

so been planted in a few other waters in an attempt to broaden the base. They are still not home free, however, as there remains evidence of some hybridization in the Silver King stock, and that is a situation the California Department of Fish and Game is trying to correct.

The master plan is as ambitious and highly commendable as it is expensive in physical effort and funding. It includes, first of all, establishing purity of the Paiute trout population in the upper watershed of Silver King Creek, above the barrier at Llewellyn Falls. This is executed through rotenone poisoning, restocking with pure strains from above barriers in tributaries, or by electrofishing to cull out hybrids, or both. Next stage is eradication of all fish below Llewellyn Falls to a man-made barrier further downstream, then stocking the intervening water with the pure strain Paiutes from those established above the falls. Finally, when that has been accomplished and the population built up to carrying capacity, the lower section will be managed as a limited no-kill fishery, once again making the Paiute trout available as a fishable resource. This, to me, sounds like a model for any native trout restoration program and could be implemented in many places throughout the West.

At this writing, however, there remain problems with the purity of stock above Llewellyn Falls. When a field crew was being organized to electrofish the stream, I was fortunate enough to join in through Steve Nicola, who at that time headed up the Department's rare trout restoration program. On the appointed date I made the long, mountainous climb to Little Antelope Pack Station, just across the first ridge of the Sierras, back of Coleville, California. En route a cougar bounded into the road thirty yards ahead of me and loped along in front before plunging into the head of an impenetrable canyon. This was the second cougar I had ever seen in the wild in the better part of my lifetime spent in the bush, though doubtless many others have seen me. It was a beautiful animal, big as a small deer, with its long, black-tipped tail looping up in a graceful arc — a lovely sight and a wonderful way to start the day.

Once over the top I found the pack station tucked into the head of a picturesque little alpine valley with corrals for the stock and quarters for the wrangler. I met Russ Wickwire, the crew leader, two other fisheries biologists with the Department, a forest service wildlife man and Elwood Davis from nearby Markleeville. All hands were hurriedly stuffing their gear into rope net bags to be lifted in by a helicopter standing by, rotor whirling, and I added my bedroll and personal impedimenta to the pile. I acquired my mount from the wrangler at the pack station. The forest service man had brought his own horse, which left three of us riding and three walking, the bulk of the gear going in by air. It would take us five hours to reach camp; the helicopter made it in five minutes, and had lifted two loads in before we got started.

Even with the pack station perched at the 8,500 foot elevation level, we still had a sharp climb to the top of the next ridge. We were in dense old-growth timber to the top — Douglas fir, spruce, Jeffrey's pine and lodgepoles — before breaking into the clear and dipping gently down a bald, open ridge to the crossing of Silver King Creek. We passed what coyotes and bears had left of a dead horse near the crest of an open ridge, our mounts shying away from the still malodorous remains. The pack station wrangler had told us that about a month before, a pack string coming out had been caught by a thunderstorm in the worst possible place — right on the crest, in the open. Lightning had found them, killing one horse, blinding another and leaving one man clinically dead until revived, ultimately, by a medic in the party. It was our pack horse, in fact, that had been blinded and had since regained the sight of one eye. He did pretty well with only one, though — about on a par with me, or maybe with a slight advantage — he had no need to thread a tippet through the eye of a fly.

Silver King Creek was quite a stream where we forded it, just below its junction with Corral Valley Creek — fifteen to twenty feet wide and clear as glass. It had been pure Paiute trout water, a barrier below denying other fish access. Now it contained practically every kind of trout under the sun *except* the Paiute, but for the few that slipped over the upper barrier at Llewellyn Falls.

Legend has it that originally there were no trout above the falls, the Paiutes occurring from the falls down to the next barrier, now washed out, and that sheepmen had carried them above Llewellyn Falls in buckets and also put them in Corral Valley and Coyote Creek, above barriers. If true, those sheepherders deserve the credit for the continued existence of Paiute trout, for they otherwise surely would have joined the Dodo.

We paused briefly at the crossing to let the horses drink and tried some ourselves, then moved through a series of long, narrow meadows called Lower Fish Valley. We climbed a steep slope, the site of Llewellyn Falls, to Upper Fish Valley and were "home" — to a cabin nestled under the lodgepoles at the edge of a broad meadow. The cabin and surrounding lands now are owned by the forest service, but stockmen had built the shelter many years ago and still use it occasionally as a line camp.

Inside the cabin and hanging on the outside walls was an accumulation of the ages. Nothing had ever been thrown away. There were broken axes, mauls, saws, peaveys, wire cutters, hammers, rusty horseshoes, buckets of assorted old nails and spikes and miscellaneous bits and pieces. I had occasion to get into this treasure trove for my mount had a loose shoe that had clattered like a castanet on the way in. I had no difficulty finding a few horseshoe nails, a hammer of sorts, and cutters. Though none of us were farriers, I had helped shoe horses during my buckaroo days, and between us we got the shoe tight.

There was a fenced pasture for the stock surrounding the cabin and there, in the open meadow part, the helicopter had left our gear. When this was safely stowed in the cabin, Russ cooked dinner — a mountain of food — and we were equal to the task of doing away with it, all of it. From then on Russ did all the cooking while the rest of us cleaned up the pots and otherwise swamped out. Once chores were done, the camp settled down. The owls hooted, the coyotes wailed their laments, and the mice rustled and rattled about in the otherwise quiet cabin.

Dawn came early. It seemed as though I had just gotten to sleep when I heard Russ rattling the cookery. After breakfast the crew assembled an imposing pile of gear for the first day of electrofishing — backpacks with electrical controls and small storage batteries, probes, dip nets, buckets and waders. The plan was to pack the gear upstream about a mile and "fish" down as far as time would permit. All fish having more than five spots on the body, indicating hybridization, would be killed. All others would be returned to the water unharmed. Accurate records were to be kept of numbers, size and degree of hybridization.

Russ explained the mechanics of electrofishing to me thusly: A team of two men operated as a unit, one carrying a backpack containing electrical controls and battery and each carrying a probe, one positive and one negative, connected to a control box by long electrical cords. The probes, one with a net attached at the terminal end, are kept constantly in the water, creating an electrical field to which the fish are attracted. Upon entering the field they become shocked and partially immobilized and can be scooped up with the net. The crews wear rubber waders and gloves to protect them from shock as they are constantly wading in charged water. The strength of the field is controlled by dials and is adjusted for each stream due to varying degrees of conductivity, which is governed by the amount and type of dissolved salts in the water. If absolutely pure, as distilled water, there would be no conductivity and the system wouldn't work. If, on the other hand, the water were briny with salts, the conductivity would be too great and the battery would soon be exhausted.

Russ said the procedure normally catches about seventy percent of the total stream population, making it an ideal method for sampling but ineffective in completely eradicating unwanted fish. The remaining thirty percent will contain hybrids in proportion to the total population and be a continuing source of contamination.

The crew donned waders and gloves, strapped on backpacks and adjusted controls for the upper limit of the section to be sampled, and our "fishing" began. There were four men in the creek with probes, one team following the other about thirty feet behind as a mop-up crew. Elwood kept the records and I followed along with buckets to carry the shocked fish back upstream to prevent their being caught twice. Every foot of water was so fished, and while the creek was not exactly stiff with fish, a good number were caught — enough to keep me busy packing them back up and away from the electrical fields.

The Paiute trout is a unique cutthroat. These were deep bodied, chunky and some not so little — up to 11 inches — considering the stream's size. Individual fish varied slightly in ground color, from quite dark on the back to light greenish yellow, shading to lemon yellow or almost orange on the lower sides and flanks. A pink streak paralleled the lateral line and gillcovers were pinkish, the belly white to grayish, setting off the brilliant orange slash marks. The parr marks and smaller auxiliary parr marks were prominent even on the larger fish, but the most outstanding feature was the almost total absence of black spots on the body of pure specimens. Those that may have been slightly hybridized had a few black spots on the caudal peduncle. Those with more than five were culled. High up, where we began electrofishing, the trout were practically all pure, but further downstream we found more with extra spots.

The entire sample probably produced about five percent hybrids. During the entire operation not a fish was harmed, except those few hybrids eliminated intentionally. I was told that really large fish are often unintentionally killed during electrofishing, their muscular contraction so violent when they hit the electrical field that the spasm breaks their backs.

A day with the electrofishing crew was a novel one for me, the first time I had seen it done. I was able to see a great number of the rare Paiute trout and to get numerous photographs, so

many, in fact, that I ran out of film. I don't intend to forsake the fly rod for the probes, however, for besides being an illegal method for ordinary fishermen to take trout, it is back-breaking work. For those who do it professionally I have the utmost admiration.

Finally I did take up my fly rod, down below the falls where it was legal to angle normally, and managed to high grade two pure Paiute cutthroats from amongst the hordes of non-native trout inhabiting that stretch. They apparently had slipped over the falls, and I released them carefully.

Later, with luck, I will fish that water again when *all* the trout will be pure Paiutes, home again in their ancestral waters.

CHAPTER 7

Trout of the Bonneville Basin

RAYS FROM A LOWERING November sun flashed on high-flying swans, white undulating lines against the dark face of the Wasatch front. They communicated in high-pitched but melodious calls, perhaps discussing their trip down from the Arctic or prospects of a feast of sago pondweed tubers in the pools of nearby Bear River refuge. Among them, surely, were pairs that had vigorously defended their tundra lake territories against me, a census-taker, and all other intruders of their High Arctic home. Now they were united into large flocks and would remain sociable throughout their winter stay in the southland.

Yet another light, stripe-like line caught my eye on the steep scarp of the Wasatch Range as I shifted easterly in my duckblind on the Bear River Marshes. The thin line — level enough to have been laid out with a transit — stood out plainly 1,000 feet above the marshy floodplain of the Bear. I marveled at the old Bonneville shoreline, marking the highest level of pluvial Lake Bonneville, once the ancestral home of Bonneville Basin trout.

My game bag was light that warm, windless, lazy day. On a mat of tules beside me lay a greenhead mallard, two bull sprigs and a gadwell hen. I had hoped for a canvasback or two but they hadn't moved from the lush sago beds — too warm and too still. But I was never bored by the lack of action, for the marsh dwellers were all about me; coots fussed around on the borders of the weedbeds, marsh wrens called from the tules and flocks of chattering blackbirds wheeled overhead. I was also surrounded by historical riches and magnificent topographical features laid out on a grand scale. Westward across the marshes were the salt flats at the north end of Great Salt Lake, a remnant only one-tenth the size of its parent Lake Bonneville. Far beyond loomed the dark silhouette of Promontory Point, seemingly detached

and floating in the shimmering haze. Near there, amid much fanfare, "The Golden Spike" had been driven a century earlier to mark the joining of rail lines from East and West.

The Bonneville shoreline is of great significance in the distribution of trout throughout the basin. The lake rose to that highest level when Bear River, dammed by volcanic action, diverted there from its original Snake River drainage. The diverted water contained Yellowstone-like cutthroats, or their ancestors. They spread rapidly throughout the old basin and entered the tributaries, eventually evolving into a separate race, *Salmo clarki utah*, the Bonneville cutthroat. With later lowering of the lake level and almost complete dessication, some of these stocks became isolated and diverged slightly from each other, but apparently not enough to warrant separate subspecies.

Lake Bonneville was the largest late Pleistocene pluvial lake in North America and, like its contemporary, Lake Lahontan, it fluctuated greatly with the waxing and waning of the mountain glaciers, cutting terraces and forming beaches when it paused long enough between its ups and downs. Surely it remained at its maximum level a long time to etch such a perfectly preserved shoreline, plainly visible 20,000 years or so later. Then it burst its seams, broke out at Red Rock Pass at the north end, and drained into the Snake, stabilizing awhile at a lower level. Apparently Bonneville twice broke out at Red Rock and for brief intervals became part of the Columbia River system. Final retreat of glacial ice led to Bonneville drying up, possibly 8,000 years ago, leaving Great Salt Lake, Utah Lake and Sevier Lake in its lowest sumps.

The possibility exists that trout also entered Bonneville from the Snake when the lake overflowed at Red Rock. If so, they would not have affected the purity of the Bonneville stock since they would have been from the same race as the original Bear River strain.

Bonneville trout were once considered to be extinct. They had run the all too familiar course — from superabundance in the early settlement days to near oblivion in modern times — dispossessed, hybridized and outcompeted. Then a few relict populations were found in remote headwater streams. Oddly, the greatest numbers of pure stocks left are in Wyoming and Nevada, on the fringes of their former range.

I first found them in Southwestern Wyoming, in the Smith Fork and Thomas Fork, tributaries of the Bear River. My camp was on Smith Fork, a classic mountain stream, above the irrigated meadows and ranches, where it issues from a narrow valley on the flanks of Wyoming and Salt River ranges. There were few signs of other fishermen. Smith Fork cutthroats were numerous, of fair size, and eager for a fly. I was especially grateful to be able to fish standing again, making conventional casts without being compelled to creep and crawl on hands and knees.

The fish I caught for inspection were, with one exception, silvery with orange lower fins — even the dorsal, caudal and adipose fins had a yellowish cast. The spots were fairly large, round and evenly distributed over the body, not concentrated on the caudal area as in most other races of interior cutthroats. This also applied to one greedy 13-incher I found in the shelter of an undercut bank. The tail of a sculpin protruding from its mouth hadn't prevented this trout from actually jumping for my fly! The exceptional fish was much duller, with brassy tinge and more numerous, larger spots. Was this one an oddball, or the typical Bonneville cutthroat? I would have to see more fish from different streams to be certain.

Thomas Fork lay just across the ridge from camp, its headwaters probably no more than four or five miles distant. But what the map showed as a road wandering that way was actually a badly washed track and too much for The Beetle. I had to go around, and during the fifty-mile backtrack I had time to reflect on how the early mountain men had left their mark on the region. Many of the creeks, mountain ranges, basins and some towns bear their names. Smith Fork and Thomas Fork are two of them. They often wintered at Bear Lake, straddling the Utah-Idaho border, wandering over the whole area on their trapping forays.

It was Jim Bridger, traveling out of Bear Lake, who first set eyes on Great Salt Lake, at first thought to be a bay of the Pacific Ocean and later considered to be the source of the mythical Buenaventura River, supposed to flow westward to the Pacific. That myth died hard. The indefatigable Jedediah Smith made two nearly disastrous trips to California before concluding that there was no such river. Smith Fork likely was named for Jedediah, although it could have been named for his nefarious namesake, old Peg-Leg Smith, who roamed the area somewhat later. Thomas, whose fork I was headed for, probably had been one of the free trappers who had thrown in with the famous partners, Smith, Sublette and Jackson.

At the turnoff heading along Thomas Fork I drove up a few miles for a look. I was back with the mini-streams. Thomas was possibly a yard wide, but there were pools, pockets and some deeper runs between shallows. The countryside was open, however, with low sage on the hillsides and a few willows along the streambank meandering through little meadows. Again I was kneeling and crawling to keep out of sight. The trout I caught were mirror images of the silvery fish predominant in Smith Fork and I concluded that they must be *the* representative form of Bonneville trout. They were smaller than those in Smith, but I managed to beach several suitable to photograph and I felt well paid for the long detour.

Another distinctive form of the Bonneville, found in East Central Nevada and extreme Western Utah, now became my interest. It is thought that they invaded those regions when Lake Bonneville filled all the connecting intermontane basins on its western fringe. They were stranded in the streams draining to the Snake Valley off the slopes of Mt. Wheeler and Mt. Moriah in Nevada and in the Deep Creek Mountains in Utah when the lake level lowered and the basins dried up.

Most of the few tiny headwaters where these trout now are found are closed to angling. In Ely, Nevada, I counseled with a fisheries biologist to learn where I might legally fish, and he advised me that my options were limited to Mill Creek and Hampton Creek.

I remembered Bob Behnke's admonishing words: "Mill Creek must be the smallest trout stream in North America."

The biologist reminded me that the year had been one of drought; Hampton Creek seemed the better bet, but a storm held me up. While waiting out the wind and rain I drove up Mt. Wheeler, through all the life zones — from Upper Sonoran to Arctic-Alpine. At road's end, across the brink of a talus-strewn canyon, an awesome glacial cirque had been gouged out, the naked rock walls rising sheer to 13,000 feet around a basin still covered by dirty snow and ice. It seemed anachronistic in the midst of all the surrounding aridity, that its melt waters, the source of Lehman Creek, had once nurtured Bonneville trout that then dwelt in it — before the time of the hatcheries.

The weather cleared and I set out for Hampton Creek, southeast across the desert basin's floor, up over Sacramento Pass, between Mt. Wheeler and Mt. Moriah. Both completely dominated the Snake Range, their green timbered slopes a refreshing contrast to the desert's drabness. On the east side I branched off north into the upper end of Snake Valley. Here Lake Bonneville, during its maximum stage, had thrust a long finger — which was when and how the Bonneville trout got here. Crossing Hendrys Creek, sustaining a remnant population of Bonneville trout in its uppermost headwaters, I dropped to the Snake Valley's floor, so barren and sere it looked as if a jackrabbit might be hard-pressed to make a living. A few miles later a dry wash with a track led up toward Mt. Moriah. According to my map, this was the way to Hampton Creek. At the base of the mountain the creek emerged from a little canyon, a trickle of water over gravel. The track in the bottom of the canyon passed an abandoned mine, ramshackle buildings and a tumble-down headframe, ending at a trail that angled away from the creek.

I walked down to a creek I could step across, sneaked up on the first little pool and flipped in a nymph. A tiny trout, all of four inches, darted out from under the bank, tapped the nymph and darted back. Such split-second rejection — when a fish seems to quickly mouth the hackle and then turn tail — has always amazed and frustrated me.

Instantaneous striking doesn't solve my problem. I have snatched the fly out of a trout's mouth far more often than they have beaten me to the draw and spit it out.

Just above, in a longer and deeper pool, I could see several trout and one was a veritable bull-of-the-woods, at least six inches! This fish held the best lie and was pickier than the smallfry companions I managed to hook before turning the big one over and putting them all down. They were odd-looking little fellows — chunky, with oversized dorsal and anal fins. Their basic ground color was brassy, with large, bluish parr marks, giving them a bluish tinge. The black spots were fairly large, round and evenly distributed over the entire body, right down to the abdomen. They most likely were pure *utah*, isolated thousands of years from their parent stock.

Upstream the fishable water disappeared into a matted tunnel of dead branches, an effective shield against fishermen, kingfishers and herons, provided by a species of willow common to the stream valleys of the West. As I hadn't hooked a trout big enough to photograph, I returned to the pool dominated by the six-inch monster. We played games for quite awhile before the trout made a mistake. Then I had my prize in the grass and in the eye of the camera. This trout beat my estimate of size, going six and three-quarter inches without stretching. I could not have been prouder had it weighed three pounds.

After all, the trout was as long as one-third the width of its home stream. What, I marveled, would a Rogue River steelhead of comparable size to *its* home water measure!

Another form of Bonneville trout I wanted to see and compare with others was isolated in the southern part of the basin. At Ely, Nevada, I was only two hundred miles from Birch Creek, said to contain pure stock, so I hooked The Beetle to the camper and headed across the desert, over the Wah Wah Mountains and through their valley to Beaver, Utah. There, forest service folk supplied a map, road condition information, and the way to the *right* Birch Creek — for there were two of them.

Early next morning I drove up the valley of the Beaver to where Birch Creek joined it or, more exactly, where they sometimes joined, for Birch now was a dry wash, the streambed as dry as a bone. Following the creek's general direction I drove up a trail so badly rainwashed The Beetle could barely navigate, even at a snail's pace. The foothill country of open sagebrush and sparse scatterings of junipers and pinon pines rose toward the Tushar Mountains, forming the divide between Beaver and Sevier drainages. Finally I came back to the valley of Birch Creek almost at its upper limit, a narrow little vale incised through the lower slopes of the Tushars. Aspens, willows and occasional junipers lined the stream banks, but the surrounding slopes were almost bare of trees, only a few patches of aspen and mahoganies breaking the monotony of gray-green sage.

I parked The Beetle on an old terrace above the creek and walked down for a look. The effects of a recent cloudburst were apparent. The deluge had washed the slope's soil severely and the creek had been ravaged and scoured. There were leaves and trash washed up on the banks and draped in the low bushes. A beaver pond was silted in completely, leaving only an inch or two of water spread over the mud. Picking my way upstream through downed aspen logs and old beaver cuttings, I watched for the flash of trout. But there were few places for a fish to hide in the badly cut up and washed creekbed. Shortly I came out of the aspens into a small, boggy meadow where the stream broke up into a labyrinth of tiny rivulets and seeps, almost concealed under rank sedges. This was Birch Creek's headwaters. Beyond, the gray-green slopes rose sharply, with streaks of aspen in the draws and mahogany thickets clustered around the knobs and rocky outcrops. Clearly I was at the end of the line for trout. The little valley above and the slopes, far and near, belonged to the mule deer and the coyotes.

I watched the water even more carefully in retracing my steps. Below the silted beaver pond I dropped my fly in a few little pools and once thought I saw a trout flash. But that was all, right to the end — less than a half-mile downstream where the flow went underground. I followed the streambed, hoping the water would resurface, but when it didn't I walked back, found a log in the shade of a juniper and ate my lunch. As I smoked my pipe I mused on the situation. I had fished too many years to believe that just because I couldn't see or catch any fish there weren't any. Convincing myself that a few just had to have survived the flash flood, I knocked the ash from my pipe, got up and began a campaign of caution and stealth.

Keeping out of sight by crouching, kneeling, crawling and creeping, dapping where necessary and making short casts where I could, I fished all the water, from pocket to pocket and pool to pool. Finally I hooked a fish, a smallish trout, which, after a few flip flops, came loose. In another pool I turned a fish over, also a smallish trout, maybe six or seven inches, and it wouldn't come again. That was all. I was skunked, thoroughly and absolutely, and somewhat humiliated. I walked back to The Beetle and put my rod away.

Thunderheads were making up again over the Tushar Plateau, tops boiling up, creamy white in the afternoon sun.

"Better get out of here," I thought, "before I get caught in another cloudburst."

Back on the rocky trail, bumping and thumping over boulders and ledges sharply defined by the earlier deluge, I rationalized my failure to catch a Birch Creek fish.

The "answers" seemed logical at the time. But the fact remained then and now, I have yet to clearly see or photograph a Bonneville trout from the southern part of that historic basin.

CHAPTER 8

Native Trout of the Alvord Basin

RUMORS OF UNUSUAL TROUT in the high desert country of Eastern Oregon finally were verified by friends who had been deer hunting there and had caught some. Consensus was they were "natives," but native what?

I looked at a map. The place in question was just over a low divide from the Lahontan Basin, that vast desert area in Northwestern Nevada once covered by waters of the post glacial Lake Lahontan. Could these trout be Lahontan cutthroats? If so, they would be a noteworthy find because pure *Salmo clarki henshawi* are mighty scarce.

Jack James, the deer hunter group's leading spirit, agreed to take me in. We piled gear in Jack's four-wheel drive pickup and away we went — across the Cascades, through the Klamath Basin, across the Warners, up through Blizzard Gap and Dougherty Slide. From there we crossed the high desert plateau of Northwestern Nevada, invaded Virgin Valley and passed the Pueblos and Pine Forest mountains. Finally in late afternoon we pushed up into the mass of the Trout Creeks whose tops are on a great rolling volcanic plateau covered with scrubby sage and bunchgrass.

We left what by then could hardly be called a road and struck off across the slopes, bouncing down through draws and gullies to end up at Jack's old camp on Little Whitehorse Creek. Years before Jack had hauled in boards and studs and made a tent frame. It was still there, embellished with great nettles growing up and through cracks in the floor. We stomped the nettles, threw down our bedrolls, then I went to the creek for water. At campside the creek was about two feet wide, a series of clear little plunge pools. As I stooped to fill the bucket, a spooked trout dashed into the next pool.

I looked around. Across the creek sheer rimrock shone red and black in the setting sun. A patch of gnarled mountain mahogany clung precariously in a turreted gash. On our side stood a grove of aspen, gray-boled with leaves quaking in cool evening breezes. Elsewhere and everywhere were endless benches with slopes of gray-green sage broken by rimrocks and isolated turrets and pinnacles of dark lava rock, remnants of ancient rhyolite flows dating from the Miocene over ten million years ago.

It seemed a most unlikely place for trout. Yet we were at 8,000 feet and the creek was spring-fed and cold as ice. So why not trout? I had just seen one, hadn't I?

That night we slept under the stars on the floor of the tent frame with the nettles. The last sound I heard was the eerie cry of a coyote. I dreamed of trout — big, native trout in a little mountain stream.

At first light I was awake in silence broken only by the creek's constant babbling. Did I only imagine its "come hither" call? The exhilaration always present when about to fish a new stream with new trout was so strong I ached with anticipation.

After breakfast we struck out toward some beaver ponds Jack suggested we explore before fishing back. The creek dropped rapidly into a canyon, the rims rising sheer on both sides. Willows appeared along the banks forming thickets so dense that in places the creek seemed to flow through a tunnel. Nearby were patches of black sage higher than our heads. The rich volcanic soil was capable of growing dense vegetation with just a little water. Further down wild rose bushes put in their appearance, becoming progressively thicker and bigger. Finally we came to the beaver meadows.

The scene was one of rank meadow grass criss-crossed with

dead aspen downfall, logs that beavers had felled years before. Ahead were the beaver ponds, a whole series of them, back-to-back! Over the years they had filled with silt and muck, however, and the only deep water was in channels that the beavers still maintained.

Over 150 years ago Peter Skene Ogden had led his fur trapping brigades out of Fort Vancouver through the desert ranges of Eastern Oregon with explicit orders of the Hudson's Bay Company to clean it out — in fact, create a "fur desert" to discourage American trappers and settlers from entering the country. Obviously he didn't quite get the job done; these beavers were descendants of those he missed.

I worked out to the nearest channel through muck and ooze. There, just above me, was a trout finning behind a willow root. A big one! Ten inches, at least. I pitched a buggy-looking nymph in the channel. The trout moved out deliberately, sucked in the nymph and when I tightened, it was fast. For a trout of those dimensions it had made a considerable ruckus before I could slide it out on the mud. I picked it up carefully, excitement surging as I held a trout of a new race — new to me at least. I carried the fish to dry land and laid it out in the full sun to get pictures from many angles before its colors faded. After a number of shots I examined the fish in detail.

I had never set eyes on any trout like it before. It was dull, coppery, almost brick red in background color, with large, round spots evenly distributed on the sides and back. The parr marks were prominent, even though this trout probably had spawned more than once. Lower fins were brownish, dusky, the belly was gray, and bright orange slash marks proclaimed its cutthroat lineage. Altogether its coloration was quite typical of cutthroats of the Great Basin.

What struck me most was the trout's head — a great long head with a big mouth — almost pike-like in proportion. It looked like a predator, but cutthroats were the only fish in the stream. Invertebrates were the sole food available, yet the long head was not due to inadequate diet. This trout was as plump as a three-pound robin.

I worked upstream, routing out a magpie that had been watching surreptitiously from the willows. It flapped across the stream, its black and white plumage in startling contrast to the somber gray-green slopes at the base of the rimrocks. In the pond I saw a trout finning below a channel bend. It was a good one, too, and within easy casting range — but how to get a fly to it? Dead willow branches were intertwined over the water, effectively blocking any presentation from my position. I considered dapping a fly from closer range.

As I stood deliberating, the water suddenly sucked and surged at my feet as a submerged beaver steamed up the channel, inches from my toes. I looked directly down on it, the water pressure matting the reddish brown fur close to its body so that the black, shoe-button eyes looked as if they were about to pop. Maybe they did pop a little when the silent swimmer saw me, but if so, it gave no other sign of alarm and continued its submerged cruise up the channel. That solved my problem with the trout for it was gone, back to its hidy-hole under the willow roots.

I continued upstream, catching a trout now and then — all as alike as peas in a pod except in size. Most were seven or eight inches, a few were nine or ten.

I felt the canyon's heat as I sat on a rock to wait for Jack. The sun made shimmering heat waves on the rimrocks and distilled the sage's pungency. In the cloudless sky a golden eagle soared high in the blue, riding thermals, losing altitude in downdrafts to maintain air speed, then wheeling to catch an updraft, becoming almost motionless at the peak of its climb.

From its superior elevation the eagle's horizons were broad and it could look, at leisure, as a man on a mountain top. During my years of flying I had to look quickly from only 100 feet as the scenes rolled by in a rush. I tried to visualize what the eagle could see from its vantage point in the thin, clear air.

To the west and northwest was the Alvord Basin, the ancient bed of glacial Lake Alvord abutting against the flanks of the Pueblo Range and the scarp of the Steens, their high rims glittering with last winter's snow. North and northeast lay the headwaters of the Owyhee traversing the almost endless sagebrush plains to join the Snake far to the northeast. East and southeast were the jumbled desert ranges straddling the joint borders of Oregon, Idaho and Nevada. South and southwest lay the serrated peaks of the Pine Forest Mountains in Nevada and the Blackrock Desert, the dessicated bed of a part of a post glacial Lake Lahontan.

Directly below it, that eagle could see me, sitting on my rock, surrounded by the uplifted mass of the Trout Creeks with thin lines of tiny streams draining off in all directions only to disappear in the desert flats. My creek ran north to join west-flowing Big Whitehorse before their combined flow vanished in irrigated hay fields. Just across the divide to the west, Willow Creek followed a parallel course and it too disappeared in the greasewood flats of the desert.

In all this vast expanse visible to the eagle above, only these two tiny stream systems held stocks of original native trout. In all other streams the natives were no more — replaced by non-native hatchery fish. One of these native stocks was unique — a separate and distinct race — extinct before it could be formally described. This trout, also a cutthroat, was found only in a few small streams draining into post glacial Lake Alvord — a total casualty to hybridization with hatchery rainbows.

How did these trout get here, surrounded as they are by thousands of square miles of aridity in the midst of nowhere? Behnke thinks they may have come from the Alvord Basin by way of a headwater transfer with Trout Creek, whose headwaters interdigitate with those of Willow Creek. There is also the possibility that they came with a headwater transfer from McDermitt Creek, a Quinn River tributary of the Lahontan Basin, into Little Whitehorse whose headwaters abut against low divides. A third possibility is that they came from pluvial Lake Alvord when it overflowed into the lower basins of Willow and Whitehorse creeks. Geologists claim that Lake Alvord never overflowed; but it did, in two places, and the evidence is there for anyone who cares to look. All of this, of course, is conjectural, and probably academic, since the trout are here, but zoogeographical considerations are always of interest when trying to explain the presence of a unique race of trout isolated in the midst of a desert.

A raven brought me out of my reverie and back to earth. It was calling raucously and posturing on a rim across the creek. It looked rough and unkempt like an unmade bed and every time it croaked it lowered its head and flared out its throat feathers. I didn't know if it was protesting my presence or merely engaging in raven chatter.

I looked away to the creek a few yards below. In a small open space between willows where the water was slow and deep, a trout appeared, intercepted a submerged tidbit and retired to its lair under the willows. There were too many obstructions for a cast, but I thought of dapping an offering in its larder. I crawled close, stripped in all line and all but two feet of leader and gently lowered the fly. At first, with the fly floating, the trout didn't show. When it sank, out came the trout to inspect it before turning back. Results were the same in a different pattern. That fish had no interest in a floating fly but investigated every submerged offering. In changing patterns again, to eliminate the floating

phase, I soaked the fly in my mouth. Sink it did, but when the trout nose-bumped the new offering, it raced for cover, scared witless. Spit on your bait for luck? Forget it!

Jack appeared and we headed up creek toward camp. The sun was really bearing down and we were hot and dry, lured on "ever upward and onward" by the brew cans cooling in the icy plunge pool by the tent frame.

Next morning we broke camp to investigate the creek's lower reaches. We loaded our gear and jounced out to the "road," branched off on another and finally worked our way down and out to the edge of a rim. There was the creek all right, but it was a long way down and it would seem further coming back.

Still, a beaver pond glittered there like a mirror in the sun so down we went, sliding and scrambling over rocks with ever a wary eye for rattlesnakes. At the bottom we found wild rose bushes had entirely replaced the willows and grew along the water's edge like a hedge. They were the biggest, toughest and thorniest wild roses I had ever seen and effectively prevented any fly fishing from the bank.

We found the beaver pond almost entirely silted in, its water merely a thin sheet — not even a channel was visible, and not a sign of trout. Hoping for deeper water just above the old dam, I followed on around. It was still shallow so I crossed below and came up the other side. There was a pool just under the dam, where the water spilled through an old break, and in it were two trout, a veritable monster and a lesser one! The monster held the choice spot, right under the break where it got first choice at everything coming through. This trout was rising regularly and often!

Fortunately, there was a small opening through which to cast. I was so close I dared not move, so stripped line and popped a short cast under the break. His Majesty came up, but missed! Swallowing my heart a couple of times, I tried again. The scrappy fish had it this time and roared around at a great rate, but the pool was so small there was really no place to go. Some snags worried me and I pressured my little Orvis to the limit.

When the frantic thrashing and splashing subsided I slid the monster onto the mud — just as the fly came loose. Flinging my rod aside, I dropped on my knees and, with frantic scooping, got the trout safe on high ground. When I looked up at last, there stood Jack. He had watched the whole ludicrous performance. I gilled the trout and held it up for Jack's comment.

"I'll be goshdarned!" was all he could get out.

The tape read 15 inches exactly, and the scales registered one pound, two ounces — of pure, undiluted cutthroat, a male still colorful from spawning, with a great maw I could almost stick my fist into. We laid the prize out in state on a rock to admire and to photograph.

Most anglers would not consider such a trout all that great. To me, the fish taken from a tiny stream no larger than those I fished as a boy for shiners and dace, was a prize equal to any big steelhead I ever caught, including a 16-pounder.

Any other trout would have been anticlimactic after that experience so we struggled back up the rim to find we had company. John McKelvey, the game warden, was squatting in the shade of his pickup waiting to check us out. John was an old-timer with a wide reputation of being able to be everywhere at once. There were few who roamed the vast expanse of sagebrush desert and rimrock who didn't eventually encounter John someplace along the line.

John allowed that my trout was the biggest he had ever seen come out of that country. We agreed we ought to have a beer to celebrate but the cooler, along with our other gear, was in the great chest in the back of the pickup. Jack discovered his keys were locked inside. We borrowed John's axe to smash the lock, a fringe benefit of being checked by the game warden.

Our plans were to camp at Willow Creek that night but once there, after bouncing over rocks and ruts, the weather changed our plans. Over the mass of the Trout Creeks loomed a huge cumulo-nimbus monster, blue-black at the bottom with the creamy white tops boiling and seething like a giant cauldron punching up toward the stratosphere. The rumble and roar was almost constant as lightning flashed along the horizon.

This was not the time or place to be caught without shelter. We drove the 40-odd miles to Denio, a little semi-ghost town straddling the Oregon-Nevada border, and took refuge in the old frame hotel. In the bar, over our brew, we told "Smiling Ed," the amiable barkeep, about *the* trout.

Ed's skepticism was evident so I went to our cooler, brought the trout in and laid its full 15 inches on the bar.

"Ha!" Ed said, "so you snuck into Summit Lake!"

A cowboy slid off his stool and came to have a look. He supported Ed's assessment.

"Ain't no trout like that around here," he drawled. He climbed back on his stool and went silent again.

The cowboy was more correct than I had realized then. Hav-ing removed that trout, I never again found one so large in that area.

Back home I consulted the experts. Bob Behnke wrote me that these trout were not Lahontan cutthroats, *Salmo clarki henshawi*, but were an undescribed race not yet graced with a scientific name. They are unique, inhabiting only the two small stream systems — and that's all there are in the whole wide world!

They have been there since the glaciers melted and maybe before, at least 8,000 years ago but possibly 100,000 years ago, or even longer. They have weathered floods, droughts, range fires and possibly glaciations; despite man's activities, they are still there — alive and well. There are no records of stocking in these two stream systems, nor any evidence of hybridization with non-native trout. I hope they hold out until the next glaciation and maybe they will survive that too.

They could use some help, however, such as special angling regulations — flies only, barbless hooks, a lower bag limit, protection of streamside habitat from livestock, and a firm stand against any road development or improvement in these watersheds.

These little trout and their tiny streams are part of our heritage, and as their entire habitat lies mostly on public lands, it would seem reasonable that we could insure their protection and survival.

CHAPTER 9

Native Trout of the Central and Southern Rocky Mountains

CAPT. BENJAMIN LOUIS EULALIE de Bonneville's anticipation while awaiting his first Rocky Mountain rendezvous with Indians and free trappers couldn't have been any keener than mine toward meeting, at long last, the Colorado cutthroats.

The setting was the same, Horse Creek and the upper Green River in Wyoming's Bridger Basin country, but the century wasn't — not that a few years mattered much to those divide-jumping trout.

The captain's aim, on leave from the U. S. Army, was to trade with the Indians and trappers and to explore the Rockies. Free trappers dubbed his post "Fort Nonsense" and, while his venture *was* a financial failure, he left his name on more than just Fort Bonneville in the West.

Mountain men gathering to trade beaver skins for booze, bullets, blankets and beads didn't fare so well, either. Seeking respite from ever-present fears of being scalped, starved, frozen or mauled by grizzlies, they sipped then, from horn cups, raw alcohol watered from Horse Creek. Few had the wit to let traders bank their earnings, and most were left with monumental hangovers, colossal debts for new outfits and, possibly, new Indian wives to warm their blankets.

Horse Creek is also distinguished as the site of the first Mass celebrated in the Rockies. It is not recorded whether Father De Smet's words penetrated the camp's alcoholic haze, but spirits still are a big consideration in that country. When I pulled into a garage in LaBarge for gas and information, my question to the attendant was: "How big is Big Piney?"

The broken-down cowboy type squinted his face into seams resembling old saddle leather. Considering a moment, he finally observed: "Big Piney's only got two bars. We got three."

Despite that negative report I pushed on, across rolling sage-covered hills bordering the valley of the Green, its banks lined with stately cottonwoods. I arrived at Big Piney as the lowering western sun highlighted a badlands belt on the far side of the valley, turrets and spires sculptured in horizontal beds of pink, ocher and gray. The dearth of campgrounds proved more acute than the shortage of bars, but I finally parked in the backyard of some kindly soul for the night.

Next morning the local tackle shop attendant advised that Daniel, about twenty-five miles up the road, would be a good base from which to fish Horse Creek. Daniel, it developed, was a one-bar town. In fact, the only other building was a general store with a gas pump out front. The campground, however, commanded a view of the jagged crest of the Wind Rivers to the northeast and the rounded knobs of the Wyoming Range on the west.

Many years before I knew there was such a special trout, I had wandered into the Colorado cutthroats' original range, packing into the Wind River Mountains and fishing the high lakes for cutthroats, all stocked fish — probably Yellowstone cutts. Only after coming to realize that the Colorado cutthroat was one of our most colorful native trout did I return to the upper Green to find them.

Pondering the complexities of trout distribution in drainage systems where, under present topographical conditions it would be impossible for them to get into, I had arrived at some bizarre explanations. I accepted the obvious without question. For example: trout in the Yellowstone from the Snake via Two Ocean Pass, still a direct water connection; trout in the upper Missouri from the Columbia via Marias Pass, a water connection in historical times. But . . . trout in the Colorado, the South Platte, the Arkansas and the Rio Grande by way of "headwater transfers" across rock-ribbed divides? That seemed a bit much, a handy way of explaining away what seemed an impossible or at least an improbable situation.

With my vast store of ignorance I imagined that toward the end of the last glacial period, during the ice melt, when the climate was cooler and wetter, trout from the Yellowstone and the Missouri were able to penetrate even to the Gulf of Mexico and came up the Platte, the Arkansas and the Rio Grande from their lower ends, later to be restricted to headwaters by a warmer and drier climate. It was in such a way that other trout from the Pacific moved south to the then cooler water around the tip of Baja, California, into the Sea of Cortez, up a few rivers in Mexico, up the Colorado and into the Gila. That may be how the Mexican goldent trout, the Apache trout and the Gila trout, all closely related, came to be where they are today. But it hardly explains the distribution of cutthroats.

Before man altered and desecrated the environment, the distribution of native fish (at least in the mountainous West and in the North) was controlled and shaped by the last major push of the ice, the stage we call the Wisconsin. At its maximum the Wisconsin ice sheet covered practically all of Canada, parts of the northern states and the higher parts of our western mountains.

Fish survived in suitable habitats south of the ice, in unglaciated pockets and in streams issuing from the snouts of ice lobes pushing into intermontane valleys. Then, as the climate warmed, the ice began to recede and the cold-adapted fish followed it back, re-invading their former range and entering new territory, aided by the proglacial lakes that formed along the ice margins. These lakes, though short-lived, were vast, covering low divides between drainages and some drained first one way and then another, contributing to a wide dispersal of fish. Some species probably found their way to watersheds where they hadn't occurred before.

Strange things happened in those times. The Peace, an Arctic watershed, drained the upper Fraser Basin across what is now the Continental Divide; glacial Miette Lake, also in the Fraser Basin, flowed east and south across the Divide to the Athabaska and North Saskatchewan; and the Columbia tapped the Thompson Basin of the Fraser. Through these avenues some species of fish passed both ways. Small wonder that trout turn up in strange places, inexplicable by present land barriers.

The Wisconsin glaciation, being the last, is the one we know most about. There were three others going back a million years or more, each obliterating the traces of its predecessor as it oozed and gouged its way across the land, and each being followed by an interglacial period with climates similar to or warmer than we now have. Trout and other cold water fish had to adapt to these vast alterations each time, surviving in glacial refuges beyond the limits of the ice and then re-invading the glaciated areas as the ice melted back. It is quite possible that at least some of the races of trout evolved to their present form and became established in certain watersheds prior to the Wisconsin, although we have little knowledge of the pattern of prior drainage in the glaciated areas.

The Colorado River cutthroat, *Salmo clarki pleuriticus*, was one of the "headwater transfer" divide jumpers. Its ancestors probably reached the upper Green, the Colorado's principal tributary, from the upper Snake, the tributaries of both abutting along their common divide in many places. From the Green they pretty well infiltrated the upper Colorado system. But they never penetrated below the mouth of the San Juan River in the state of Colorado, which rules out an ascent from below, for there are tributaries below the San Juan that could have provided suitable habitat but contain no native trout.

My travels in seeking them now had been around the south end of the Wyoming Range and into the Bridger Basin, then up the broad valley of the Green. I had no definite locale in mind, except that somewhere in the Green's tributaries flowing east from the Wyoming Range there must be some relatively pure strains of Colorado cutthroats.

The valley of lower Horse Creek was wide, flat ranchland with hay meadows and pastures. Small bands of antelope stared as I passed, curious and unafraid. Sage hens yielded the right-of-way reluctantly, lumbering off the track to crouch in the roadside weeds and grass. As I approached the mountains, Horse Creek veered away to the south, then split into two forks, North and South Horse creeks, and when the water swung back to the road again I was on North Horse Creek and right at the gate of the mountains.

Here, as I approached the road's end, the valley pinched down, bordered by steep timbered slopes with occasional willow flats along the bottom. A forest ranger drove in with a horse trailer as I was rigging up. We talked about the country and its fish as he unloaded and saddled up. Before he rode off he suggested I try Lead Creek, a small tributary I had crossed on my way up. He said Lead Creek had the purest stock of Colorado cutthroats in the area, a bit of information I filed for future reference.

Clambering down toward the water I sensed that old surge of excitement that attends fishing a new stream with the prospect of catching a new race of trout. North Horse Creek was a sight to gladden one's heart, a beautiful stream about thirty feet wide, chattering away over a freestone bed, the water absolutely clear and cold as ice. I elected to explore downstream first and to concentrate on the best spots on the way back. The few trout I hooked on my downstream wet fly weren't really big enough to identify as pure Colorados or hybrids. Much of the stream was shallow, its bed scoured by recent flood, but in pools behind logjams and in deep runs against willow-bordered cutbanks I turned a few good fish.

The afternoon of intermittent sun gave way to clouds and I could hear thunder muttering and grumbling back in the hills. I started back, hoping to fish the best lies before the storm hit and one in particular, tucked in a tight bend against a high bank with a wide gravel bar on my side. Of the trout rising near the pool's head I judged one to be a nice fish by its swirl. It came for the floater I tied on but missed, then ignored my second drift but took on the third try and struggled all over the pool. When I worked this trout onto the gravel bar, it measured 14 inches, heavy and deep, but hardly a Colorado. Though bright orange on belly, gillcovers and cheeks, its markings were those of a fine-spotted Snake River cutthroat. I got the hybrid's picture anyway and hurried on. Halfway back I got caught. Behind the thunder rattling and booming down the canyon came sheets of rain. A nearby spruce thicket provided no shelter so I made for The Beetle and then for the one bar in Daniel.

Morning, crisp and bright, revealed new snow adorning peaks of the Windrivers, and I could see white also on the far ridges of the Wyoming Range. Lead Creek, my day's objective, required retracing the route of the day before. I noted the antelope and sage hens had weathered the storm and also were enjoying the sun's warmth. The trail the forest ranger told me about turned onto a narrow rocky track, over a low ridge through spruce thickets and lodgepoles to the edge of a great willow flat. Somewhere in that willow jungle was Lead Creek. Rank sedges hid old beaver canals, holes and burrows that I found only by stumbling into them. When I found Lead Creek I spent several hours poking about and wallowing around through the willows, but the only thing I scared up was a cow moose. She went across the flat in a swinging trot, throwing her head from side to side to better see what had spooked her.

I gave up, too, hot, sweaty and exasperated. I would have to find my Colorado cutthroats elsewhere.

Rummaging through unpublished manuscripts on trout back in my camper, I found Bob Behnke's statement unequivocally locating a pure population of Colorado cutthroats in Rock Creek, a tributary of LaBarge Creek, which empties into the Green just below the village of LaBarge. Clearly I hadn't done my homework properly and the folly of having left a three-bar town for a place having only one was underscored.

LaBarge was only fifty miles back down the road, so I retraced my route, turned The Beetle up LaBarge Creek and, finally, to the junction of Rock Creek. A few hundred yards upstream, a man and his son were skidding poles up a trail with a team of horses to build a fence around the creek's upper section. The Wyoming Fish and Game Department was trying to prevent cattle from trampling down the stream banks, they said, and I also learned from them the location of the barrier that had been built to keep the native Rock Creek cutthroats isolated from the LaBarge Creek hybrids.

It was heartening to hear that Wyoming really was committed to protecting remnant populations of native trout.

I was glad I hadn't worn my hip boots as I labored up the trail, for as I paused for breath and looked back, the valley literally seemed to fall away behind me to a few scattered aspens, spruce and pine in the narrow bottom. The upper slopes, bare except for scattered mahogany thickets, finally flattened into a hanging valley of sorts. There I found the barrier, a wooden structure with a vertical drop of several feet, the boundary between possible hybrids and pure Colorado cutthroats.

The tiny stream, almost obscured by rank, drooping sedges, was unfishable until I came upon a beaver dam with a pool at its downstream base. I could see a trout nosing about where the water trickled under the dam, alert for anything that might come its way, but I couldn't cast or even raise my rod from where I crouched. I backed away and came up the other side where I could toss in a nymph. The fish turned to meet the fly and gulped it. The trout made for snags at the dam's base, but I held on easily and soon had the creature on the grass.

It was a ten-incher and a perfect example of a pure Colorado! The fish's back and upper sides were brassy golden, shading to yellowish lower down and finally to pink on the belly. The gillcovers were carmine and the slash marks the reddest I have ever seen on a cutthroat. The coal black spots were large and round, profuse on the caudal area, becoming smaller and fewer further forward, with spots both above and below the lateral line. Altogether this was a beautiful fish and I took a number of phtographs for the record.

Then, crouching low, I came up and peeked over the dam. It was an old one but still in good repair, impounding at least a quarter of an acre of water, deep and dark between the thick beds of milfoil. Against the far shore, where dead trees and bushes thrust their gray skeletons above the surface, a few trout were rising. I managed a long cast and hooked a good trout, a 12-incher, colored exactly like the first except this one's belly and gillcovers were blood red and even its lower fins were red-tinted. I filmed this specimen, too, before moving on, for the ruckus had put the other trout down.

Just above was another dam and another pond with trout cruising in open water, but I failed to hook any and moved up to yet another dam and smaller pond still holding good trout. I caught only one from this last of the beaver ponds, then explored upstream, hooking smaller fish in miniature plunge pools. They differed from their larger kin in having less color — white bellies, pink gillcovers and, of course, parr marks.

It appeared that the larger the fish the brighter the colors, and I wondered what a two-foot pure Colorado would look like.

Puzzled by my failure to solidly hook half of the trout inspecting my fly, I returned to the middle pond to experiment. From a perch where I could see into the depths I waited until a nice trout cruised into view, investigating everything that looked interesting. The trout came, slowly and deliberately, to the nymph I sent out, took the offering in its mouth, chewed on it a few times, spit it out and moved on. Perhaps four seconds had elapsed, ample time to strike had I been so minded, but I hadn't felt a thing and wouldn't have known that I had a taker had I not seen the entire affair.

Another trout came nosing to the nymph in the same leisurely way, took the fly and mouthed it, but in raising my rod, I pulled the fly out of its maw and the fish dashed off.

Is pure chance as important as timing in hooking a fish? I wondered.

As the sun neared the western ridge top I started back down the mountain too, satisfied that I had finally found, caught and photographed the real, pure strain of Colorado cutthroats. It was even more satisfying to know that others also will experience that feeling, now that Wyoming cares enough about these fish to build barricades to keep them pure and to fence headwaters to enhance their habitat.

But for a single encounter, two miles above sea level in the shadow of the Mummy Range, I was one hundred years too late to find the greenback cutthroat, *Salmo clarki stomias*, a more recent relative of the Colorado, with the same divide-jumping propensities. That occurred in a tiny unnamed creek, near a stream designated by a forest service sign as "Never Summer Creek." How the greenback got there makes our ultimate meeting still more interesting.

Somewhere in the neighborhood of Colorado's South Park, high on the backbone of the continent, ancestors of the greenbacks crossed from the headwaters of the Colorado to the headwaters of the South Platte and from there across another divide to the Arkansas, changing their affiliation from the Pacific to the Atlantic. This likely occurred during unstable drainage when the last ice sheet melted back. When things got straightened out, they found themselves unwitting victims of circumstances, as not even fish would willingly move from Pacific to Atlantic. Fortunately, they didn't have far to go. Ecological barriers blocked their downstream progress and they remained in the spectacularly beautiful high country of the Southern Rockies.

The greenbacks have had a rough time since man first began to introduce species of fish where they didn't belong. They have been hybridized by other cutthroats and rainbows and displaced by brown trout and eastern brook trout until, finally, there are only a few remnant populations persisting in tiny headwater streams overlooked by the fish stockers.

The state of Colorado more recently has had an active greenback restoration program, but many efforts have ended in failure. They are persisting and, should they continue to persevere, ultimately will restore this unique trout to a viable population. They are too late, though, to help the yellowfin cutthroat, *Salmo clarki macdonaldi*, which lived in harmony with the greenbacks in Twin Lakes, Colorado. It was said to have been a deep water form, much larger than the greenbacks with small "star" shaped spots on a silvery background and with yellowish fins. Seven preserved specimens are all that remain of this subspecies of cutthroat for with the introduction of non-native trout before the turn of the century it disappeared along with the greenbacks from Twin Lakes and as this was the only place in the world where it occurred, the yellowfin joined the ranks of the Dodo. You or I or future generations will never see or catch a yellowfin, thanks to the untiring efforts of the fish culturists.

I came into the greenback country from the northwest, down the Green River, over the Uintas, across the Colorado Plateau, crossing the Continental Divide at Rabbit Ears Pass and, finally, North Park to a campsite at the foot of the Medicine Bows. From there the headwaters of the Cache la Poudre lay just across Cameron Pass, ancestral greenback waters, and within easy striking distance.

Late August produced beautiful, bright warm days and cold, frosty nights, perfect weather to be in the mountains. At first light I drove up and across Cameron Pass and down to the Poudre, ten miles from the summit. Such an idyllic mountain stream amidst alpine grandeur didn't fit my recollections of the South Platte system where its passage across the High Plains is in uninspiring, muddy channels.

And while I hadn't expected to find the Poudre an unfished stream, for most of Colorado's population lives along a belt at the east foot of the Front Range, the evidence of fishing pressure was considerably more than I had wished for. Discarded bait cans, empty packets once holding snelled hook rigs, and snarls of monofilament cluttered the valley's well-traveled trail. Thankful I was there on a weekday, at least, and out of the way of weekend mobs, I left my walking shoes on and hiked upstream for nearly two hours.

The pools below me eventually looked too inviting and I reasoned that I had gone far enough. I was wrong. The fish were non-native — rainbows, eastern brook and a few hybridized cutthroats — and my steps back to The Beetle were leaden with disappointment.

Once again I turned to the expertise of Bob Behnke. He had told me of a tiny unnamed stream, draining into the Cache la Poudre, which contained trout that, if not pure natives, were only slightly hybridized and looked to all outward signs like good greenbacks. Another early morning departure put me back up Cameron Pass, but off on a side road, about twenty-five miles from camp. When I reached road's end I was almost at the boundary of Rocky Mountain National Park.

I found Never Summer Creek there, well-named, for though it was still August, the grass was white with frost and shell ice had formed around the puddle margins. Summer is always brief above 10,000 feet, of course, even at forty degrees north latitude.

Oriented by Never Summer Creek, I backtracked to the un-named creek Behnke had mentioned — so small when passing under the road in an unobtrusive culvert, it was little wonder I had missed it. Waiting until the sun had burned off some of the frost, I followed tiny plunge pools upstream but found no fish until reaching a meadow, lush and green, spongy and wet underfoot like Arctic tundra. A trout in the first long pool saw me first and I used more caution in approaching the next, on hands and knees. My nymph hesitated midway in its first drift and when I raised my rod I was fast to my first greenback.

It was only a chunky eight inches, with spots round and large, the biggest ones larger than the pupil of its eye. The spots were largest and most concentrated on the caudal area, becoming smaller and less numerous forward, but well distributed over the sides as well. The trout's belly, lower fins and gillcovers were salmon covered with the back and sides greenish yellow. The slash marks were crimson and although it was a small fish there were no parr marks of immaturity. I had finally hit pay dirt. Quickly, before they faded, I recorded the fish's colors on film.

Another fish at the head of a tiny pool and one from an undercut bank were almost identical to the first in size, spotting and coloration, a good sign of purity of stock. Finally satisfied I had fished almost to the little stream's source, I returned to a dry knoll in the meadow and sat awhile to warm my soggy knees and elbows, for my serpentine progress upstream had been damp and cold. The sun felt especially good as its warmth seeped through me.

Summer was almost gone in this "never summer" country. Only a few purple asters and yellow cinquefoils still bloomed. Most flowering plants already had set their seeds. A pervading stillness enveloped the land — not a breath of wind or call of bird — and the meadow seemed to be brooding under the somber, spruce-covered ridges, as if waiting for the mantle of white soon to cover it and the frost to seal its seeps.

But spring would come again in due time. Flowers would bloom, the birds would sing and the greenbacks would spawn in their home creek. I thought of other meadows in other mountains, and of the trout that led me to those high, beautiful places.

All life, plant and animal, is similar at the high altitudes of the mountainous West. Yet each mountain range, each meadow, is different from the other. Sometimes the differences are subtle, hardly discernible. Yet each has its own character, something unique, and each has its own trout, all differing somewhat.

Were it not for the trout and their differences I would never have seen this meadow, or multitudes of others. I would not have known the high crags of the divides, the awesome glacial cirques and the tumbling clear streams that drained them.

I have still other trout to find, fortunately, to lead me to the high places again. The quest is not over, will never be over. When my legs someday fail to bear me, I will have my memories of the high places and my dreams of the trout that call them home.

CHAPTER 10

Rio Grande Cutthroats · 1

A FAR-FLUNG INTELLIGENCE system is helpful in seeking clues to the whereabouts of relict native trout populations. The nature of my old job and my hobby put me in contact with people who poke around in the wild places, in remote wilderness areas far from roads and easy access.

Thus I learned of the trout in the tiny streams rising in the high country of the Jemez Mountains of New Mexico. Don Stanley had been up there hunting and had seen these fish in the extreme headwaters of the Rio Puerco, a stream so small and fragile that its uppermost pools were isolated from one another, the water going underground in between.

The Rio Puerco is a western tributary of the Rio Grande, so it seemed plausible that these trout might be the Rio Grande cutthroat, *Salmo clarki virginalis*, possibly pure strain or nearly so. Plans were laid, then and there, to probe this mountain wilderness and to meet those trout on their own turf.

The following June found Jack James and me in Albuquerque where Don lived, in between his jaunts into the mountains. Don had arranged with a rancher friend to pack us in, once we had checked in with the New Mexico Fish and Game Department. The Albuquerque district supervisor, Tom Rogers, was a friend of Don's, a typical old-time lawman, a game warden of the old school, long-geared and laconic, full of dry wit and desert humor.

Rogers looked like a man more at home astride a horse than an office chair. The placard on his desk read: "I'm a tobacco chewer. If you don't blow on me, I won't spit on you."

Fair enough! I put my pipe in my pocket.

Tom called in Mike Hatch, a fisheries biologist, and Mike assured us there were indeed pure Rio Grande cutthroats in the Jemez Mountains, pointing out on a map the streams where they occurred, the Rio Puerco among them.

At Don's house we sorted gear into pack boxes, culling and high-grading with a heavy hand, hoping to get by with just one pack horse. That meant just so much food per man per day, mostly freeze-dried to save weight, and the clothes on our backs plus spares in case of a drenching. Also, jackets, slickers, foot gear, cookery, bedrolls, tent, cameras, maps and fishing tackle. And axe, ropes, shovel, horse gear. Lastly, of course, a reasonable supply of strong spirits in case of snake bite or other terrors of the trail.

Dawn found us on the road, our gear in the back of a pickup and Don's black mare in tow in a "horse pullman," up the valley of the Rio Grande, northwest through the Jemez and Zia Indian reservations, through desert plains and broken, contorted country where junipers and pinons struggled to maintain life in the harsh and arid land.

Our turnoff, a mere track, climbed through oaks and ponderosa to the trailhead on San Jose Creek and rendezvous with Bill Humphries and his neighbor, Gary Nelson, with a truckload of horses. With Don's mare we each had a mount and one to pack.

We saddled the horses and surveyed the mound of gear to be loaded on Ichabod, the pack horse. The pack boxes, already balanced, were slung from the saw bucks, the rest hefted and placed according to weight and bulk with a tarp thrown over the lot. Then bill uncoiled his lash rope, threw it over and around, made his hitches and tightened it up with a mighty heave. Ichabod objected to this, laid back his ears, lashed his tail and looked around in disapproval. But the load was on and secure and we mounted up and started out.

Gary headed the procession as we began our long climb into

the San Pedro Parks, one of the few remaining strongholds of the Rio Grande cutthroats, the race named *virginalis* by Girard in 1856. The trail crossed and recrossed San Jose Creek, and at every crossing Gary's mount reared and shied. Only a good dig with the spurs would persuade the horse to cross. It was a desert-bred animal and had never seen running water before. The other horses plodded across without protest, their hooves making sucking sounds as they dragged them out of the mud.

I was riding "drag," the last one in the string, and so I was enveloped in a haze of dust along the dry benches. I could smell it, along with the slightly astringent scent of aspens mixed with the smells of sweating horses, wet saddle blankets and leather. The sounds also fit the setting — the tinkling song of the brook, the clop of horses' hooves and the creaks of saddles and pack.

From my vantage point at the rear I could see the string move up the trail, the horses cautiously picking their footing, the riders swaying slightly with the motion of the animals, ducking occasionally to dodge a branch, and the pack on Ichabod lurching a little with every step. I thought of the mountain men a century and a half back in time. They had come up here with their pack strings, probably over this very same trail, their goals the tiny headwater streams on top, as were ours.

The sights, sounds and smells were the same then as now, though they had beaver traps in their packs and carried flintlock rifles while our working tools were fly rods and cameras. But the scene was the same.

We switchbacked over the nose of a ridge and stopped to let the horses blow. I looked back down the gash in the mountain through which we had come, to the sere plains below, across the Jicarilla Apache Indian lands simmering in the hot, yellow glare of high noon as far as the eye could span to the blue horizon. Up here it was a different world. Cool, fragrant aspen leaves quaked in the high, thin air. I could see the whole gamut of life zones at a glance, from Lower Sonoran on the desert, to the Hudsonian (where we were), and everything in between. The distance was not great but the contrast was extreme.

The horses had their wind at last, and we continued, breaking out on a long, sloping meadow at the top. The creek was stilled, broken into trickles and seeps from sidehill bogs where grew rank stands of hellebore. It looked like a good place to noon so we dismounted, secured the horses, found some convenient logs to sit on and munched our sandwiches.

Almost immediately a gray jay sailed in on silent wings and perched on a nearby spruce bough, waiting expectantly, ready and willing to share lunch with us. Share it he did, accepting our offerings with utmost confidence. These gray ghosts are symbolic of wilderness areas, common across North America wherever boreal forests occur. They will invariably seek out travelers and campers at mealtime, the proverbial uninvited guests. They are quiet, trusting souls, in contrast with other members of the jay tribe, and their presence is seldom detected until they are there with you, often at arm's length.

The Cree Indians and Metis living in the subarctic around James Bay had an intriguing legend about these bits of fluff. They assured me these were not just birds, but actually the souls of lost trappers and voyageurs. Therefore the Cree would not harm them, although everything else that moved in the bush ended up in their cooking pot if they could arrange it. The common name "whiskey-jack" probably is an Anglo corruption of the Cree name, *weeska-jonish.*

Lunch over, we made minor adjustments to our saddle girths and Ichabod's pack and were off again on top of the San Pedro Parks. The trail was almost level through dense strands of fir and spruce and then through open vegas, mountain meadows with brilliant displays of spring wild flowers. For being mountainous it was gentle country, a vast rolling plateau, probably the worn-down stump of a huge granitic batholith that had bulged up through the earth's crust eons ago. Probably it had never been glaciated, had never felt the grinding crush of the cordilleran ice lobe that had stalled just short of this uplifted mass.

When we came out on a long, winding vega to the headwaters of the Rio Puerco, the tiny channel meandering through the meadow was dry; there had been almost no snow the winter before and no runoff. In another vega, the headwaters of the Rio de las Vacas, there was water. We turned up a side draw to a majestic stand of old growth fir and made camp close to all we needed — wood, shelter, water and graze for the horses.

Bill and Gary brought out their fly rods which were stout enough to land a marlin, and when I tagged along to the Vacas, Bill looked dubiously at my little Orvis, commenting, "You don't laugh at me, I won't laugh at you."

The creek made tight little meanders, all of two feet wide at the pools and only half of that in between. The fitful, gusting wind added to our challenge. The wind took my tentative first cast and my fly landed on the grass along the bank. On the next cast the wind slackened and the fly found the grass on the other side. Bill's eyes twinkled but he didn't laugh in commenting, "Little bit early in the day for trout to be out in the meadow."

I agreed. Should have waited until dark, I thought. Then, at least, no one could see me flogging the meadow. So I got down to business — down on hands and knees — and crawled close enough to lash out a short line and hit the water.

I carefully examined the first six-incher I made contact with. Too many spots, I thought, and too round. I ran a fingernail over the base of the tongue. No teeth. Hybrids, probably Yellowstone blood mixed with rainbows. Damn the hatcheries! The consolation that they were stream-bred wasn't enough to keep fishing what ichthyologists call a hybrid swarm.

A timely hail from camp summoned us to chow. Jack and Don had been busy at the fire and we completely demolished their culinary efforts as well as making serious inroads into our supply of snake bite cure. Bill and Gary hurried to get down and off the mountain, leaving Icahbod and these parting words, "Ich don't amount to much, but you can ride him, pack him and, if things get really tough, eat him."

They rode off, completely immune to any rattlesnakes lurking along the trail. Fortunately for Ich and for us, too, we didn't have to resort to Bill's last option.

When the fire burned low we turned in to escape the cold that creeps in at 10,000 feet when the sun sinks behind the ridge. Every star glittered in the black dome overhead, some looking close enough to pluck. The wind soughed through the old growth firs and the horses nickered from time to time. I heard it all for I had neglected to bring an air mattress and sleep came slowly and then only at brief intervals. My contours just didn't mesh with those of the ground.

We were up at first light, a crackling fire boiling the coffee, cooking powdered eggs and frying bacon while Don gathered up the horses. Agreeing to concentrate on streams known to have pure stocks of *virginalis*, Jack prepared to hike over a low divide to the top of Clear Creek while Don and I decided to backtrack to the Rio Puerco, cutting it lower down where there might be some water.

Saddling up after camp chores, I tied to Ich's left side, facing forward, a saddle scabbard I always use to pack my fly rod by horseback. All went well until I tried to slip the metal tube into the scabbard. Ich would have none of it, rearing back and pulling against the halter rope with all the strength he could muster to the accompaniment of cracking hitch poles and much shouting.

The ruckus spooked the black mare and she did the same, pulling loose the stump to which she was tied and racing off across the meadow, kicking at the stump each time it bounded into the air. When things quieted we retrieved the horses, tied them to more secure moorings and this time I reversed the scabbard so the rod case could be slipped in from the rear. What Ich couldn't see, he didn't object to.

Don and I came to the Puerco lower than where we had crossed the day before, but it still was dry so we continued down until a few wet places turned into a trickle and a few sidehill springs contributed more until it was almost a creek or at least a rill. Further exploration would be afoot so we tied the horses and strung our rods. Our tiny stream, purling through a narrow wooded valley, was joined by a tributary from the south and we proceeded more cautiously but still scared some little fellows dashing from the shallows back to their hidy-holes.

Don suggested we might find bigger water and bigger fish below and when the valley opened into another meadow there was a glint of water at the far end. A beaver pond! Surely here would be trout of greater dimensions. Picking our way across the meadow through knee high clumps of shrubby cinquefoils until the water backed into the grass, we viewed a half-acre of open water with occasional rings of rising trout. I crept out to a small point, knelt in the wet grass and mire, but every time I got enough line in the air to reach rising fish my backcast hung up on the cinquefoil. I backed off to dry ground to reappraise.

I considered the far side where I could reach fish rising close inshore if I could find an opening for a backcast, and I found it in a small cove with a corridor between boles of old growth fir that had shed lower limbs. There I sat at water's edge, waiting for cruising trout.

A raven sailed overhead and peered at me, croaking. It and a companion, maybe its mate, had kept me under close surveillance ever since we had come to the meadow. No doubt they kept all resident creatures advised of our whereabouts and what we were up to.

But the trout didn't heed their warning and continued rising. I got out my pipe and tobacco pouch and had the bowl tamped half-full when a trout cruised into my cove. It was a dandy, maybe a foot long! I quietly put the pipe down, picked up the rod and sailed out a cast. The nymph touched the water, the trout whirled, glided up and engulfed it. When I tightened, the fish was hooked solidly; fortunately, for there were snags edging the cove. But this fish was unable to bore out of the cul-de-sac and soon was in hand.

A beautiful male still flaunting nuptial coloring, this trout was a real, undiluted Rio Grande cutthroat in all respects. Its carmine-plated gillcovers, cardinal slash marks and bright orange tints along the belly contrasted with the gray-green over the back and along the sides. Jet black, large irregular spots clustered in profusion near the tail, becoming fewer and smaller along the back. I ran a fingertip across the base of its tongue, feeling the sharp little prickles known to ichthyologists as basibranchial teeth.

Overcoming waves of elation, I laid this beauty out on the canvas of my creel, fins and tail spread to best advantage, uncased my camera and took shots from all angles at stops below and above the aperture indicated by the light meter. Maybe one or two would be nearly as perfect as the fish.

I retrieved and lit my pipe and took up my vigil again. The next fish to enter the cove took the same nymph but this one was a female, about the same size but more silvery and less highly colored than the male; I photographed it to record the color variations between the sexes. The scenario was repeated, but this one I gently unstuck and steered back to the depths, wishing it well, more growth and many successful spawning seasons.

When I resumed my now well-worn seat at water's edge and glanced over the pond, a broad wake was cleaving the placid surface in my direction. At the apex of the lines of wavelets was a wide brown head, tilted up slightly and topped by two rounded ears. As it moved slowly closer I could see the beady black eyes had me in focus. They belonged to the rightful owner of the property, undoubtedly, the patron. Pausing momentarily abreast of my cove, the beaver made a final inspection with its near eye, then plunged with a mighty surge, its tail whacking the pond's surface like a rifle shot. Gone, too, were the trout. Don came along about now.

"Somebody shoot at you?" he grinned.

"Maybe old beaver was trying to tell us something," I mused, "like 'Andale!'"

So go we did. The sun was riding low in the west anyway. Topping the trail's first steep pitch, we stopped to blow and Don, looking back toward the pond aglow in the sun's slanting rays, commented, "Most beautiful trout I ever saw. Sure glad we came up here."

I managed a nod and a grunt as we continued on into the horses'

sight. They nickered softly in welcome, glad to be untied and headed for camp and pasture.

Yet another stream within our reach, the Rito Resumidero, was a tributary of the Rio Puerco, but a different one — a Rio Puerco that flowed to the northeast and into the Chama. Streams bearing the same name are not uncommon; there are uncounted Willow, Bear, Deer and Trout creeks, among others, but it is unusual to find two hog rivers with their headwaters on opposite sides of the same mountain!

Early in the morning we saddled up and were away, this time without the excitement of a mini-rodeo. Jack elected to walk again with Don and I astride the horses, Ichabod being quite content as long as he couldn't see the rod case out of the corner of his eye.

The trail to the Resumidero climbed out of the valley of the Vacas, skirting Vega del Oso and crossing Oso Creek, a mere rillet at this point. Presently we broke out on a high open bench overlooking Vega Redonda, a vast basin bordered by steep slopes and sheer cliffs. The view was magnificent and we stopped a while to look and marvel.

Farther on, the trail dropped down to a saddle at the north end of the Vega, then picked up a wee tributary of the Oso and on down to its junction with the parent stream. We were lower now, back into the long needled ponderosas and the oaks.

We found the Resumidero where it started, at the joining of Oso and Corralitos creeks. Between the two they created a fair-sized stream all of a yard wide and with a moderate volume of water.

Jack went back up the Oso, exploring for trout and whatever else might turn up. Don and I tied our horses and walked down the trail paralleling the Resumidero to fish back up to the junction. In about a half mile we left the trail and cut back to the stream, or rather to where the stream should have been, for it was gone . . . vanished . . . gone underground.

We started back up the creekbed, knowing water had to be some-somewhere ahead. In a couple of hundred yards we found it, first wet places on the gravel, then isolated shallow pools and shortly thereafter flowing water. The Rito Resumidero was alive and well again clear as glass.

We found a few nice pools amid heaps of great boulders and along water-worn ledges of bedrock, but the trout were few and the few we saw were small. So we didn't take any. We reasoned that if what we had seen was any indication of the total trout population then every single one should be left for breeding stock.

Jack had preceded us back to camp. He too had seen only a few trout in his progress up the Oso and we hoped that the few that were there would proliferate. Fortunately the rainy season was almost at hand so at least there would be more water. But it takes more than mere water. Trout just don't emerge from the mud as swallows were once said to do.

After our camp supper of freeze-dried beef stroganoff we set out to gather the horses which had been turned out to graze. At dark we returned to camp, horseless, to discuss probabilities. In an earlier time frame in that country we would have figured that the Utes or Apaches had them and we were lucky to have our hair still attached to our skulls. Times had changed and at first light Don was backtracking the main trail while Jack and I searched nearby, agreeing to meet at the Puerco beaver pond about noon if we hadn't found the horses before then. Naturally I took my fly rod.

When I arrived at the beaver pond, before Jack, the trout were rising and I sneaked around to my cove. A trout cruised in but apparently only for a siesta as it resisted all offerings for ten or so minutes. When the trout finally stirred and accepted my nymph the feel of steel woke it all at once. When the fish had recovered from the shock and the fight I released it. Jack came up the far side just as I lost another trout and my tippet in another part of the pond..

"Found some tracks back in the timber but lost them in a vega," he said. "They were headed this way."

Tracks were all I had seen too and probably they had not been made by our horses. I recalled a time in my youth, hot on the trail of a deer in New Hampshire's snowy hills, when I reported that night in camp all the tracks I had seen. An old-timer looked at me quizzically, shook his head and observed, "Them tracks makes awful thin soup."

Make mighty poor saddle stock, too, I thought, as Jack rummaged in the recesses of his jacket pockets and came up with a fistful of jerky to share with me. As we gnawed on the squaw candy, a cowboy rode toward us and asked first about fishing and then about cows.

I allowed fishing was fair and Jack reported seeing ten head the day before, including "a big, brindled brute with horns like a longhorn."

The cowboy beamed.

"Ha," he chortled, "wondered where the old heifer was!"

When I asked if he'd seen any horses, he reported spotting a black and a bay, both hobbled, "back up the trail about a quarter mile."

We thanked our visitor profusely and wasted no time moving uphill as fast as the thin air of 10,000 feet would allow, huffing and puffing, and still munching on our jerky. The cowboy's estimate turned out to be a "mountain quarter" — nearer a half-mile — or maybe just the difference between being mounted and afoot.

We rounded a bend, spotted the horses, removed the hobbles and started for camp. They had been hobbled so long they crow-hopped a ways before realizing their fetters were gone. Don rode into camp before dark on a horse he had borrowed from Bill Humphries down on the flatlands. He had put in a long, hard day, and we felt a little sheepish telling him how our horses had almost found us while we fished at the beaver pond.

Next day we broke camp and returned to the hot, dry desert. I looked back at the brooding mass of the Jemez and remembered how it felt to be up there — in the cool, fragrant stands of old growth fir and spruce, the vegas green and bright with wildflowers, the tiny sparkling streams, the beaver pond and, above all, the beautiful trout.

I'll be back, I thought. Someday I'll make it back.

In Albuquerque we again called on Mike Hatch of the Department of Fish and Game to report what we had found. Mike listened patiently to our superlatives regarding the beauty of the Rio Grande cutthroats of the San Pedro Parks, then he said, "Wait until you see those in the headwaters of the Pecos! More highly colored . . . and the biggest spots you can imagine, like on green-backs!"

He got out a map and showed us exactly where. So we were hooked again. Don said he would make arrangements with a packer he knew. All that Jack and I needed to do was to be back in Albuquerque next spring at the right time. He would let us know then.

CHAPTER 11

Rio Grande Cutthroats - 2

THE INTERVENING WINTER was a wet one, all to the good following a year of drought, but it also meant a later departure for the Pecos Wilderness, as the Sangre de Cristos had shared in all the western mountains mantles of white. Don set rendezvous at mid-June, late enough for snow-melt but early enough to beat the violent thunderstorms spawned over the Southern Rockies in July.

Mid-June found Jack and me back in Albuquerque where Don had everything in readiness. We drove up the Rio Grande Valley to Santa Fe this time, then southeast following the route of the old Santa Fe Trail, across Glorieta Pass and on to the village of Pecos. Turning due north we followed the Pecos River, a beautiful stream but containing only brown trout and hatchery rainbows.

Climbing steadily we left behind the sagebrush, junipers and pinons for the oaks and ponderosas. At Tererro, consisting of a store and a few buildings where our packer headquartered, we learned our horses were further up the road in a meadow near trailhead. We found the meadow, the horses, and Hughie, the packer's son who would take us in. Hughie had a compadre, an old, leather-faced, broken-down vaquero. Between them they had our string ready in record time, pack horses tied head to tail, and we mounted up and were away.

Topography surrounding the trail we now rode contrasted sharply with that where we had been just the year before. The Jemez had been gentle mountains, steep-sided but plateau-like on top. We now were ascending the southern terminus of the Front Range of the Rockies — the Sangre de Cristos — the ancient core of the backbone of North America. Snow-capped peaks pierced the sky to the north and northwest, some over 13,000 feet, their names as intriguing as their mysterious mass — Santa Fe Baldy, Pecos Baldy, the Truchas (north, south and middle), and Cerro Chimayosos.

The life zones were similar to those of the Jemez, except here we could look up into the Arctic Alpine as well . . . the topmost, the roof of the world. We wound along the rim of Mora Canyon, snatching glimpses of the Rio Mora 2,000 feet straight down. Then it was up over Hamilton Mesa, a broad-backed hump whose top was an open plain, a vega carpeted with bunchgrass and brilliant with spring flowers.

Hughie stopped the string to let the horses blow. Being a trifle rump-sprung, I dismounted to ease my aching joints. The entire basin of the upper Pecos spread out before us, an amphitheater rimmed on three sides by glittering peaks, awesome sheer precipices and frowning timbered ridges. Naked rocks and dark forests contrasted sharply with the immaculate white of serrated peaks. The basin sloped gently toward the center to the main Pecos. Drainage lines fanned out through the furrows in the blue-green forested slopes. Each furrow contained a tiny stream and, in some of these, at their headwaters, we would fish for the big-spotted Rio Grande cutthroats.

The horses rested, the riders satiated with grandeur, we pressed on off the flank of the mesa and into the timber. We wound down the slope to the Pecos, a beautiful trout stream but too low down for natives, and continued to its junction with the Rito del Padre and the once-upon-a-time site of Beatty's cabin. It was gone now, like the old prospector who was said to have fought off grizzly bears with foot-long knives, his only weapons. His diggings were hereabouts, but no one knows if he found anything. Perhaps his search for gold was only an excuse to live in this magnificent country — the trout at his doorstep were the real treasure. The entire upper Pecos watershed was stiff with pure, big-spotted Rio Grande cutthroats then — not brown trout, not rubber hatchery trout.

The trail forked, one following the Pecos, the other going up the Padre. We followed the Padre past a gash in the canyon wall where the crystal clear Rito Ceballosos gushed into the equally clear Padre. Where the Rito de los Chimayosos joined in we again forked, following the Chimayosos until we found what we sought, a streamside meadow, good graze for the horses, water, wood and shelter, and a flat place to pitch the tents. After a year of planning we had arrived. This was the threshold to the world of the big-spotted *Salmo clarki virginalis*, where those few that were left still lived.

Hughie left us after unloading the horses and taking a bite of lunch. He also left us three horses to ride and promised to be back at the appointed time to pack us out.

When the weather is fine, making camp is a pleasant chore, and so it was — warm and bright, with just enough breeze to shake the greenery on the aspens. We fashioned a lean-to with a tarp to store our saddles, pack boxes, grub and cookery. We made a table of sorts and a fireplace, put the tents up, laid out our bedrolls and brought in a supply of firewood. We lit a fire, put on the coffee and relaxed to assess our surroundings.

This meadow in a bend of the Chimayosos was almost level and carpeted with lush grass and sedges. It abutted against a steep, open slope on the north, an old river terrace terminating in a bench on top, where the trail wound through a scattering of open-grown firs and aspen with tough, wiry bunchgrass underfoot. On the creek's far side the ground rose abruptly, the steep slopes clothed in dense spruce and fir.

The Chimayosos was quite a stream at campsite, ten to fifteen feet wide in places, with numerous pools and pockets among the boulders and against the ledges. Chattering merrily on its way to join the Padre, it looked to be a perfect trout stream . . . had it only held natives instead of the ubiquitous browns. Don couldn't contain himself; he strung his rod and in a few minutes was back with a plump brown trout for the frying pan. It was a lovely fish, stream-bred and reflecting golden hues in the afternoon sun. But here it was out of place, like a leghorn rooster in a grouse covert.

Our camp was well-placed to reach the waters where the big-spotted cutthroats were reported to be, but we would need to go to the utmost headwaters above the natural barriers that enabled

these trout to persist without competition from the browns. There were only four of these tiny streamlets. Above our camp, the extreme headwaters of the Chimayosos was one, and its tributary, the Rito Azul; then the headwaters of the Rito del Padre and the uppermost stretch of the Rito Maestas that joined it lower down. And that's all there were . . . Nada mas.

I spent a restless night in my tent under the blue spruce. The creek babbled incessantly, loud and clear, but the sound alternately faded away, then mounted again as a gusty wind surged fitfully through the tree tops. I thought of these unique, big-spotted cutthroats in their four tiny creeks and of what might be done to insure their survival, to broaden their base.

Why couldn't a barrier be placed in the main Pecos at a suitable site in the canyon? Then, electrofish the waters between the natural barriers in the four creeks and the man-made barrier below to salvage what natives there might be. Next, treat everything between the barriers, including the tributaries, to remove all fish. Finally, once the exotic fish were eliminated, repopulate the waters with pure native stock from above.

It would be expensive, but it could be done, and at a fraction of the annual cost of producing rubber trout in hatcheries. I was aware of the rising groundswell of sentiment to manage suitable waters for wild fish. So, why not take that one extra step and manage for wild, *native* fish?

Having worked out that seemingly simple solution I dozed off and the next thing I knew it was dawn. The wind had died and the creek was talking louder than ever as I crawled out of my nest to look around. I snapped some dead branches from a spruce to kindle a fire. The horses heard me and nickered in greeting, anxious to get to their grazing. A doe mule deer and two yearlings, probably her last year's fawns, paused on the trail. They watched intently, every sense alert, their great ears aimed in my direction. After a minute or two, with a toss of their heads and a flick of their tails, they moved on, unhurried and unafraid.

As the fire began to pop and crackle, the rest of the camp came alive. Don went out to tend the horses and Jack rummaged around in the grub boxes. This was the day we had been waiting for. We planned to scout around, to explore in several directions separately, each of us on our own. When breakfast was over and the camp chores done, the sun's rays hit the top of the ridge. It was time to go. I set out for the Chimayosos headwaters on foot because it didn't look far on the map. But my map showed only horizontal distances, not the ups and downs.

I walked the trail on a bench above the creek, finally winding down again where the Azul joined in. The trail left the Chimayosos to follow the Azul so I took to the brush in the canyon which shortly became a maze of downed timber where a past storm had ripped through laying down giant trees like jackstraws. It was a case of crawl under, climb over, or go around — quite a task with fly rod in hand. By the time I had scrambled up through the chaotic jumble to a hanging valley above I was hot, scratched and exasperated. But the scene I had scrambled to was well worth the effort. The valley flattened, opening into a wide basin reaching to the furrowed slopes of the Truchas, their peaks burnished silver in the rays of the morning sun.

Concentrating on the stream with such a grand backdrop was like trying to fish the Snake River under the brooding mass of the Tetons. Gradually I became accustomed to the scene and could keep my eyes off the peaks and on the stream, four feet wide, flowing gently, burbling over shallow riffles and coasting through deeper runs into still deeper pools. The fish were few and I had no takes until I came upon a pool so deep the bottom was not visible even in the sparkling clear water. It was unfishable from three approaches because of brush and branches. I detoured to a ledge jutting into the pool from the far bank and pitched a short cast. On the third toss a great form materialized from the depths and turned back. When the fish turned I tightened and it was hooked fast, but not for long. The scrappy trout raced, splashed, made one jump and was gone; a good fish, too, possibly a foot or more. Fifty yards upstream I hooked a ten-incher that I "saved," as the Nova Scotians say, and laid it out on the sedges for the camera.

A gorgeous trout it was, greenish-blue along the back, shading into orange tints along the belly. The gillcovers and slash marks were brilliant crimson and the lower fins were tinged yellowish. Ichthyologists describe the size of spots in relation to the size of the pupil of the trout's eye, but these spots were almost as large as the eye itself! They crowded densely on the caudal portion, thinning and becoming smaller toward the head. Most of these were above the lateral line. The adipose fin was margined in coal black with one black spot exactly in the center.

Every time I see a new race of trout for the first time I think it is the perfection of beauty. Here was another to defy superlatives.

I sat there, contemplating my fish in the splendor of his mountain wilderness, thinking of this trout as the end result of thousands, perhaps hundreds of thousands, of years of evolution. Its ancestors had survived drought, floods, forest fires, headwater transfers and glaciation. Primordial progenitors roamed along the eastern shores of the North Pacific, entered the Columbia, ascended the Snake and, by some geological event, came into the headwaters of the Green and thus into the Colorado system.

By further headwater transfers those fish pioneers crossed the Continental Divide into the Rio Grande and into the Pecos; or, perhaps they went by way of the Arkansas and then into the Pecos, depending upon its possible relationship with the greenback cutthroat. During possibly several glacial periods ice lobes certainly pushed their snouts down this valley where I sat. The trout reinvaded after the ice melted.

So here it was now, 1,500 miles as a crow flies from its mother ocean and the brackish waters of the Columbia estuary, its ancestral home. It had traversed rain forests, deserts and lofty mountain ranges. It was perfected by eons of natural selection and adversity — a biological masterpiece — as beautiful as the wildflowers in the surrounding meadows.

Don and I tried the Rito Azul the following day and took the horses. They seemed better able to cope with the two-mile-high elevation, particularly in climbing. Our trail led back up the Chimayosos to the Azul junction and then climbed steeply along the canyon edge through cool shadows of dense stands of Englemann spruce and Douglas fir. On top and back into the sunlight of a rolling vega we pulled up to let our horses blow.

The stream, at trail level now, had shrunk to a streamlet meandering through miniature forests of lush hellebore, yellow-flowered cinquefoil and scattered shrub willows. A gentle breeze rippled through the bunchgrass, the harebells and gentians nodding their blue heads to the rhythm of the swaying grass. We tied our horses in an island of spruce where clumps of Indian paintbrush made splashes of orange-red in the greenery.

Surely this would have been a likely place for Eve to have conned Adam into that fateful chomp of the apple. But this garden had a trout stream and so was better than Eden!

The sun was warm on our backs as we stripped the saddles from our mounts and strung our rods. A pair of Clark's nutcrackers swooped overhead to see what was afoot in their domain, their strident calls seeming exceedingly loud in the exquisite alpine setting. We walked to the creek where the trail crossed. Don started down, hoping to find more and bigger water, and I went up to search each tiny run and pool.

I didn't, as far as I know, even scare a fish so I wandered back to the horses to meet Don. We found streamside shade for lunch and discussed the situation while munching on cheese and bread. Don had caught one trout and had seen a couple more down below. There, he said, a tributary augmented the flow considerably, and I elected to work through the canyon and hike back to camp from the Chimayosos. We resaddled the horses and Don rode out, leading my mount behind.

At timber's shade I entered the creek not far above the tributary where the Azul gained a more respectable volume. Just below the meeting of the waters Don had mentioned, I saw a trout, a sizeable fish holding in a slow run. I drifted a nymph toward it. The fish took on the second drift but came loose as so often happens when fishing downstream with a tight line. This was a good fish and I wanted it badly so I circled in from below where a big spruce offered cover. The trout was back in a few minutes and I dropped a nymph to the feeding lane. When it took again I nearly had the trout on the bank when we parted company. The spruce I lurked behind had its roots in the water and the trout dashed under them almost at my feet.

Since the trout hadn't seen me yet I waited and, sure enough, eventually it began to feed again. Another float or two and I had it pinned again. But it came loose and raced back under the roots. This time it was really spooked.

Under other circumstances I would have looked for another, but that hefty fish, by standards of the tiny creek, was the only one I had seen. After another long vigil behind the spruce it cautiously ventured out, slowly working back out to the feeding lane. On my third drift the fish made a move and I had it on again, for the *fourth* time. One doesn't often encounter a trout with such suicidal tendencies, I thought gratefully as I managed to work it away from the hidy-hole under the roots.

It had spectacular markings and was *big*, about 11 inches. This trout was more profusely spotted than those from the Chimayosos and more highly colored; its sides were washed with orange tints with three large orange blobs along the lateral line. Even some of the spots that should have been black as tar were orange. The gillcovers were bright orange and the prominent slash marks were crimson. It had spawned not long before, most likely, and still wore nuptial colors.

I photographed this specimen from all angles, in bright sun and shade; I wanted to get enough shots to insure one or two good ones, at minimum. Reflected glare from a wet fish is always a problem; I arrange them just so with the angle of the sun to minimize this glare. Using a polarizing filter helps but doesn't solve the problem by itself.

I sat there in the shade with a sense of well-being, happy with my conquest of the dazzling trout. The stream still purled along gently, as if holding back from the plunge to the canyon below. The altitude was well over 11,000 feet, the air thin and spicy with the pungency of spruce and fir. Overhead a few fluffy, popcorn cumulus clouds floated in blue sky; it was too early for the big, black thunderheads, which would come later in July.

I lit my pipe and lolled back against a mossy log, watching the blue smoke waft away through the blue-green bower. This was fabulous country with a colorful history dating back to the early 17th century when the first Spaniards founded their settlements in the Rio Grande valley to the west, the towns of Santa Fe and Taos. The river had been called Rio Bravo then and the Indians had roamed these mountains, the Utes and the Apaches, raiding the Spanish settlements and the peaceful pueblos along the river.

Later came the mountain men, the beaver trappers, many of whom headquartered in Taos. Possibly Kit Carson had worked this very stream for pelts as this was very near his home ground. I thought it very appropriate of the Spaniards to name the peaks from which this tiny stream drained the "Truchas," for truchas is trout in Spanish. Trout there were and still are, the real thing, the same race that crossed the Continental Divide eons ago. Exactly how they did this we may never know. Was it a headwater transfer from the Colorado? No matter, cross these trout did and though their remaining populations are few, their habitat shrunk to a few tiny streams, nevertheless they still persist.

The lowering sun roused me from my reverie. I had a ways to go and more exploring to do. The going got rougher as the ground fell away into the canyon, the stream bouncing and tumbling around huge boulders, logjams and ledges to form bubbly pools under the low barriers. The trout in those pools were cutthroats, probably washed down from above. I caught a few and released them. At the bottom where the Azul met the Chimayosos I found the trail back to camp.

After early breakfast and camp chores, Don and I saddled our mounts and headed for the Rito del Padre, cutting across a ridge and intercepting the main trail further up. Our path wound along a bench and steep sidehill, open but for scattered patches of aspen.

Below us the riffles of the Padre sparkled in the sun, but we pressed on as the stream here had been taken over by brown trout. The natives we sought were higher up.

When the trail dropped off the sidehill we forded the Padre and then its tributary, the Rito Maestas. Further on it switchbacked over a steep ridge, the edge of Padre Canyon. I was glad that my horse was mountain-bred for the footing was bad and only thin air lay between us and the bottom. The horses were lathered, their sides heaving when we broke out on top, so we pulled up to let them blow and to survey the scene.

We were on the crest of a terminal moraine where the snout of ice lobe grinding down the valley had stalled and melted back, leaving the great heap of glacial debris, a reminder from the Pleistocene. Above us the creek meandered through a green vega interspersed with narrow tongues of timber jutting in from the sides. We rode into the meadow and where the trail crossed the creek we tied our horses and strung our rods.

The view was spectacular against the Truchas with the long, sheer ridge culminating in the dome of Cerro Chimayosos, indeed the utmost headwaters of the Pecos system, above the brown trout and the domain of the big-spotted natives. The Padre was three to four feet wide and absolutely clear; the meadow reaches were deep, slow runs and undercut banks. Where the low-timbered ridges encroached, the stream tumbled in a series of cascades and plunge pools. There were trout . . . lots of them. Most were seven or eight inches, but there were a few ten, 11 and even 12 inches. We took a few for photographs; these were also highly colored, with bright orange bellies, gillcovers and slash marks, blue-green on their backs and sides. They had huge, irregular black spots concentrated toward the tail. All were the same, almost identical in coloring and spotting pattern, a characteristic found only in genetically pure strains.

The best trout I saw (at least the largest) is still there, or so I hope. It occupied a small plunge pool under a logjam where the lip of the fall was in the center forming a small eddy on each side, so small and shallow I was about to pass it up when I saw the trout. It lay in the part nearest me with hardly enough water to cover its back, investigating every item that swirled in the eddy. This trout was a foot long, *at least*, maybe more.

I sank to my knees behind a fir, for the trout was close; the morning sun behind me was an advantage. I dapped a fly into the eddy, then another and another of different sizes and patterns, practically the complete repertoire of my flybook. Each was duly investigated and refused. After using up several tippets in frequent fly changes, I gave up and carefully backed away from the pool.

Later I told Don about the choosy monster and on our way back to the horses we approached the pool carefully. I crawled up to find the fish still there and motioned Don to have a try. He made a couple of daps which the trout investigated before sliding into the fast water and disappearing. We had lost the advantage of the sunlight's angle and were perceived, no doubt, and now the game was over.

The following day the same trail took us toward the Rito Maestas, the last of the four little creeks known to have the big-spotted Rio Grande cutthroats, then we turned east on an old game trail. We tied the horses in a lush, open meadow, more cienaga than vega, for it was squishy and wet underfoot. Don opted to go above so I started down. There were a series of tiny pools in the stream small enough to step across. By kneeling upstream I could fish each of these crystal steps in the watery staircase with a very short line, the pool's levels not far below eye level.

There were trout in almost every one and I hooked several, a little less brightly colored than those in the Padre, but with the same huge spots and distribution pattern. I kept one for photographs and now had a complete series on film, one from each of the four little creeks.

We made the most of our last day in the high Pecos country, exploring the tiny watershed to its uppermost reaches and the lower canyon as well. Our ride out was an exercise in sheer beauty, all downgrade and easy on the horses. Through the meadows resplendent with spring flowers we moved between stringers of spruce, fir and patches of aspen. Then along the Padre to the junction of the Chimayosos and so back to camp.

CHAPTER 12

Redband Trout

"REDBAND TROUT? NEVER HEARD OF 'EM."

Thus spoke a grizzled old-timer as he impaled a fresh worm on a snelled Eagle Claw hook, pulled some strands of green algae from the two split shot sinkers and flung the rig back in the current.

"Nuthin' but rainbows in this crick," he added.

That was that, no doubt about it. The fact that he had three redbands strung on a willow stick and was plying his worms in ancestral redband water meant nothing to him. After all, any damned fool knows there are only two kinds of native trout — cuts and 'bows. Who ever heard of a redband?

To avoid an argument I couldn't possibly win, I hurried on upstream. I couldn't fault the old-timer as I myself had fished for, and caught, redbands in many different places for almost 40 years, secure in the belief I was catching ordinary rainbows. Some were odd-looking rainbows, to be sure, with tendencies toward orange and yellow tints on the lower sides, white tipped fins, brassy slash marks and wide, red bands along the lateral line. What I didn't know was that there are two kinds of rainbows, a coarse scaled coastal form and a fine scaled interior form, the redband.

I had caught redbands on the headwaters of the Fraser River (Kamloops trout) and elsewhere in British Columbia throughout the Caribou District and the Chilcotin. In Oregon I found them in the Klamath Basin, Klamath Lake, the Williamson River and in the stream's tributary to the desert basins of Eastern Oregon.

I remember one particular encounter with these fish. In British Columbia while searching for a place I could be reasonably sure of finding "pure Kamloops," I went to the Clearwater, a tributary of the North Thompson which drained into Kamloops Lake.

What better place to find Kamloops trout? But the trout I caught confused me. They were beautiful fish with the brightest, widest crimson bands I had ever seen on a "rainbow." Still, they didn't fit the book descriptions I had read concerning what a Kamloops was supposed to look like. I didn't realize then that these descriptions were of lake-dwelling fish and the trout inhabiting a lacustrine environment were silvery, their bright colors and spotting pattern muted and obscured by heavy deposits of guanin.

I wasn't the only one to be confused. This group of trout had baffled ichthyologists for almost a hundred years. Some classified redbands with the cutthroats while others included them with the rainbow tribe. And the experts frequently changed their minds. It wasn't until the early 1970s that the confusion began to be resolved. Now, Bob Behnke has re-christened the entire group of redbands, including golden trout, as *Salmo gairdneri* and they are back with the rainbows again, but as a different subspecies. They are no longer bastards and have a name as respected members of the society of trouts.

The group is wide-ranging from Central British Columbia to Southern California, but are found only in river systems that breached the Cascades: the Sacramento, Klamath, Columbia, Frazer, and possibly the Skeena. Even in these regions, redbands are confined to areas east of the mountains and some occur in streams that disappear in dessicating basins of the high desert.

With such a broad range it is to be expected that the various populations would be quite diverse; such is indeed the case. The group includes the Kamloops trout and its relict form, the mountain Kamloops; the trout of the mid-Columbia basin (which may prove to be the same race); the trout of the Oregon desert basins; those of the upper Sacramento; and the golden trout of the high

Sierras. There are even anadromous races — redband steelhead no less! Some of these trout are as yet undescribed so upon completion of further research two or more subspecies of redbands may be named.

A distinguishing characteristic of the redband trout is its physiological makeup; some desert populations exhibit astounding tolerances to adverse environmental conditions that would be absolutely lethal to other trout. Some, like the Kamloops, are efficient predators and grow to great size. It is time to consider the native redbands and forget about the ill-adapted, domesticated hatchery fish.

When I learned of the reality of the redbands not too many years ago, I determined to find some and see for myself what they looked like. A study of my expanding supply of technical papers and unpublished reports revealed that Sheepheaven Creek, a disrupted tributary of the McCloud River, harbored a relict population of redbands. This was a pure strain, uncontaminated by non-native fish or coastal rainbows.

As I was familiar with the general drainage area, I got out some maps and though these failed to show a Sheepheaven Creek, one did reveal a Sheepheaven Spring. I had heard that the creek originated in a spring so this had to be the place. When the next trout season opened in California I was there to find the redbands. The trail had taken me up over the Siskiyous and down through Shasta Valley, skirting the white cone of Mt. Shasta and its mate, Mt. Shastina, snuggled against its shoulder, white plumes of snow drifting from their summits.

After passing the village of McCloud I tried first one forest road and then another and got lost. I wasn't lost, really — Sheepheaven Spring was — so I backtracked on an overgrown logging road turning off on a sidetrack to the site of an old deer hunting camp and there I found the spring, a boggy sump at the bottom of a slope choked with willows. A rusty old pipe, about a two-inch bore, ran into a tiny streambed. The flow, hardly perceptible, was slimy with thick, green algae. Trout here? I'd see. Downstream, however, seeps from a sidehill meadow augmented the flow enough to clear the algae and form a trout stream — even if only a mere six inches wide!

As I strung my rod I hoped no one would come along and see me. Surely they would think me a candidate for a mental hospital. For why would anyone in his right mind fish a tiny rill on opening day when the McCloud River, only a few miles to the south, was stiff with hatchery rainbows, fat from a diet of pellets and easy living in concrete tanks?

The only witness, thank goodness, was a pileated woodpecker chopping away at a venerable red cedar, dropping great chips into an already sizeable pile at the foot of the tree. Occasionally the bird peeked around the trunk at me. Reassured that I was more-or-less behaving normally, it continued hammering away.

My gear assembled and camera strapped on, I set out for the spring seeps downstream, proceeding slowly and cautiously from there, watching for fish. I didn't see a one in the few tiny pools and riffles, but an old logging road winding off the sidehill caught my eye. I climbed out of the brush to follow it, sneaking back to the creek occasionally to inspect the most likely looking spots.

Even a sizeable pool formed by a downed log backing up the flow was fishless as I continued to the bitter end where the water disappeared underground. When it didn't surface again further down, I returned to the last pool, sat down at the base of an old sugar pine and lit my pipe.

The area had been a refuge during glacial times and so had escaped the crunch of ice. There were species of plants here found only in other glacial refuges. The redbands were relicts also, having invaded the tiny watershed before there were barriers in the stream — before the rainbows came. By the time 'bows ascended the McCloud, the barriers were in and the rainbows couldn't get up all the way.

I wondered how long the redbands had been there, just how many advances of the ice and warm interglacial periods they had weathered. This was a dry year, to be sure, with low stream flows but during all those eons of time they had surely survived droughts worse than this. They still must be here, I reasoned, even though I hadn't seen one . . . yet.

The cold, frosty spring morning gave way to warmth as the sun approached its zenith. I could feel the rays warm on my back and only then did I see the trout in the pool. It had darted out from under some willow branches, snatched a tidbit and gone back. Then I saw another and still another. There were three trout in that tiny pool.

Apparently the water had warmed to a point inducing action. My trout had begun to feed. I looked to my gear, freed the fly from the keeper ring and crawling a little closer, tossed a short cast. The fly was no sooner on the water than all three trout came. The largest, a six-incher, was first and had the fly. I hoisted it out of the water.

What a jewel! This fish's greenish-brown back harbored large black spots above the lateral line. Eight large, elliptical parr marks, almost black, were bisected by a brick red stripe, with supplementary, smaller roundish parr marks above and below. The gillcovers were carmine, the lower sides and belly washed with orange and yellow. The lower fins were orange, the ventrals and anal were cream-tipped, as was the dorsal. The adipose fin was margined coal black. This looks like a golden trout, I thought, like those from the west side of the Kern plateau in the high Sierras.

Some might wonder at my enthusiasm over a six-inch trout. But looked at relatively, a six-inch trout from a pool only a foot wide is quite a fish. This wasn't a baby trout, either. It was fully mature and had probably spawned more than once. I enjoy catching big fish as well as the next guy, but bigness in itself does not necessarily mean quality. I fish for native trout in their native habitat because they are where they belong, because they are beautiful and because they are found in majestic surroundings.

How does one measure such beauty? Surely not by the pound or by the yard. Beauty may, indeed, rest in the eye of each beholder. But who could deny that this symmetry of form, delicate blending of colors and pattern . . . this aura of perfection evolved over the millenia . . . did not possess a quality unmatched by sheer grossness or footage?

All this I had to try to get on film before it faded, so I stretched the tiny trout out on my creel, spreading the fins and tail to best advantage. Hoping I had made the correct exposures, I started up the creek slowly and cautiously. In a riffle at the tail of a tiny pool I took another fish. It was as like the other as two peas in a pod and I released it. Still further up I saw a trout rising, a bigger one, in a little pool under a maze of dead willow branches. Crawling up from behind, I sank to my belly in the sedges and watched.

I was so close to nature that I had to part the greenery before my eyes to see the pool. The trout came up at intervals, causing the water striders (Jesus bugs we small boys had called them for their water-walking ability) to skitter about wildly on the surface film. The dead willow branches over the pool were so intertwined that only by extending a foot or two of leader from the rod tip was it possible to try a dap. But now the spiders had foiled me; every time I tried dapping, the fly would hang up in a spider web. Finally I reeled the fly to the tip guide and poked around with the rod tip to clear a path through the spider webs to the pool. This was successful but the trout spooked in the process and I saw it no more.

Up the streamlet at the pool formed by a fallen log I could make a proper cast. There was clear backcast space behind me and the pool was yards wide, rather than inches across. After cautious inspection of my fly from several rising trout, a veritable monster dashed out on my last drift by the log and seized the fly. I gauged it to be a ten-incher before it flopped, twisted loose and vanished under the log. I had caught enough, however; I had my picture and I knew what a redband looked like. This was what I had come for.

Back at my rig I noted that the woodpecker had gone, but not before adding considerably to his pile of cedar chips. What a home it had, with a view over the meadow, the spring and the forested slope beyond. A southern exposure, too, from a scented cedar interior. If there is anything to this business of reincarnation, I mused, maybe I'll opt to be a woodpecker . . . if I get the choice.

That night I again got out my manuscripts and technical papers, and did some more homework. Sure enough, the redbands of Sheepheaven Creek and the native golden trout of the western tributaries of the Kern were considered to be races of the same species. Their coloration was similar and their spotting pattern identical. They were both very fine scaled and both had an extra row of teeth on the tongue. This characteristic is found in no other trout.

These trout were both glacial relicts found only in the extreme opposite ends of the great central valley of California, a linear distance of over 400 miles. Maybe geologists could learn something about ancient earth happenings from the distribution of native trout.

Some years after my encounter with the Sheepheaven Creek redbands I found others, inadvertently. Searching for cutthroats in the John Day country I found redbands as well, both species living in the same streams. While they had partitioned the water between them (the cutthroats preferring the upper reaches of the watershed while the redbands were lower down), there was nevertheless a zone of overlap. Yet there was no mass mixing, each species preserving its own genetic integrity; this unusual relationship must have prevailed for thousands of years.

Redbands show great diversity in color and spotting pattern throughout their vast range. Compared with the golden trout of the Kern and those from Sheepheaven Creek, the John Day fish were much more profusely spotted; they had spots extending even to the belly and their colors were less intense, less vivid.

They shared, however, the white tipped ventrals, anal and dorsal fins, numerous auxiliary parr marks and the crimson band along the lateral line.

I also found redbands on the back side of the Strawberries in the headwaters of the Malheur. Years ago I had fished the lower Malheur, where it had cut through high desert country between sheer rimrock walls; the streamside growth was sage and yellow-flowered rabbit brush. Here on the south slopes of the Straw-berries the streams were crystal clear mountain brooks, cold as ice, tumbling down through green stands of lodgepole, spruce and fir.

Legend has it that Peter Ogden, while leading a group of Hud-son Bay trappers, paused by the river one hot summer day so that he and his men could wash the trail dust from their hides. While they were skinny dipping the Paiutes stole their horses and all the rest of their gear, leaving them afoot and naked. Where-upon they christened the stream Malheur.

The Malheur has given me a bad time, too. I had been fishing Big Creek, one of its uppermost tributaries draining out of the Strawberry Wilderness Area. First I had lost my knife, a prized possession of many years. Then I slid off an old "buckskin" log, smooth and slippery, almost tearing off a boot foot from a new pair of hippers. But I did catch some trout, beautiful redbands and some small bull trout. The redbands were almost mirror images of those from the John Day drainage — colorful, profuse-ly spotted and active as jumping beans. I remember one in par-ticular, a 13-incher, that fouled my leader in a mat of green beaver cuttings and I beached the whole works — trout and willow sticks. After I managed to sort out the trout from the beaver's prospec-tive dinner, I took a photograph.

The largest redband I ever hooked weighed seven pounds and came out of the Williamson, Klamath Lake's largest tributary. At that time I had never heard of a redband and I thought it was a rainbow, but a mighty odd-looking rainbow. Though not a spawner, it was quite dark and colorful, with tinges of yellow and orange on its sides and light, brassy slash marks. This fish had probably ascended the river from Klamath Lake, as it was the type of locale from which specimens were described by Girard in 1858 as *Salmo newberryi*.

During the late '40s I fished the Williamson frequently and I thought it the most productive trout stream I had ever seen. Des-pite massive introductions of hatchery rainbows, the native red-bands had persisted and so, with luck, maybe they always will.

CHAPTER 13

Golden Trout of the High Sierras

THE TROUT LAY POISED IN midwater where the creek narrowed and deepened. The stream was less than two feet wide, shaded by a canopy of willows forming an arch overhead. I backed slowly and carefully away, circling around to come in from behind on hands and knees.

When I thought my position close enough I peeked over a screen of rank sedges. The trout was still there, shifting position frequently to intercept whatever food was drifting down. It was a big fish for this water — maybe ten inches, or even 11.

This trout had chosen its lie well, almost impossible to cast to, and probably the reason it was so big. But I had to try. At worst I would hang up in a willow. The cast had to be low to clear the branches yet to one side so as not to line spook the fish.

All right then. I switched the leader under the canopy. The fly bumped a twig, hung up briefly, but by luck dropped into the water. The trout turned and took, then bore hard for submerged roots. Frantically stripping in line, I pulled the fish downstream, free of the snags, and eased it onto the gravel by my knees.

Wow! So this was a *Salmo gairdneri roosevelti*. Jordan and Evermann described it as the "... *real* golden trout, the most gorgeously colored trout in all the world." And they were right. Never had I seen such intense blends of greens, carmines, yellows and black, yet it wasn't garish; nothing clashed and the total impression was exquisite beauty beyond words.

The blendings were subtle; the back was greenish bronze shading into yellow on the lower sides. There was carmine on the belly from anal fin to chin and a wide crimson streak bisected eleven elliptical parr marks. Its cheeks were yellow, the gillcovers carmine. The dorsal, pectoral and anal fins were cream-tipped and there were large, round black spots restricted to the caudal peduncle. Superlatives weren't powerful enough.

I had to be quick with the cameras. The sun was already halfway past the zenith and I needed the strongest light to capture such color. Then I sat back and just looked at the fish, first one side and then the other. I had seen many beautiful races of native trout, but this one beat them all and surpassed even the other races of golden trout of the Kern Plateau, the ancestral home of them all.

Riding in that morning from my camp on Tunnel Meadows had been, until now, a High Sierra adventure without equal. The trail bordered the south fork of the Kern, here a wee meadow stream, past huge open-growth lodgepoles. Then it was up over a low divide and into the drainage of Golden Trout Creek which I forded twice before tackling the steep climb out.

Scrambling up over the switchbacks to the summit caused my mount, John, to heave and puff and I pulled up to let him blow. John was a good horse, dependable and strong, but he had a one-track mind. He thought only of oats and the oat bin was back in camp. Hence, all the way out he had to be prodded, thumped and cajoled. But on the way back it would be another matter, like hang onto your hat and watch out for low limbs!

As we angled down the stony slope I could see the flat below, Volcano Meadows, green and lush under the August sun. When we broke out of the timber to the flat I rode to the creek to have a look. Nameless on the map, I dubbed it Volcano Creek in honor of its meadow. It was a fair-sized stream as tiny headwaters go, a yard wide in places, meandering through the meadow in lilliputian oxbows. There were few pools or deeps, however, and I continued up, startling small trout from the shallows as I went.

Soon the meadow narrowed, the steep slopes pinched in and I

was in lodgepole and spruce country again. The creek forked now, the main trail following the valley of the Right Stringer, but I followed the Left Stringer on a lesser trail used mainly by cows and deer.

A mile later the creek swung sharply from my left, bouncing down the slope through a maze of huge boulders and ledges, at times disappearing completely in the rubble. There was still a trail of sorts following the course of the creek and I urged John up, scrambling and slipping on the steepest parts.

When we topped out we were both breathless — John from the lack of wind and I from the sheer grandeur of the scene. We were poised on the rim of a hanging valley, a place so beautiful, so still and so brilliant in the thin clear air it seemed any sudden sound might shatter it like a pane of glass.

The somber mass of Kern Peak, the highest pinnacle of the Toowa Range, reared skyward at the far end of the little meadow, completely dominating the scene. At the foot of the mountain abutting against a talus slope was a tiny tarn, azure under the blue vault above. It was the source of the Left Stringer, the outlet seeping through a field of boulders, gathering into a rill. Then, picking up the trickles of springs, it became a trout stream, however small, winding through the narrow meadow, green with sedges and spangled with blue harebells, yellow monkey flowers and purple fireweed.

There were small scattered islands of alpine spruce and I tied John in one; then I strung my rod and walked to the creek where I spied the trout.

Afterwards I explored the meadow and the stream, taking a few more trout and watching them scamper for shelter when I slipped out the barbless hook. All were carbon copies of the first, identical in coloring and spotting pattern. When I reached the tarn I sat awhile on a lichen-splotched boulder to absorb some warmth and beauty.

The guttural croak of a raven was the only sound, muted and far away. Suddenly a small flock of yellowlegs wheeled in and settled on the far shore. They bowed a few times, preened a little and then took a short, one-legged nap. Yellowlegs were the last birds I expected to see there. Normally lowland marsh dwellers, they somehow had found their way to this alpine glen in their migration. As suddenly as they had arrived, they departed, southbound. Maybe their next stop would be the flats of the Colorado delta in Mexico.

I departed, too, and found John snubbed to his tree. As we clattered and slid down the trail we had two things going for us: gravity and John's vision of the oat bin. We made the trip back to camp in record time.

I had come to this High Sierra paradise the easy way. I flew in. Bob White operated a flying service out of Lone Pine on the floor of Owens Valley just under the sheer eastern wall of the Sierras. On the other side near the headwaters of the Kern's south fork he had an airstrip at Tunnel Meadows. An adjacent tent camp offered air service patrons shelter for a dollar a night per head. The camp also doubled as a pack station, with horses for the dudes to ride and a packer for trips to the more remote areas.

All that was required was to present your body at the airstrip at Lone Pine with a supply of grub and necessary gear. Within a few minutes, presto! You were away from the heat of the valley, hordes of tourists, heavy traffic, and up, up and away into the cool, clear air of the mountains, under the lodgepoles and alongside the crystal waters of the south fork of the Kern, golden trout waters, the primordial home of the goldens.

All was in readiness when I arrived at the Lone Pine airport on a clear August morning, thanks to prior arrangements. Bill, the pilot, stuffed my gear in the back seat of a Cessna 206 and off we went in a continuous climb to clear the crest of the mountain wall. I could see Mt. Whitney, the highest peak in the "Lower Forty-Eight," and its companion peaks looming large and white to the north. Over my shoulder the hot, barren depression of Death Valley, the lowest point in North America, was visible.

Obviously, there had been prodigious shifts in the earth's crust to produce such extremes in topography, and recently — a mere few million years ago as geologists reckon time — when the great Sierra batholith was raised and then tilted to the west to expose the sheer fault scarp as the east face of the range. It may still be rising, to a lesser degree, as earth tremors still rack the fault zone.

Once over the top, Bill throttled back and we slowly lost altitude toward Mulkey Meadows, the source of Mulkey Creek, winding its tenuous way to join the Kern's south fork, the origin of the first "coffee pot" transfer of golden trout during the last century. Whereas the east face of the cordillera had been sheer, naked rock, the country fanned out beneath us was infinitely more gentle, more plateau-like, a kaleidoscope of green meadows and dark-timbered ridges with serrated snowcapped peaks in the background.

Tunnel Meadow came into view as we crossed the low ridge beyond Bullfrog Meadow. The south fork of the Kern meandered down the center. There, also, was our airstrip. I was sitting on the right side of the aircraft, in the "idiot seat," and was thankful I had an experienced pilot on the left. The strip looked mighty short and narrow for a ground elevation of 9,000 feet. A wrecked aircraft lying just off the far end and a great heap of bits and pieces of numerous other aircraft piled up just off to the side were mute reminders that this was no place for pilot error.

Bill never batted an eye. He slid the Cessna on the strip with hardly a rumble and stopped it well short of the boundary. As we turned back and off to the side, Duane Rossi stepped up and greeted us. He ran the camp for Bob White and did the horse wrangling and packing. My gear was piled into a cart and pulled by a diminutive tractor to my quarters, an eight-by-ten wall tent by a concrete fireplace and a grill and a wire cage to keep my grub safe from the depredations of golden mantled ground squirrels, deer mice and whiskeyjacks.

Camp facilities were pointed out — the woodpile, the water supply and the Chick Sales house, and I was settled in for a whole month. I had planned this quest for years and at last I was right in the middle of the original golden trout waters of the Kern Plateau.

I stored my gear in the tent, secured my grub in the wire cage and kindled a fire. As the coffee pot simmered I spread out my maps and made plans. The south fork of the Kern right at my doorstep came out of a meadow to the northeast. This was walking distance. Mulkey Creek, which we had flown over on our approach to the airstrip, could be explored better by horseback. Golden Trout Creek was just down Tunnel Meadow and then over a ridge to the north. I could walk there. Volcano Meadow and the Left Stringer, a southern tributary of Golden Trout Creek, looked to be a horse operation.

To reach the western tributaries of the main Kern River where it cut through the Kern Plateau in a gorge would require a pack-in and a spike camp. All this looked reasonable and I had the time. The Left Stringer and *Salmo gairdneri roosevelti* would be my first venture.

I wasn't totally alone. There were other people about, but not many. Some came to fish, but most came to enjoy the mountains, the pure spicy air, and respite from crowds and traffic. There were backpackers going to and fro on the trail by the meadow. Some strode along mightily, others barely moved, each step an effort. I envied their energy and determination.

After my experience on the Left Stringer and an introduction to *Salmo gairdneri roosevelti*, I was anxious to see the other races of goldens. California Fish and Game folks had told me Mulkey Creek was the place to find pure *Salmo gairdneri aquabonita*, the first of the races of golden trout to be described. Arrangements for a mount early the following morning were made.

Duane was as good as his word; at daybreak I was awakened by the muffled drum of hoofbeats and the whoops of the wrangler as the remuda was herded into the corral. Scrambling out of my bedroll and into some clothes, I hurriedly lit the fire, got the coffee brewing and a pot of oatmeal started. My water bucket was covered with a thin film of ice and the meadow was white with frost. A mighty short summer, I thought, for this was still August.

I gulped breakfast, gathered my gear and hastened to the corral. John was already saddled and looked rather dejected as I strapped on the saddle scabbard containing the fly rod and tied my slicker and lunch on behind. "Another day, another dude," he probably thought. The horse made no violent objections, however, when I climbed aboard and urged him up the trail.

Our route led past the upper end of the meadow and then we were back in among the lodgepoles along the creek. The stream here, the south fork, looked to be good trout water, but being so close to camp it was heavily fished. Shortly the stream and the trail made a sharp bend to the north; we began to climb and the creek began to tumble with many inviting plunge pools and holes against logjams.

The trail forded the stream and, looking with the light, I could see an occasional trout dash for cover. The creek then swung west and the trail cut east over the low divide to the headwaters of Mulkey Creek.

As we crossed the ridge I was struck with the peculiar nature of the surrounding forest. It was almost a pure stand of lodgepole pine, some huge as lodgepoles go. There was practically no ground cover on the forest floor, not even grass. The soil was coarse and gritty, decomposed granite so loose and porous that the snowmelt and rainfall passed through with scarcely a pause.

The only plants to survive these harsh conditions, except for the lodgepoles, were little xerophytic things widely scattered and forming tight rosettes, husbanding their juices and telescoping their seasonal life cycle to a very brief span. I had seen these same tiny plants, or near relatives at least, living out their short summers on dry sand ridges in the Arctic. In contrast, the meadows and stream margins were moist and lush, green with grasses and sedges and bright with wildflowers.

From the divide we dropped to Bullfrog Meadow, the western extension of Mulkey Meadows. Bullfrog was wet and marshy and as John squished across the soggy turf a few small frogs leaped out in mindless terror, venting frantic croaks. We cut a point of timber and intercepted Mulkey Creek near the lower end of the meadow. The stream was four to six feet wide, flat and shallow and badly degraded by excessive livestock use. There were cattle aplenty and the stream margins showed it, being devoid of cover and with stream banks trampled.

The few small trout spooked from the shallows as we followed the creek down had no place to hide. We were running out of meadow, so I rode John into a side draw and tied him to a lodge-pole. The slopes drew closer and the meadow terminated as I continued down afoot. The stream gained velocity, flowing across granite ledges and around large boulders forming pools and deep runs that looked like trout water. I proceeded more cautiously, keeping back from the water, searching for fish in likely looking pockets. A boulder partially blocked the current in a bend and the gravel was scoured away around its base, forming a pool. I sneaked around from the side, kneeling to keep my profile low. When my fly drifted through the deep by the boulder, I saw a flash, one of Skues' ". . . little brown winks under water."

The refused fly, a nondescript, bedraggled nymph on a No. 12 hook, was replaced by a No. 14 tied-down caddis, one of my favorites. Next drift, the wink and the pluck were simultaneous and an eight-incher, big for the water, dashed into the riffle above before I could draw it to the bank.

Once again I felt that special thrill when I catch and see a race of native trout new to me. This was an exquisite gem, as are all goldens — a symphony in color and form. It must be seen on its own ground to be fully appreciated, for its beauty matches that of its surroundings.

This was *aquabonita* and well named. The specimens were described by Jordan in 1892 from descendants of trout from this very stream. It was different from *roosevelti* only in the spotting pattern and intensity of coloration. All of the colors were there, but paler, less intense. The black body spots were more numerous, scattered along the back and sides above the lateral line as well as on the caudal peduncle. It was absolutely beautiful, nonetheless, and trying to compare the two was like trying to compare two sunsets.

After a number of shots with the camera, some taken with the trout barely immersed under water, I worked cautiously downstream, my fly searching the little plunge pools and the deeps around the boulders. The stream wasn't exactly "stiff with fish," but I caught several, mostly six- or seven-inchers, their small size commensurate with the size of the stream. All were photo images of the first I had caught, indications of genetic purity. My barbless hook simplified their release.

Downstream the slopes shouldered in and soon I was in a canyon among huge boulders. Then the creek slowed and widened, forming a long, deep pool. The lower end was obstructed by a mass of boulders and jagged rock. Circling the deep I came to the dropoff, the ridge through which the canyon cut terminated. The higher portions were sheer rock walls while the lower half was at a 45-degree angle in an accumulation of talus. Massive rocks and boulders completely filled the original stream valley.

No water was visible or even audible. But somewhere down there it was working through those rocks to the valley floor below to emerge again as a full-blown stream. Here was a barrier, indeed. No fish could work its way through that mass of rubble.

I wondered how this had happened. Perhaps by the slow weathering of the rock walls above, a boulder at a time. Or, by a cataclysmic rending and shaking, the whole mass crashing down with a thunderous roar. Either way, I reasoned, the entire Sierra Nevada range is fraught with fault zones, some active in the not too distant past.

No matter. The pure golden trout of upper Mulkey Creek had gotten there first, and the barrier would prevent any other fish from invading their domain, insuring their genetic integrity. I was happy with the barrier.

Clambering back to the deep pool, I squatted on a rock at the lower end where the creek disappeared. I watched the clear, green depths for a sign, finally sensing movement by a ledge, a mere shadow that shifted ever so slightly. My nymph sank slowly, drifting by the ledge. There was a slight stir and a wink; I tightened, turning the shadow over. This time it truly disappeared; I had muffed my chance.

Back up the canyon at the draw I found John had wound his rope up tight and was waiting impatiently for me to untangle him. Once he was unwound, I led him to the creek for water and then we had lunch together. While I worked on slabs of bread and cheese, John grazed the lush sedges, chomping noisily on the succulent fare. I smoked my pipe, watching him with half-closed eyes, nearly asleep in the warm sun. It would take four hours to fill that paunch of his, however, and I couldn't wait that long. I slipped his bridle on, lashed the tie rope to the saddle and mounted up, heading for camp. John needed no urging, stepping out briskly, ever mindful of the oats at the end of the trail.

Another stream within my range was Golden Trout Creek, just over the divide from the south fork. What a name! It conjured up inviting visions of beautiful trout, the official state gamefish of California. Ever since reading Charles McDermand's *Waters of the Golden Trout Country*, I had longed to go there, to see and to fish. Now it was within easy walking distance and I started out early on a frosty morning, cameras and lunch on my back and fly rod in hand. At the meadow's edge, down the south fork, the horses paused in their grazing to watch me pass, John no doubt glad he was not part of my expedition. The trail forked after a mile and bore right, beginning to climb almost immediately. The easy grade grew steeper and steeper and I paused often for breath in the oxygen-scarce air. At the very top was a tiny spring in the head of a little draw. The water I drank was so cold it hurt my teeth.

The steep climb was behind me and I rested and smoked by the spring, knowing the rest would be easy, listening to the breeze singing in the pines and watching a red-tailed hawk soaring overhead. Knocking cold ash from my pipe I angled down through the timber and across a barren ridge, the starkness broken by a scattering of lodgepoles, huge old trees, gnarled and twisted. At the bottom I came upon the "tunnel" from which Tunnel Meadow was named.

At this point it was an open ditch dug by Chinese laborers during the gold mining days to divert water from Golden Trout Creek to the south fork of the Kern. Some enterprising soul envisioned irrigating meadows below to grow garden truck to sell to the miners. He failed to realize that at this altitude nightly frosts would freeze his potatoes and everything else, so the effort was a complete bust. A pity, I thought, that promoters of irrigation projects haven't learned much since.

The trail followed the ditch a ways and then swung to Golden Trout Creek and across a shallow ford. The stream was the largest of any I had seen on the Kern Plateau, six or eight feet wide and absolutely beautiful in character and setting. There were riffles and pockets, pools and deep runs. The water was colorless, like liquid air. The bottom pebbles shimmered as jewels scattered helter-skelter under the restless currents.

At the ford I left the trail and worked upstream, along a bot-

tom timbered with pine and spruce. In contrast to the dry, sparsely timbered slopes, the little valley was carpeted with grasses and sedges, the shades of green punctuated with splashes of bright color — blue lupines and gentians, yellow cinquefoils and orange paintbrush. It seemed sacrilegious to tread on such beauty.

Just looking was enough as I startled many small trout in the first stretches of water. At a larger pool a cast by a boulder at the head brought an instant response, but I missed.

"Slow down," I cautioned myself.

Pausing just a hair at the take on the next drift, the trout was hooked when I tightened. Three others spooked from shallow margins barely covering their backs when I worked the trout through the pool.

The hooked trout was an *aquabonita* type, colorful as a sunrise and unharmed by the barbless hook — just scared. At the next pool I searched the slow shallow margins before casting to the most likely looking spot. Sure enough, there was a trout lying motionless on each side. I cast to the larger of the two. It proved to be a *roosevelti* type, with spots only on the caudal peduncle and tail. The two types occurring together in Golden Trout Creek cause ichythyologists to consider them color variants of one subspecies — *aquabonita*, and to conclude that the race described by Evermann in 1905 as *roosevelti* is no longer valid.

However, the waters of the south fork and of Golden Trout Creek were mixed in the past by the "tunnel" and probably the trout populations mixed also. Yet in one tiny tributary of each watershed, the Left Stringer and upper Mulkey Creek, both isolated by barriers, the two types are pure and distinct, and so to me they are separate and discrete races.

I released small trout right up to Whitney Meadows where the stream divided into several small tributaries. The trout were abundant, which was gratifying as the trail often passed close to the water. Both types were common as well as some that appeared to be intermediate.

Once, while creeping up on a meadow run, I startled a water vole which jumped off the bank into the water with a loud plop, swam up the creek like a small, short-tailed muskrat, and disappeared under an undercut bank. The spectacle of what appears to be an ordinary meadow mouse leaping into the water and swimming away never ceases to amaze me as often as I've observed them along the meadow streams of the high western mountains. Recalling that nature abhors a vacuum, I mused that the vole certainly filled an odd ecological niche for a mouse.

And so it was with the golden trout — pre-glacial relicts, adapting perfectly to their own tiny streams on the roof of North America.

During succeeding days I explored most of the tiny creeks in the watersheds of the Kern's south fork and Golden Trout Creek, sometimes afoot, the more distant ones by horseback. I usually found goldens, but a few little stringers appeared to be troutless.

I came to know two trout exceedingly well in the course of those forays. Both were goldens of considerable size with the largest possibly a foot or more. Both were in the south fork where it meandered through Ramshaw Meadows; in this water they had to compete with brown trout which had invaded from below.

The first trout lived in a pool just under a beaver dam and shared its quarters with two large browns. I crawled up to this pool through a screen of low willows and had seen the fish finning in midwater, shifting frequently as they intercepted tidbits in the flow through the dam. I made a short cast, too short, and was ignored. With more line I cast to the golden again. It rose leisurely, gulped the nymph, then bolted toward the roots of the willows under my feet. In seconds the surges stopped and I was fast to a willow root instead of the fish.

Later in the day I tried again with the same result. I couldn't shorten line fast enough to hold this fish out of the willows. Thereafter, on every trip through Ramshaw Meadows, I tried to fool this fish. But it had learned the lesson well; every time I raised my rod to cast, the trout would dash under the willow roots. When I left the mountains weeks later that trout was still there.

The other golden, of the same dimensions, lived downstream in the shelter of an undercut bank. Willows made this trout impossible to cast to; the only way to present a fly was to creep up and dap. I hooked it twice in as many days but it shook loose each time. After those near misses this trout became exceedingly cautious. Each time thereafter when I made my first dap, the trout would come out, turn, look up on the bank instead of at my fly and, seeing me kneeling there, would vanish. This fish was an exception to the adage that a trout's memory lasts only twenty minutes.

The trouting possibilities within a reasonable range of camp exhausted, I set my sights on the main Kern and its western tributaries, once the stronghold of yet another race of golden trout, *Salmo gairdneri gilberti*. Massive introductions of hatchery rainbows beginning before the turn of the century had all but wiped out this race of goldens. Now they are found in only a few tiny tributaries above barriers.

California Game and Fish folk told me that Coyote Creek would be the most accessible water from Tunnel Meadow containing a virtually pure stock of this race. According to my map, a trail followed Golden Trout Creek down to the brink of Kern Canyon and then to the main Kern to a point near the mouth of Coyote Creek. There I could set up a spike camp. Duane agreed to pack me in and pick me up again in a few days.

The pine straw was stiff with frost underfoot on a cold, bright August morning as I lugged my gear to the corral. Duane had the stock saddled and ready, and I proceeded to lash my accoutrements on the back of old Jake, a Roman-nosed gray with a malevolent eye. As Duane heaved the diamond hitch tight, Jake gulped a deep breath and held it, an old hand at this game. With the pack apparently secure, I led Jake back and forth a time or two for Duane's inspection. Then we climbed aboard and headed out, I on John and Duane on a rat-tailed Appaloosa. The Appaloosa was a good walker and set a brisk pace down the trail.

Crossing the low ridge at the meadow's end, we dropped to Golden Trout Creek, forded it and followed the flank of a timbered bench. Out of the sun the air was crisp and cold and I was glad when we found the sun and its warmth as we skirted Ground Hog Meadow.

When the creek swung back to us it was bordered on the far side by a malpais — a lava flow so fresh it looked like it had been poured yesterday. No vegetation softened the rough chunks of scoriaceous lava, reddish-black and porous with gas holes. This barrier had sealed off Volcano Meadow and preserved the purity of the *roosevelti* type goldens I had found in the Left Stringer.

We passed Little Whitney Meadow, forded the stream again and came to the brink of the canyon where Golden Trout Creek plunged in a series of white-plumed cataracts to the main Kern 2,000 feet below. The canyon itself is a geological wonder, splitting the Kern Plateau in a monstrous gash. The river that cut it flowed due south from its headwaters just under the Kings-Kern divide and at right angles to the typical Sierra drainage. Geologists believe the river and its canyon follow a zone of structural weakness, an ancient fault, and that it was deeply incised before the Sierra mountain mass was tilted to the west. Whatever the reason, it is a rent in the mountain on a grand scale.

The forest's character changed abruptly as we descended numerous switchbacks. The lodgepoles were replaced by Jeffrey pines resembling ponderosa but having larger, more robust cones and denser foliage. The trail was steep and the horses picked their footing carefully, slipping and sliding on the loose rocks and dirt. We broke out at the bottom on the flood plain of the Kern, a boulder-strewn flat with a dense thicket of manzanita, clattered across a wooden bridge spanning a large rushing stream, and found a suitable campsite near the mouth of Coyote Creek.

We unpacked old Jake and set up my tent on a pine straw-covered flat beneath a towering Jeffrey pine. I scraped the forest litter away, arranged some rocks for a fireplace and in short order had a fire going and the coffee pot on. It was hot on the canyon floor, and compared to the heights on the rim the air seemed close and oppressive. We had dropped steadily since leaving Tunnel Meadow and we were less than 6,500 feet above sea level. We lunched in the pines' shade on bread, cheese and salami and then Duane left me, riding the Appaloosa and leading the others, heading back for Tunnel Meadow and the long climb out.

"See you in five days," he called, "and watch out for rattlesnakes!"

I soon had the camp in order, gear stowed, bedroll laid out, and the grub pack slung from a high pine bough. My camp was right on the border of Sequoia National Park and I didn't relish a visit from tourist-oriented bears. All shipshape, I jointed and strung my rod and started up the creek, looking for trout and trout-holding places. Coyote Creek was a beautiful little stream, maybe a yard wide. The slope was fairly steep and Coyote tumbled a bit, but there were small pools and deep runs that should hold trout.

Seeing no fish I began fishing anyway, drifting the wet fly in likely places. A taker, a seven-incher, was unceremoniously hoisted for a look. It was a hybrid, more rainbow than golden, and I banged it on the head for the pot. I have no qualms about killing hybrids. Someplace ahead there had to be a barrier where I could get above the hybrids, so I continued on, taking a fish now and then. All showed hybrid influence.

The slope steepened as I moved up. Massive boulders crowded the streambed and there were some deep, fishy-looking pools containing plump trout of varied appearance. The distant roar of a cataract spurred me up and around ledges and boulders. Soon I stood at a plunge pool where the creek fell in a vertical drop of over 100 feet. This was it! No rainbow or any other fish could pass beyond here.

It was too late in the day for a climb to the top and I returned to camp, cleaned my fish and got a fire going. The trout brown-

ing and curling in the pan attracted yellowjackets. They moved up in force. And they were hungry yellowjackets, almost frantic at the smell of food. Soon the pan contained more fried yellowjackets than trout, so when the fish were barely done I forked them onto a plate and retreated behind the mosquito bar of my tent. I had no desire to share my dinner with yellowjackets.

At first light I was up, hoping to beat the yellowjackets to breakfast. This I managed and was on the trail to the canyon's western rim before the sun peeked over the eastern escarpment. The trail, gentle at first, steepened shortly, climbing the grade in a series of switchbacks. I carried only my fly rod, one camera and lunch. As I toiled along, I wished mightily for a horse.

From numerous vantage points the view up and down the canyon was monumental. The great rift ran straight as an arrow due north and south, almost sheer in places, as though the forces of nature had tried to split this granite batholith and had almost succeeded. I paused often to puff and marvel. Eventually I reached the top and the trail leveled off and crossed the creek. I was now only a mile from my camp as the crow flies, but almost 2,000 feet higher and well above the barrier.

Coyote Creek was a more sedate stream on top, meandering through the forest, sliding over gravelly riffles and coasting slowly through pools and runs. The water looked thoroughly trouty and my anticipation was high as I knotted on a small wet fly and began explorations.

Not seeing any trout, I searched the pools and deeper runs. In an eddy behind a slanting log I touched the first fish, a gentle pluck, but my timing was wrong and I only pricked it. Upstream I hooked another in the tail of a pool and this one, an eight-incher, I drew through a riffle below and onto a bar. Like other goldens, this one was a spectacular fish, similar in general coloration. But there *were* differences. The band along the sides and the color of the belly were more orange than red, the red color terminating just below the pectoral fins. The spots were larger and more numerous with some occurring below the lateral line. Round, auxiliary parr marks were present along the lower sides and the conformation of the fish was chunkier, deeper-bodied, with the head and jaws larger in proportion. I hastened to capture it on film before the delicate colors faded.

All of the golden trout of the Kern Plateau are now thought to be of redband extraction. This one in particular, *gilberti*, resembles closely the redbands of Sheepheaven Creek, 400 miles to the north. Possibly eons ago, before rainbows invaded headwaters of the Sacramento and the San Joaquin, the entire western slope of the Sierra Nevada range was populated with ancestors of these trout. Lucky we are that these few relicts survive, for our world would be poorer without them.

I fished up the creek slowly and carefully; the water was small and the trout spooky. The Coyote flowed almost due east, heading up just under the serrated peaks of the Great Western Divide. Yet here the land was gentle, almost level, the thin spicy air a blend of forest scents. I caught a number of trout, the smallest about five inches and the largest almost nine. I photographed two and released the rest. All were marked like the first one I had caught; if there was any hybridization, it didn't show.

I lunched under a spreading fir by the stream and had a smoke. A breeze soughed through the blue-green canopy and the creek murmured at my feet. Shafts of filtered sunlight bounced off a riffle, a kaleidoscope of dancing lights. A woodpecker tapped on a snag deep in the forest. As my senses were busy absorbing all of this I reflected on the joys of fishing these beautiful little waters, catching and seeing their dazzling little trout. That was my excuse for being here, really, if an excuse were needed. In the process of seeking out the fish I had become a part of it all, rather than merely an onlooker, and I learned much about my fellow creatures and the world they lived in. I also learned much about the anatomy of a trout stream, for it was all there to see, in miniature, all visible at the same time.

A cloud drifted across the sun and the lights went out on the riffle. The air had become cooler, almost chill. I picked up my rod and started back, just looking rather than fishing. When I came to the trail crossing I continued on down the creek, hoping to come out on the canyon rim and the dropoff. Soon the slope steepened and the stream began to plunge over ledges and around huge boulders. A few trout showed here and there in the glass-clear pools but there were not many and, as the going was getting difficult, I retraced my steps before ending in a cul-de-sac. Trail walking was easy, all down hill, and I soon was back in camp, the yellowjackets there to greet me. They had assembled in droves and I again retreated to the shelter of the tent to eat my freeze-dried supper.

My spike camp stay permitted exploration of the main Kern, both upstream and down; this was first class trout water of the classic type and big enough to be considered a river. It was assumed until recently that rainbows were the original trout of the Kern and that the goldens in the tributaries above the barriers were derived therefrom. Now it has been shown that the original specimens from the Kern on which the name *gilberti* was based were in fact golden trout, and that the rainbows had been introduced.

The fish I caught in the Kern were certainly rainbows, no question, and looked exactly like McCloud River rainbows. And well they should, for that was their origin — a McCloud River hatchery.

Duane rode in on the fifth day with a spare mount and a packhorse and retrieved me from my yellowjacket empire. I didn't get stung, but the miserable beasts tried to eat me, much as they will chew on a deer carcass hanging from a meat pole. It was a new experience for me, to be chomped on by hungry yellowjackets, and one I could do without. To be successful in finding and photographing the golden trout named *gilberti*, however, was well worth it.

Identification of Color Plates

1. **COASTAL CUTTHROAT TROUT**. *Salmo clarki clarki*. Dean River, British Columbia, August, 1983.

DISTINCTIVE CHARACTERISTICS: Silvery background, numerous black spots, small to medium, irregular in shape and evenly distributed over the body (except on the belly). The only other trout colored and marked similarly is the fine-spotted Snake River cutthroat, on which the spots are smaller and less numerous. Fresh sea-run fish are mint bright while the landlocked forms or fish that have been in fresh water for some time are more brassy and have rosy tints along the lateral line. Slash marks vary from faint brassy in sea-run fish to bright orange or red in landlocked forms.

NATURAL RANGE: Eel River in California north to Prince William Sound, Alaska, including the larger offshore islands — more common northward. Seldom occurs more than one hundred miles inland from the coast.

2. **WESTSLOPE CUTTHROAT TROUT**. *Salmo clarki lewisi*. Dupuyer Creek, Montana (Upper Missouri Basin), June, 1977.

DISTINCTIVE CHARACTERISTICS: Differs from the Yellowstone cutthroat, whose range abuts, by the numerous small to medium, irregular-shaped black spots, which are largely absent along the mid sides below an arc extending from anal to pectoral fins. This race also has the genetic potential to develop high coloration (red, orange or yellow) on the lower sides and belly, most evident in larger fish and in males during spawning.

NATURAL RANGE: Upper Columbia River Basin above barriers, particularly Clark's Fork, Flathead and Kootenay drainages; also in the Spokane, Salmon and Clearwater. Isolated populations are found in the Blue Mountains of Oregon (upper John Day River) and in the Fraser and Columbia drainages in British Columbia. It also occurs east of the Continental Divide in upper Missouri and South Saskatchewan tributaries.

2A. **WESTSLOPE CUTTHROAT TROUT**. *Salmo clarki lewisi*. Upper Twin Creek, Montana (South Fork Flathead River Basin), September, 1978.

This specimen, taken above a barrier, is considered to be "pure strain." Being a small fish, it is not as colorful as the male shown in Plate 2 but the pattern and arrangement of the spots are classic westslope.

3. Formerly called the **MOUNTAIN CUTTHROAT**, *Salmo clarki alpestris*, this trout is now considered to be an aberrant form of the **WESTSLOPE**, *Salmo clarki lewisi*. Six Mile Creek near Revelstoke, British Columbia.

DISTINCTIVE CHARACTERISTICS: In color and spotting pattern this trout is almost identical to the westslope, although the spots are typically smaller and less profuse.

NATURAL RANGE: Isolated populations are found in Kootenay and Shuswap Lake tributaries in British Columbia (upper Columbia and Fraser River systems).

4. **YELLOWSTONE CUTTHROAT TROUT**. *Salmo clarki bouvieri*, Cottonwood Creek, Wyoming (Salt River tributary), August, 1977.

DISTINCTIVE CHARACTERISTICS: The trout illustrated has typical large, mostly round spots well distributed over a brassy background. Although some individuals, particularly males, exhibit rosy or purplish areas along the lateral line, this subspecies does not have the capability to produce the reds, oranges and yellows of the westslope race.

NATURAL RANGE: Snake River and tributaries above Shoshone Falls to Palisades Reservoir and above Jackson Lake, the area between these last two points being occupied by the fine-spotted cutthroat. It is the native trout of all the upper Yellowstone and tributaries downstream as far as Tongue River. It has been widely planted outside its natural range.

(Continued on page 97)

Color Plates

1. COASTAL CUTTHROAT TROUT. *Salmo clarki clarki.*

2. WESTSLOPE CUTTHROAT TROUT. *Salmo clarki lewisi.*

2A. WESTSLOPE CUTTHROAT TROUT. *Salmo clarki lewisi.*

3. WESTSLOPE, *Salmo clarki lewisi.* Photo by F. Tony Pletcher, Vancouver, B. C.

4. YELLOWSTONE CUTTHROAT TROUT. *Salmo clarki bouvieri.*

82

4A. YELLOWSTONE CUTTHROAT TROUT. *Salmo clarki bouvieri.*

5. SNAKE RIVER FINE-SPOTTED CUTTHROAT. *Salmo clarki* subspecies.

6. HUMBOLDT CUTTHROAT TROUT. *Salmo clarki* subspecies.

6A. HUMBOLDT CUTTHROAT TROUT. *Salmo clarki* subspecies.

7. LAHONTAN CUTTHROAT TROUT. *Salmo clarki henshawi.* Photo by California Department of Fish and Game.

7A. LAHONTAN CUTTHROAT TROUT. *Salmo clarki henshawi.*

8. PAIUTE CUTTHROAT TROUT. *Salmo clarki seleniris.*

9. BONNEVILLE CUTTHROAT TROUT. *Salmo clarki utah.*

10. BONNEVILLE CUTTHROAT TROUT. *Salmo clarki utah.* (Snake Valley form).

11. WHITEHORSE-WILLOW CREEK CUTTHROAT TROUT. *Salmo clarki* subspecies.

12. COLORADO RIVER CUTTHROAT TROUT. *Salmo clarki pleuriticus.*

13. GREENBACK CUTTHROAT TROUT. *Salmo clarki stomias.* Photo by Terry Hickman.

14. RIO GRANDE CUTTHROAT TROUT. *Salmo clarki virginalis.*

15. PECOS strain of the RIO GRANDE CUTTHROAT TROUT. *Salmo clarki virginalis.*

16. REDBAND TROUT. *Salmo gairdneri* subspecies. Photo by California Department of Fish and Game.

17. REDBAND TROUT OF THE MID-COLUMBIA BASIN. *Salmo gairdneri gairdneri.*

17A. KAMLOOPS TROUT. *Salmo gairdneri kamloops.* Photo by F. Tony Pletcher, Vancouver, B. C.

17B. MOUNTAIN KAMLOOPS TROUT. *Salmo gairdneri whitehousi.* Photo by F. Tony Pletcher, Vancouver, B. C.

18. VOLCANO CREEK GOLDEN TROUT. *Salmo gairdneri roosevelti.*

18A. VOLCANO CREEK GOLDEN TROUT. *Salmo gairdneri roosevelti.*

89

19. SOUTH FORK KERN RIVER GOLDEN TROUT. *Salmo gairdneri aquabonita.*

20. GILBERT GOLDEN TROUT. *Salmo gairdneri gilberti.*

21. APACHE TROUT. *Salmo gilae apache.*

22. GILA TROUT. *Salmo gilae gilae.* Photo by Dr. John Rinne, U. S. Forest Service, Tempe, AZ.

23. COASTAL RAINBOW TROUT. *Salmo gairdneri irideus.*

23A. STEELHEAD TROUT. *Salmo gairdneri irideus.*

23B. EAGLE LAKE RAINBOW TROUT. *Salmo gairdneri aquilarum.* Photo by California Department of Fish and Game.

23C. KERN RIVER RAINBOW TROUT. *Salmo gairdneri.* Photo by California Department of Fish and Game.

24. RIO YAQUI TROUT. *Salmo* species.

25. MEXICAN GOLDEN TROUT. *Salmo chrysogaster.*

26. RIO DEL PRESIDIO TROUT. *Salmo gairdneri* subspecies.

27. RIO SAN LORENZO TROUT. *Salmo* species.

28. LAKE TROUT. *Salvelinus namaycush.* Photo by F. Tony Pletcher, Vancouver, B. C.

29. EASTERN BROOK TROUT. *Salvelinus fontinalis fontinalis.*

30. ARCTIC CHARR. *Salvelinus alpinus* subspecies. Photo by Norval Netsch, Anchorage, AK.

31. NORTHERN DOLLY VARDEN TROUT. *Salvelinus malma malma.*

32. SOUTHERN DOLLY VARDEN. *Salvelinus malma* subspecies. Photo by Norval Netsch, Anchorage, AK.

33. BULL TROUT. *Salvelinus confluentis.*

34. ATLANTIC SALMON. *Salmo salar.* Photo by Gary Anderson, Atlantic Salmon Federation.

**4A.	YELLOWSTONE CUTTHROAT TROUT.** *Salmo clarki bouvieri.* Sedge Creek, Yellowstone Park, Wyoming.

This particular trout, found only in Sedge Creek above a thermal barrier, is considered to be a variant of the Yellowstone cutthroat. Note that the black spots are largely confined to the caudal area.

**5.	SNAKE RIVER FINE-SPOTTED CUTTHROAT.** *Salmo clarki* subspecies. Snake River, near Moose, Wyoming, August, 1977.

DISTINCTIVE CHARACTERISTICS: An undescribed race, this trout has the smallest spots of any native trout north of Mexico. The spots are irregular in shape, very numerous and well distributed over the body. The silvery ground color has a yellowish wash with a pinkish tinge along the lateral line. Fins and tail are yellow or orange. It most resembles the coastal cutthroat and to a lesser degree the Gila trout.

NATURAL RANGE: That section of the Snake River and most of its tributaries lying between Jackson Lake and Palisades Reservoir. It still occurs there in good numbers and has been introduced into many other waters of the West.

**6.	HUMBOLDT CUTTHROAT TROUT.** *Salmo clarki* subspecies. Gance Creek, Nevada (disjunct Humboldt tributary), July, 1978.

DISTINCTIVE CHARACTERISTICS: Generally a rather dull-colored trout, typical of the Great Basin, the brassy ground color becoming almost brick red in larger fish. Spots are large and round, most numerous on caudal peduncle. Parr marks persist with age with auxiliary parr marks present along lower sides. Compared with the Lahontan cutthroat, the spots are fewer and less evenly distributed over the body.

NATURAL RANGE: Upper Humboldt River Basin in Nevada, persisting in only a few remote headwaters.

**6A.	HUMBOLDT CUTTHROAT TROUT.** *Salmo clarki* subspecies. Frazier Creek, Nevada, July, 1977.

The trout illustrated here is considered to be "pure strain" and being larger and more mature than the Gance Creek specimen, it shows more typical adult coloration.

**7.	LAHONTAN CUTTHROAT TROUT.** *Salmo clarki henshawi.* Heenan Lake, California.

DISTINCTIVE CHARACTERISTICS: The usual dull brassy coloration of Great Basin trout is evident in this race, although at spawning time males may develop rose or reddish tints along the lateral line and on the gillcovers. The spots are round, fairly large and well distributed over the body and frequently there are numerous very small spots on the abdomen.

NATURAL RANGE: Lahontan Basin and tributary streams in California and Nevada, excepting the Humboldt River. At present this trout is maintained in Walker and Pyramid lakes by hatchery input, although the stock may be somewhat hybridized. Pure strains still occur in Summit Lake, Nevada, and in headwaters of the East Carson River, California.

**7A.	LAHONTAN CUTTHROAT TROUT.** *Salmo clarki henshawi.* East Fork Carson River, California, September, 1979.

The specimen illustrated is from a population considered to be essentially pure strain. Being much smaller than the Lahontan cutthroat shown in Plate 7, the parr marks are evident and the brassy color is just beginning to develop.

**8.	PAIUTE CUTTHROAT TROUT.** *Salmo clarki seleniris.* Silver King Creek, California (East Fork Carson drainage), September, 1979.

DISTINCTIVE CHARACTERISTICS: Pure strains of this unique trout typically have no black spots; specimens with a total of five or more spots are considered hybrids. Parr marks are retained into adulthood as in golden trout. Otherwise, it is similar to the Lahontan cutthroat from which it was derived.

NATURAL RANGE: Silver King Creek and tributaries, Sierra Nevada of California. Carson River drainage.

**9.	BONNEVILLE CUTTHROAT TROUT.** *Salmo clarki utah.* Smith Fork, Wyoming (Bear River drainage).

DISTINCTIVE CHARACTERISTICS: Silvery ground color with large, round black spots well distributed over the body. Resembles Yellowstone cutthroat but is silvery rather than bronze or brassy.

NATURAL RANGE: Streams tributary to the Bonneville Basin in Utah, Idaho, Wyoming and Nevada. Pure populations are now extremely rare.

**10.	BONNEVILLE CUTTHROAT TROUT** (Snake Valley form), *Salmo clarki utah.* Hampton Creek, Nevada (Snake Valley basin), July, 1977.

DISTINCTIVE CHARACTERISTICS: This isolated race has smaller and more numerous black spots than other forms of *utah.* The ground color also tends to conform more with other Great Basin trout, being more brassy than silvery.

NATURAL RANGE: A few perennial streams draining to Snake Valley on the Utah-Nevada boundary.

**11.	WHITEHORSE-WILLOW CREEK CUTTHROAT TROUT.** *Salmo clarki* subspecies. Willow Creek, Oregon (Trout Creek Mountains), August, 1978.

DISTINCTIVE CHARACTERISTICS: The brassy background, sometimes almost brick red or brown and the rounded black spots well distributed over the body are typical of this race.

NATURAL RANGE: Willow Creek and adjacent Whitehorse Creek, Trout Creek Mountains, Oregon — the only two streams where this trout occurs.

12. **COLORADO RIVER CUTTHROAT TROUT.** *Salmo clarki pleuriticus.* Rock Creek, Wyoming (Green River drainage), August, 1976.

DISTINCTIVE CHARACTERISTICS: Yellowish or brassy background color, rounded black spots concentrated posteriorly becoming fewer and smaller forward along the back and sides and the high colors along abdomen and gillcovers. The coloration of the abdomen can be red, orange or yellow and apparently is an expression of size and age, juveniles having white bellies which become progressively more colored with size.

NATURAL RANGE: Upper Colorado River and tributaries. Lower down in the system where the water becomes warmer and more turbid, the range is discontinuous.

13. **GREENBACK CUTTHROAT TROUT.** *Salmo clarki stomias.* Island Lake, Colorado.

DISTINCTIVE CHARACTERISTICS: Why this trout was named "greenback" is a mystery as the back is no more green than in many other races of trout. The large spots separate it from the Colorado cutthroat from which it was derived, typically the largest spots of any race excepting the Pecos strain of the Rio Grande cutthroat. Like the Rio Grande and Colorado cutthroats, the greenback can be highly colored.

NATURAL RANGE: Upper South Platte and Arkansas River drainages. Rare now as pure populations.

14. **RIO GRANDE CUTTHROAT TROUT.** *Salmo clarki virginalis.* Rio Puerco, New Mexico (Rio Grande drainage).

DISTINCTIVE CHARACTERISTICS: Black spots concentrated on the caudal peduncle, occurring more sparingly forward above the lateral line. This race also has the capability to produce high colors on lower sides, abdomen and along the lateral line. Another feature noted in all Rio Grande cutthroats is a bluish tinge in the lining of the mouth and on the membrane under the maxillary.

NATURAL RANGE: Upper Rio Grande River and tributaries. An isolated population occurs in the Sacramento Mountains of New Mexico in a stream once tributary to an ancient course of the Rio Grande.

15. **PECOS** strain of the **RIO GRANDE CUTTHROAT TROUT.** *Salmo clarki virginalis.* Rito del Padre, New Mexico (Pecos River headwater), June, 1978.

DISTINCTIVE CHARACTERISTICS: This trout is similar in all respects to other Rio Grande cutthroats except for the huge spots. Only one other cutthroat, the greenback, has spots this large.

NATURAL RANGE: Upper Pecos River Basin in New Mexico. Presently restricted to only four tiny headwaters.

16. **REDBAND TROUT.** *Salmo gairdneri* subspecies. Sheepheaven Creek, California, June, 1969.

DISTINCTIVE CHARACTERISTICS: All redband trout, with the exception of the golden trout of the Sierra Nevada and the Kamloops and Mountain Kamloops of British Columbia, are currently lumped together as *gairdneri.* Being so diverse in intensity of coloration and spotting pattern, however, new subspecies will undoubtedly be named. Even so, all have certain shared characteristics: prominent red band along the lower sides, traces of "cutthroat slash marks" varying from bright orange to faint brassy, a cheek blotch, oval parr marks with small, round auxiliary parr marks above and below and cream-tipped dorsal, anal and pelvic fins. Compared with coastal rainbows, they also have smaller scales and fewer pyloric caeca and in some cases vestigial basibranchial teeth.

NATURAL RANGE: The trout illustrated on this plate is known only from Sheepheaven Creek in Northern California, a tiny, disjunct tributary of the McCloud River, Sacramento drainage.

17. **REDBAND TROUT OF THE MID-COLUMBIA BASIN.** *Salmo gairdneri gairdneri.* Big Creek, Oregon (Malheur River headwater), August, 1980.

DISTINCTIVE CHARACTERISTICS: Compared with the Sheepheaven Creek strain, the spotting is much more profuse, covering the entire body even to the abdomen. Coloring is less intense, more "rainbow" like. Most specimens have faint brassy slash marks but some Deschutes River fish have the slash marks brilliant orange.

NATURAL RANGE: Upper and mid-sections of the Klamath and Columbia River systems (below barriers), and in some interior drainages (dessicating basins) in Eastern Oregon.

17A. **KAMLOOPS TROUT.** *Salmo gairdneri kamloops.* Lardeau, River, British Columbia.

DISTINCTIVE CHARACTERISTICS: The trout illustrated is a 21-pound male from the Lardeau River, British Columbia, a tributary to Kootenay Lake, where it undoubtedly grew big and fat on Kokanee salmon. The Kootenay strain is the largest of the redbands and one of these stocked in Jewell Lake, B. C., reached a weight of 52.5 pounds. These redbands are not spotted as profusely as those of the mid-Columbia but most closely resemble the Deschutes River "redsides." Lacustrine and sea-run forms are more silvery and show less color than stream-dwelling fish except during spawning.

NATURAL RANGE: Frazier River and tributaries above Hell's Gate and the Upper Columbia Basin in British Columbia. It is probable that the "rainbows" native to headwaters of the Peace and Athabaska rivers were derived from the Kamloops through headwater transfers. The Kamloops trout has been widely introduced beyond its original range.

17B. MOUNTAIN KAMLOOPS TROUT. *Salmo gairdneri whitehousi.* Headwaters of Wahleach River and Lake system, British Columbia.

DISTINCTIVE CHARACTERISTICS: This race is not considered a valid subspecies by some ichthyologists who state that the difference between it and the Kamloops are environmentally produced rather than genetic. Be that as it may, the mountain Kamloops is different, primarily in having smaller **scales**, higher coloration and the retention of parr marks into adulthood.

NATURAL RANGE: The mountain Kamloops generally occurs above barriers in headwater tributaries of the Frazier and Columbia systems in British Columbia.

18. VOLCANO CREEK GOLDEN TROUT. *Salmo gairdneri roosevelti.* Left Stringer of Volcano Creek above barrier, California (Golden Trout Creek tributary), August, 1975.

DISTINCTIVE CHARACTERISTICS: This race, not considered a valid subspecies by ichthyologists, is the most intensely colored, most beautiful of all races of golden trout. It differs from other goldens in having black spots restricted to the caudal peduncle and in more intense coloration. Otherwise it has all the typical characteristics — cream-tipped anal, dorsal and pelvic fins, crimson stripe, yellow lower sides and red abdomen. All races of goldens retain the parr marks into maturity.

NATURAL RANGE: Golden Trout Creek and tributaries (Kern River drainage), California. Now restricted to Volcano Creek above a barrier as a pure population.

18A. VOLCANO CREEK GOLDEN TROUT. *Salmo gairdneri roosevelti.* Left Stringer, Volcano Creek, California, August, 1975.

This specimen, from a dark-shaded pool, shows the intense coloration this race is capable of.

19. SOUTH FORK KERN RIVER GOLDEN TROUT. *Salmo gairdneri aquabonita.* Mulkey Creek above barrier, California (South Fork Kern River tributary), August, 1975.

DISTINCTIVE CHARACTERISTICS: Similar to *roosevelti* but the black spots extend to the head above the lateral line and coloration is less intense.

NATURAL RANGE: Upper South Fork of Kern River and tributaries, California. This is the golden trout propagated in hatcheries and has been widely planted at high elevations throughout the western states.

20. GILBERT GOLDEN TROUT. *Salmo gairdneri gilberti.* Coyote Creek above barrier, California (Kern River tributary), August, 1975.

DISTINCTIVE CHARACTERISTICS: Coloration is the same as in other golden trout but the colors are less intense, the belly being orange rather than red and extending from the base of the pelvic to the pectoral fins only. The black spots are typically larger, more profuse and in some populations extend below the lateral line.

NATURAL RANGE: Main stem of the Upper Kern River and its western tributaries. Now only a few isolated populations occur above barriers.

21. APACHE TROUT. *Salmo gilae apache.* Little Bonito Creek, Arizona (Black River tributary, Salt River drainage), April, 1972.

DISTINCTIVE CHARACTERISTICS: Very pronounced yellow ground color, including the fins, the anal, pelvics and dorsal being white-tipped. There are no red tints in this race and the black spots are fairly large, round and well distributed over the body. The iris has two small black spots on either side of the pupil, giving the impression of a black horizontal band across the eye. Having fewer vertebrae than most trout, it has a short, chunky appearance. Juveniles are much darker, probably due to the large, dark parr marks.

NATURAL RANGE: Headwaters of the White and Black rivers in the White Mountains of Arizona, Salt River drainage, and also headwaters of the Little Colorado. This distribution is unique, being sandwiched in between disjunct populations of the Gila trout. Now very rare as pure populations.

22. GILA TROUT. *Salmo gilae gilae.* Main Diamond Creek, New Mexico.

DISTINCTIVE CHARACTERISTICS: Differs from the Apache trout in having much smaller and more profuse black spots and in having a brassy tinge over the body rather than the pronounced yellow coloration. The Gila trout also develops pink or rose colors along the lateral line, completely absent in the Apache.

NATURAL RANGE: Upper Gila River Basin, including headwaters of the San Francisco. Disjunct, widely separated populations occur in the Salt River drainage — the Verde and Aqua Fria rivers. Now very rare as pure populations.

23. COASTAL RAINBOW TROUT. *Salmo gairdneri irideus.* Illinois River, Oregon (Rogue River tributary), September, 1978.

DISTINCTIVE CHARACTERISTICS: Fresh sea-run fish (steelhead) are bluish-green on the back with bright silvery sides. The black spots, often X- or crescent-shaped, do not occur below the lateral line except for a few that sometimes spill over on the caudal and pectoral areas. In fresh water they become darker and a rose blush develops along the lateral line. Landlocked populations have a more compressed body and the black spots are well distributed on both sides of the lateral line which also sports a "rainbow stripe."

NATURAL RANGE: Northern Baja, California, north in coastal drainages to southern tributaries of the Kuskokwim River in Alaska. At least three disjunct populations occur in Mexico as far south as the Rio del Presidio at 24° north latitude. Thus the range extends nearly from the Tropic of Cancer to 61° north within 5° of the Arctic Circle. This is the race that has been introduced world-wide and is still present in most of its original range.

23A. STEELHEAD TROUT. *Salmo gairdneri irideus.* Dean River, British Columbia, August, 1983.

DISTINCTIVE CHARACTERISTICS: The trout illustrated, a two-year salt female, probably weighed 10 or 11 pounds. Note the typical steelhead spotting pattern (no spots below the lateral line except a few above the pectoral fin and just forward of the tail).

NATURAL RANGE: The natural range of steelhead extends from Southern California to the Alaska Peninsula, although each river system probably has its own unique physiological race and in some cases two or more, depending on the section of the river used for spawning and whether summer or winter run.

23B. EAGLE LAKE RAINBOW TROUT. *Salmo gairdneri aquilarum.* Eagle Lake, California.

DISTINCTIVE CHARACTERISTICS: This trout is currently considered to be a rainbow but it does show many redband characteristics. Due to its position in the Lahontan Basin, the lake should contain cutthroats; therefore, the trout's ancestry may actually contain cutthroat as well as rainbow and/or redband. Whatever its origin, this trout is peculiarly adapted to the highly alkaline waters of Eagle Lake. Note the crescent-shaped black spots above and below the lateral line.

NATURAL RANGE: Native only to Eagle Lake, California.

23C. KERN RIVER RAINBOW TROUT. *Salmo gairdneri.*

DISTINCTIVE CHARACTERISTICS: The taxonomic status of this trout is still in question. Formerly classified as *gilberti,* it was thought to be the ancestor of the golden trout on both sides of the main Kern River. Re-examina-tion of early collections, however, has led Dr. Robert J. Behnke to believe that the original trout of the main Kern was the golden trout now confined to a few headwaters of its western tributaries and that the Kern River rainbow is the result of hatchery introductions. There are other ichthyologists, however, who hold to the native rainbow origin. It is shown here because of its clouded status.

NATURAL RANGE: If this trout is indeed endemic to the main Kern River, the race is restricted to its mid and upper sections.

24. RIO YAQUI TROUT. *Salmo* species. Rio Gavilan, Chihuahua, Mexico (Rio Yaqui tributary), May, 1983.

DISTINCTIVE CHARACTERISTICS: Very small X-shaped black spots confined to the area above the lateral line and long, narrow, rectangular parr marks. Specimens from the upper Tomochic, the Yaqui's southernmost tributary, were bright lemon yellow on the lower sides. They differ from the Mexican golden trout in having a white belly rather than orange and they lack the banded appearance of the eye. This trout is said to be similar to those of the Rio Mayo and is as yet undescribed.

NATURAL RANGE: Uppermost tributaries of the Rio Yaqui, Chihuahua, Mexico. Similar trout from across the Continental Divide in the Rio Casas Grandes drainage were probably stocked there from Yaqui sources.

25. MEXICAN GOLDEN TROUT. *Salmo chrysogaster.* Rio Loera, Chihuahua, Mexico, April, 1983.

DISTINCTIVE CHARACTERISTICS: Numerous very small black spots above the lateral line; parr marks bluish and oval in shape with many auxiliary parr marks along lower sides; the belly and lower fins are bright orange; the dorsal, anal and pelvic fins are white-tipped and black spots of pigment are in the iris on both sides of the pupil, giving the eye a horizontally-banded appearance. There is a faint rainbow stripe and the lower sides are light yellowish. This trout has the fewest number of vertebrae and pyloric caeca of any North American trout of the genus *Salmo.* While all Mexican trout have slight brassy slash marks, they are most pronounced and colorful in *chrysogaster.*

NATURAL RANGE: Known only from the uppermost tributaries of three Pacific drainges: Rio Fuerte, Rio Sinaloa and Rio Culiacan, Chihuahua and Durango, Mexico.

26. RIO DEL PRESIDIO TROUT. *Salmo gairdneri subspecies.* Taken from an unnamed tributary of the Rio del Presidio in latitude 23° 48′ N. (about 20 miles north of the Tropic of Cancer), Durango, Mexico, April, 1983.

DISTINCTIVE CHARACTERISTICS: This is the most rainbow-redband-like trout of any in Mexico. It has a prominent rainbow stripe, white-tipped anal, dorsal and pelvic fins, round parr marks and numerous auxiliary parr marks. The black spots are large, oblong in shape, with their axis aligned vertically.

There is some question as to whether this trout is actually native to the Rio del Presidio or was stocked there. It does, however, have more vertebrae than any others of the rainbow clan.

NATURAL RANGE: Known only from headwaters of the Rio del Presidio, Durango, Mexico. If actually native there, it is the most southerly of all naturally occurring North American salmonids, over 4,000 miles south of the most northerly known form of Arctic charr.

27. RIO SAN LORENZO TROUT. *Salmo* species. Rio Truchas, Durango, Mexico (San Lorenzo tributary), April, 1983.

DISTINCTIVE CHARACTERISTICS: This trout appears to be akin to the redband-rainbow complex. The black spots, as well as the parr marks, are smaller and more numerous than in the Rio del Presidio trout while both share the white-tipped anal, dorsal and pelvic fins. There is also some question as to whether it is actually native to the San Lorenzo or if it was stocked there.

NATURAL RANGE: Known only from the Rio Truchas, a headwater of the San Lorenzo, Durango, Mexico.

28. LAKE TROUT. *Salvelinus namaycush.* Shuswap Lake, British Columbia.

DISTINCTIVE CHARACTERISTICS: The only trout in North America that has whitish spots only — no black, red, pink or yellow spots. Typically the background color is dark (green, gray or brown), and the spots are large and profuse. It also has a markedly forked tail.

NATURAL RANGE: Northern North America, from Atlantic to Pacific, south to New England, New York, the Great Lakes, Minnesota, Northwestern Montana and Central British Columbia. Restricted to the mainland, mostly in lakes, but occurs in some of the islands of the Arctic Archipelago. This vast area is practically coincidental with that covered by late Pleistocene glaciation.

29. EASTERN BROOK TROUT. *Salvelinus fontinalis fontinalis.*

DISTINCTIVE CHARACTERISTICS: To many, the eastern brook trout is the most beautiful of all freshwater fishes and it may well be. Its jewel-like markings and vivid coloration have been described so often that anything written here will be repetitious. However, the blue-haloed red dots, creamy white spots, white-margined lower fins, worm-like vermiculations of the back and dorsal fin are all distinctive. Its background colors depend upon the habitat — fresh sea-run fish are bright and silvery while those in fresh water and particularly from peat-stained streams and ponds are quite dark, tending to vivid yellow, orange or red on the lower side and abdomen.

NATURAL RANGE: Eastern North America from the Southern Appalachians to Northern Labrador and Quebec. West of Hudson Bay from Seal River south to Great Lakes drainages and some tributaries of the upper Mississippi. Widely introduced in Western North America in mountain lakes and streams.

30. ARCTIC CHARR. *Salvelinus alpinus* subspecies. (Landlocked form of Western Alaska), Schreder Lake, Alaska.

DISTINCTIVE CHARACTERISTICS: This charr is closely related to the Northern Dolly Varden to which it bears a close resemblance. Both have pink spots along the sides and in the Arctic charr the spots are large — larger than the pupil of the eye while in the Dolly Varden the spots are smaller than the pupil of the eye. Note slim caudal peduncle and forked tail.

NATURAL RANGE: Circumpolar. In North America from Western and Northern Alaska around the rim of the Arctic and south to New England. The Alaskan, Canadian Maritime and New England populations are relict landlocked forms but from the Mackenzie River to the Eastern Arctic, it is anadromous as well. This charr is our northernmost salmonid, recorded in the Queen Elizabeth group of the Arctic Archipelago at 82° 34' north latitude.

31. NORTHERN DOLLY VARDEN TROUT. *Salvelinus malma malma.* Goodnews River, Alaska, July, 1981.

DISTINCTIVE CHARACTERISTICS: This trout and the Arctic charr are very similar in appearance, the Dolly having smaller and more numerous pink spots along the sides, typically smaller than the pupil of the eye, the caudal peduncle is thicker and the tail margin straight. It also has a significantly lower number of pyloric caeca but this feature is not apparent without dissection.

NATURAL RANGE: Eastern Siberia and Northwestern North America. In Alaska it occurs in north slope drainages of the Alaska Peninsula north and east around the coast to the Mackenzie River. Both landlocked and anadromous forms are present.

32. SOUTHERN DOLLY VARDEN. *Salvelinus malma* subspecies (Possibly *lordii?*), Anchor River, Kenai Peninsula, Alaska.

DISTINCTIVE CHARACTERISTICS: The charr illustrated is a sea-run fish, quite silvery with blue halos surrounding the pink spots. Landlocked forms are generally darker and the spots may be yellow, orange, whitish or light pink. It closely resembles the Northern Dolly, *Salvelinus malma malma,* but has significantly fewer vertebrae and gillrakers. Probably the best way to distinguish between the two would be locality where taken: if north of the Alaska Peninsula, it would be a Northern Dolly; if south of this point, a Southern Dolly.

NATURAL RANGE: From southern drainages of the Aleutian Islands and the Alaska Peninsula south to the Columbia River, but not abundant south of Puget Sound. Both anadromous and landlocked populations occur.

33.   **BULL TROUT.** *Salvelinus confluentis.* Big Creek, Oregon
      (Malheur River drainage), August, 1980.

DISTINCTIVE CHARACTERISTICS: Greenish to brownish back and sides,
spots usually quite small and numerous, well distributed over the body and
they are usually orange or yellow. In cross section the body is quite round,
the head long and somewhat flattened. Tip of lower jaw in larger specimens
has a pronounced fleshy knob with a corresponding notch on the upper jaw.

NATURAL RANGE: Western North America from the McCloud River in
California north to upper Skeena River drainages in British Columbia;
particularly widespread in the mid and upper Columbia Basin. East of the
Continental Divide in headwaters of the North and South Saskatchewan and
upper Mackenzie system.

34.   **ATLANTIC SALMON.** *Salmo salar.* Adult salmon, caught
      on the Grand Cascapedia River, Quebec.

DISTINCTIVE CHARACTERISTICS: Atlantic salmon are silvery-sided fish
with greenish- blue backs when fresh and in from the sea, becoming darker
during their spawning runs in fresh water. Black spots are rather sparse,
mostly above the lateral line, highly irregular in shape and said to resemble
the Cross of St. Andrews.

NATURAL RANGE: Coastal streams and adjacent ocean on both sides of
the North Atlantic from Galicia in Spain northward around North Cape into
the Barents Sea, the British Isles and Iceland. In North America, Atlantic
salmon probably originally occurred from the Delaware River northward
into Ungava Bay in Labrador. In the United States dams and pollution
eliminated salmon from all streams except for a few rivers in Maine but
restoration programs are slowly making some progress and a few salmon
now run into the Connecticut and even the Hudson.

CHAPTER 14

Native Trout of the Lower Colorado System

MY "SOMEDAY" HOPES OF tracking down rare Apache trout in their wild, ancestral homeland had been triggered by earlier news reports of last-ditch efforts to save the then undescribed species. Accounts said the Apache Indians and U.S. Fish and Wildlife Service had banded together for the try. Return of a viable population might permit a limited fishery.

My "someday" finally arrived late one April when I set up camp under an open grove of ponderosas on a bench within sight and sound of the White River, a tributary of the Salt. I was within the Fort Apache Indian Reservation in Arizona, over a million and a half acres of wild mountain country and plateau land lying between the Mogollon Rim and the Salt and Black rivers. Apache trout still held out in a few tiny headwaters, possibly inhabiting about one percent of their original range.

It was not that other waters of the reservation were unsuitable for Apache trout; other streams contained ample stocks of non-natives — browns and hatchery rainbows. The White River at my doorstep was beautiful trout water, but the natives had long since become victims of hybridization. They had been out-competed, sacrificed to the rubber trout philosophy of instant fishing.

I had come into this mountain fastness of the Apaches from the desert, across the arid plains of Western New Mexico and Eastern Arizona, through the Painted Desert and the Petrified Forest. It is a vast country of far horizons, bold mesas, and vivid-ly colored badlands eroded into fantastic shapes. It is beautiful in a grand way, but harsh and forbidding; I was happy to be back in the forest again, among the oaks and ponderosas, and to hear the wind in the trees and the song of running water.

Some reservation waters were closed to any and all fishing to protect the Apache trout; to learn where I might fish legally for pure natives, I pow-wowed with tribal officials in White River and with federal fisheries biologists at Pine Top, a small village just north of there. I found that pure Apache trout had been stocked in Christmas Tree Lake to provide a sport fishery, but I was too early. The few small streams where I might try included Little Diamond Creek and its tiny tributary, Coyote Creek, and also a tributary of the Black River, Little Bonito Creek.

I decided to try Little Diamond first since it was nearest my camp. A branch of Big Diamond, a tributary of the White, it joined the main stream just above my camp. Armed with the necessary tribal permit and fishing license, I set out through ranks of stately ponderosas, their cinnamon-hued trunks gleaming in the dappled lights that filtered through the needled canopy. When the track swung away from Main Diamond over a low divide and into Little Diamond's drainage, I found a wide bench above the creek and parked The Beetle.

A pickup truck pulled up as I was pulling on my hippers and assembling my rod; I was being scrutinized by three Apache women. In the exchange of greetings, they informed me they didn't have a man and were in need of one. I explained that I was after Apache trout, not Apache women. They giggled a bit and left me, saying they would be back. I retreated hastily down the slope toward the creek.

When I broke out of timber at the foot of the slope, I was in a long, narrow meadow through which Little Diamond meandered and burbled, a beautiful little stream, maybe a yard wide, sparkling clear, and open enough for conventional casts.

By a half-submerged log midway of a pool I hooked a fish, a lovely wild brown trout of about ten inches, good-sized for the water but a far cry from a native. Upstream in a bend I plucked an eight-inch rainbow, or mostly rainbow, from the tailwaters of a riffle. I hooked others, but none that even slightly resembled pure Apache trout.

From its junction with Little Diamond, I followed Coyote Creek up a ways, but it was a mere rill, a tiny trickle. If it contained trout they must have been of minnow-size; even a six-inch fish couldn't have turned around in water that small. I returned to Little Diamond and fished up until the sun's slanting rays warned me to return while there was still light. I found no barrier and no Apache trout; only browns or rainbows or rainbow-Apache hybrids.

Descending on a dim trail within a timber fringe bordering the stream, I saw in the dust lots of deer tracks and, now and again, the splayed track of a wild turkey. I strained to see a shadowy form dashing across the trail ahead of me. It flashed through an open glade, neck ramrodded straight out, its whitish-blue head glowing eerily in the half light, and beard swinging wildly as it fled — a sight to thrill an old turkey hunter to the marrow.

It was almost dark when I reached the point at which I had entered the valley and I had to pick my way carefully through the timber. As I labored up the slope I heard a pickup start and drive off. My Apache belles had returned, as vowed, and had just left.

Fisheries biologists at Pine Top were as disappointed as I was that I had found no Apache trout in Little Diamond and its tributary, Coyote Creek. They suggested I try Little Bonito where a new logging road afforded fairly easy access. Little Bonito, a tributary of Black River (the Black and White rivers making up the Salt), was within the ancestral range of the Apache trout. I was advised to fish Little Bonito high up, above the rainbows and the hybrids.

On a clear, cool morning I moved through White River Village and past old Fort Apache, then southeasterly across an open plateau with scattered stands of ponderosa pines. Ragged clumps of junipers and pinons appeared as the country sloped gradually toward Black River and into grazing country. I passed several stock watering holes called "tanks" — Seven Mile, Navajo Pit, Chino Spring — and when I reached Corn Tank I turned northeast, climbing again into open groves of ponderosa, or what was left of them. The area had been logged recently and there were more stumps and slash than trees.

The new logging road, still under construction, dropped off into the valley of Little Bonito, crossed the creek and ended abruptly in piles of broken rock and heaps of gravel. I parked The Beetle and hurried up Little Bonito, little enough to flow easily through a metal culvert under the new road. I was impatient to leave the scene of raw cuts and fills, piles of logs, roots bulldozed into windrows and other signs of man's heavy hand. The little valley, narrow at first with steep timbered slopes crowding in, opened into a fairly wide flat with aspen glades alternated with patches of pine. What a contrast to the devastation below.

Little Bonito meandered through miniature parks, the sun's rays accentuating the greens, blues, oranges and yellows of spring blooms. The stream glided through the dappled shade of streamside forest and back into the light again. There were little pools, riffles and slick runs and the sound of water in motion. Best of all, in that beautiful, idyllic setting, there were fish. The creek was alive with them, scooting in all directions whenever I showed myself. Employing more stealth, I caught several of fingerling size, odd-looking creatures, indeed, but definitely Apache trout: *Salmo gilae apache*. They were dark-hued, rather than yellowish as are adult Apache, probably due to the profusion of parr marks, but all had the genetic "bandit mask" — a black, horizontal band across the eye caused by two large black spots on the iris on either side of the pupil.

I hooked and released several of the little bandits upstream but found none large enough to photograph with adult characteristics. Reluctantly I left the lovely vale, hoping to find bigger water and bigger fish below. Beyond the devastated area, Little Bonito looked better again as it was joined by another little tributary — not as lush and pristine as that higher up but still beautiful. Downstream a big trout and I spotted one another simultaneously and I marked the place well for another try at such a grand fish on my return.

Still further down, at the head of a wide pool where a little island of rocks and gravel split the current, the water had scoured two plunge pools. Each of the little deeps held trout. They looked to be a foot long at least, each feeding actively in its own little pocket. At the pool's lower end I knelt at water's edge, stripped line and switched a cast to the nearest fish. The fly fell into the little chute and drifted naturally. The fish moved over and I raised the rod, feeling the solid weight of a good fish. After a few runs and considerable thrashing against steady pressure, I had the fish in the shallows at my knees.

Here was the real thing, an adult Apache and an amazing fish, chunky and deep-bodied like a bass. Its basic color was yellow, with the brassy yellow on the back becoming lighter, almost lemon yellow, on the sides and belly. Even the head, cheeks, gillcovers and maxillary were yellow, and its overly-large fins were dusky yellow; the dorsal, anal and pelvic fins were margined in creamy-white. Medium-large black spots were evenly distributed above the lateral line, a few spilling over below, particularly on the caudal area. The most unique feature was the black bar across the eye, the bandit mark, and the total impression of a blend of gold and black was striking.

Once this amazing combination of color and form was on film I turned my attention to the other trout, now recovered from the scare and feeding again in its niche. This one took the same fly, a No. 12 Adams fished wet and was a photo image of the first. With fully mature Apache trout on film in all their gold and black splendor I sat back and relaxed with a smoke. The combination of sounds and scents — wind in the trees, tinkling water, buzzing insects, spicy scents distilled from pines — joined with the sun's warmth to produce such a soporific effect that I hated to break the spell. Finally though, when my pipe burned down, I arose and explored downstream, just looking more than fishing, then turned back. I did try for the grand fish noted and marked on the way down; it moved once but refused to take and I left the Apache in peace.

I have never been back to Little Bonito Creek. The area was logged shortly after I was first there and even though I was in the same general area a few years later I had no desire to view the shambles. I have often wondered, though, if those native Apaches survived the degradation of their habitat.

My near return was about a hundred miles further southeast, in the Mogollon Mountains in New Mexico. We had just come out of the Pecos Wilderness in the Sangre de Cristos and, having a little more time, I went with Don Stanley into the Mogollons where possibly we might find Gila trout: *Salmo gilae gilae*. At that time the Gila trout were on the endangered species list and none could be killed. Most streams where they occurred — a few tiny headwaters of the Gila River — were closed to fishing entirely, but we learned of one that was still open.

We planned a brief expedition, cutting it a bit thin, but at least I would get to see some of the Gila Wilderness and, with luck, maybe even see a Gila trout. I had once been within sight of the Mogollons but had never been in them and just the name was intriguing. Who hasn't heard of the "Muggyown Rim" and the "Muggyownes," as the rim and the mountain mass are called locally?

We were traveling light out of Albuquerque in Don's pickup on a clear June dawn with only the clothes on our backs, rain gear, fishing tackle, cameras and a cooler of cowboy Kool Aid — Coors beer. Packing rain gear through the desert and into desert ranges seemed odd, but the rainy season was imminent and we could expect violent thunderstorms.

Our route lay down the Rio Grande towards El Paso, then swung west across dry plains sparsely covered with bunchgrass and creosote bush, a typical Lower Sonoran life zone. Isolated desert ranges loomed dark and brooding in the distance, shimmering through the heat waves as the sun climbed toward the zenith. We passed through little desert towns, dusty, windblown and sere, looking as though they had seen better days. At Datil we branched off to the southwest, passed Horse Springs and skirted a bolson, a vast, parched basin that probably had been a lake during the post-glacial period. As we neared the Continental Divide, we were back into ponderosas and oaks, then dropped into the valley of the Tularosa River, a tributary of the San Francisco, to green fields of alfalfa and straggling lines of cottonwoods along the stream bank. This was Gila River drainage where Gila trout probably had dwelled in years past.

At the district ranger station in the village of Reserve we obtained maps and a permit to enter the Gila Wilderness, then followed numerous small canyons through pine-clad foothills where tufts of beargrass thrust their creamy-white spikes toward the sky. In the valley of the San Francisco we came to the village of Glenwood and found a motel, just under the turreted mass of the Mogollons, to serve as our headquarters during our forays into the Gila Wilderness.

Cumulus clouds had been building during the day and by late afternoon had grown to masses of cumulo-nimbus, blue-black at their bases with creamy white tops boiling and surging into the stratosphere. About dusk one drifted over us and suddenly the full force of its fury broke overhead. Blasts of wind, thunder and lightning and driving sheets of rain completely obliterated the landscape. We were glad to be in the shelter of a motel room rather than cowering in a tent in the forest.

The next morning, en route to the trailhead, rain still fell lightly as we climbed steadily through a gap in the mountain wall before dropping into the village of Mogollon, a ghost town from the robust mining days of the past. From Mogollon we climbed again, topping out at over 9,000 feet on a narrow, winding ridge, the densely forested slopes falling away steeply on both sides. After several miles we dropped into Willow Creek and a campground with a few buildings: our trailhead and the boundary of the Gila Wilderness. Donning gear against the light rain we moved easily up the trail, an old cart track, another vestige of mining days. The climb was continuous to the divide between Willow Creek and Iron Creek, to a small plateau on top, almost level, supporting an open stand of cinnamon-boled ponderosas. In the very middle was a small shallow lake where, years ago, someone had dammed a spring head. On the far side of the water five adult mule deer, startled and alert, watched us intently before bounding away through the pines.

We moved out, too. The path descended abruptly in a deeply incised draw to Iron Creek, shallow and flat at this point, about four or five feet wide, with much filamentous green algae waving in the clear current. As we continued upstream for an hour, which we reckoned to be about two miles, the algae thinned out and the water looked better, not so flat, with occasional pools and little cascades.

It was mid-morning, the rain had ceased and the sun peeked through breaks in the clouds. Now was the time. We strung our rods by a pool under a logjam and as I knotted on a small nymph I noticed a large, yellowish blaze on a tree trunk a few yards away. We had not seen any sign of man since leaving the trail and I walked over to have a look. A bear had ripped the bark completely off one side of a spruce two feet through. I could see the claw marks and it was so fresh the resin was still oozing, forming little droplets on the naked wood.

Don interrupted my conjecture of the bear's present whereabouts with a shout, "This pool is full of fish!"

He was crouched behind a logjam. The main current had scoured a deep around three big rocks just downstream from where it surged around the end of the logs before flattening at the pool's tail. It looked fishy, sure enough, but I could fish it better from the other side by crossing above the logs and circling in from below. Kneeling on a little bar, I switched a short cast to the deep around the rocks, hooked a tiny fish and drew it, splashing, to the shallows at my knees.

It was a Gila trout — a little gem all of four and a half inches long, but the first one I had seen. It was chunky for its length, with prominent elliptical parr marks, rosy tints along the sides and finely speckled, small black spots. The dorsal, pelvic and anal fins were yellow-tipped. I gently unstuck the fish and sent it scooting back to the pool. Then I took three more small trout from that hole by the rocks, but all were browns; there was not another Gila in the bunch.

We moved up the creek, Don on the opposite side, fishing the pools and pockets alternately. The pools were beautiful and the trout were extremely wary in the glassy tailouts. Getting into casting position on our knees was difficult. We caught several trout from six to 11 inches, but all were browns.

Believing there must be a barrier higher up where the browns could not go, we pushed on, but we never found that barrier and we didn't catch another Gila trout. Were we high enough? We were within two miles of the extreme headwaters, but our time was running out and we turned back to get out before dark. It began to rain again as we worked our way down through spruce thickets in the creek bottom and open groves of ponderosas along the bordering slopes. Distant thunder rumbled across the ridges, but the violence of the storm center passed us by, and when we reached the trail the clouds broke briefly. Dusk settled as we topped the divide to descend to Willow Creek, but the old cart track was wide and easy. We reached the pickup in pitch dark, but not too dark to locate and slurp a few cans of cowboy Kool Aid.

As we threaded our way back along the forest road toward Mogollon I reflected on the Gila Wilderness and its trout streams. The country looked the same as it always had within man's memory — a wilderness of beautiful uncut forests, sparkling waters, no pollution, no diversions, no vestiges of man except for the trails. But what of the native trout that once abounded? They were almost gone, on the brink of oblivion. They existed only in a few tiny headwaters of the Gila system and had been transplanted to one or two other streams nearby. Practically the entire population had been replaced by less desirable, non-native trout.

Was this fisheries management or conservation or was it something perpetrated in ignorance or thoughtlessness? It had cost almost nothing to destroy the native fishery, but it would be a monumental task to restore even a small part of it.

Don and I concluded it was a sad day for all native trout everywhere when man learned to propagate salmonids in a hatchery and then plant them, will-nilly, in waters that had no need of planting.

Don has fished the high Pecos streams and tramped the Mogollons for the last time. In the autumn following our trip he was thrown from his horse and killed. Charles Ritz, in concluding *A Flyfisher's Life*, invited all good fly fishers to look him up in heaven. He will know where the best trout are lying. Don, a fine gentleman and a good fly fisher, is sure to be there now, and no doubt has made contact with Ritz and gotten the word. I visualize him fishing those high celestial streams for heavenly trout —trout that once were native here. There must be lots of them, for there are precious few remaining on this earth.

Good fishing, Compadre!

CHAPTER 15

Rainbow Trout · 1

THE READER AT THIS POINT may wonder what I have against rainbows, perhaps suspecting that I have a built-in prejudice against *Salmo gairdneri irideus*. This is far from the mark. Rather, I had an early love affair with rainbows that endures to this day. But, over the years, this affection has been refined to embrace *native* rainbows only. Any trout or any salmon, when stocked in waters where it doesn't belong naturally, becomes a non-native, an exotic, and to me at least has lost its shine, that certain indefinable charm that goes with native fish in their rightful waters.

I applaud the introduction of rainbows, or any trout for that matter, in waters that cannot support a native trout fishery; that is, as long as they then can't infiltrate waters that do harbor native trout. And I think it is great that famous trout fisheries have been established where none existed before, as in certain waters of the Southern Hemisphere. But the trout I caught in New Zealand and in African streams were just fish to me. They didn't really generate the same enthusiasm they would have if they had been natives.

I live in rainbow country within easy range of three famous rainbow-steelhead streams: the Klamath, the Rogue and the Umpqua. In my opinion the rainbow-steelhead, the summer run fish, is the finest gamefish to ever breast a stream, not excepting the Atlantic salmon, *Salmo salar,* testimony to the contrary notwithstanding.

In my first year of trouting, over a half-century back in time, I aspired to own a Goodwin Granger fly rod. The nearest I came to this was acqusition of a Granger catalog, the cover depicting a leaping rainbow, resplendent in brilliant colors arcing to the fly. I tacked the masterpiece to the wall over my desk while a fresh-man in college. When my mind flagged over dull facts and figures of studies I could glance up and momentarily be refreshed, my soul refurbished. It is possible I spent more time admiring *Salmo irideus* as it was then known, than I devoted to my books. I have always regretted the passing of the name *irideus*, but now Bob Behnke has revived it as the subspecific name of the coast rainbow to differentiate this coarse-scaled form from the redband, both subspecies of *gairdneri*. Someday the name of the rainbow will be changed again, for the Siberian race, *mykiss*, was named first and it is now known that this form is identical to the coastal rainbow of North America.

With all due respect, however, to Dr. Gairdner, a naturalist of the Hudson Bay Company at Fort Vancouver in whose honor the rainbow was named by Sir John Richardson in 1836, *irideus* rolls off the tongue easier and is more descriptive. The practice of naming a species for a person has been widespread and is, no doubt, one way to bestow immortality. A friend of mine, though, had a louse named for him and he wasn't sure whether he was honored or not.

I caught my first rainbow in Joe's Brook, a tributary of the Passumpsic in the Connecticut River drainage of Vermont, almost 3,000 miles from its native waters. That was in the late '20s, and although the rainbows I caught were assuredly of hatchery origin, they were better fish then, not so highly domesticated and planted as fry or fingerlings. Fish culturists had not yet dreamed up the practice of planting "catchables."

Joe's Brook was a beautiful little stream tumbling over polished granite bedrock and boulders through a forest of beeches, birches and hemlocks. We caught few trout that measured the size limit of ten inches and I was disappointed they didn't quite look like the leaping beauty on the catalog cover. But they were rainbows, the first I had ever seen. We also fished larger streams, the Ammonoosuc, and the Wild Ammonoosuc, eastern tributaries of the Connecticut River flowing out of New Hampshire's White Mountains, but the few rainbows we hooked were small, mostly parr, and again didn't quite measure up to my expectations.

The next spring I was fishing with Bob Tweedy in Vermont's Waits River, not far above its confluence with the Connecticut. The Waits, in its lower reaches, was a fair-sized stream, meandering sedately through meadows and pasture lands. By early afternoon the mid-May sun was hot and oppressive and Bob opted for a skinny dip. While he splashed and wallowed in the lower end of a long, wide pool, I plied the fast water at the top with my three-fly cast. The improbable happened and I was suddenly fast to a grand fish, the biggest, fastest trout I had ever felt. It was everywhere at once and completely out of control. I could only hang on, oblivious to the shouted advice of my naked companion running up and down the water's edge. Finally the trout tired, I worked it through the shallows and onto a shingle beach, then scooped it with both hands up into the grass.

Glancing up, I saw we had a witness on the bank above the pool. A grizzled farmer, hearing the ruckus from the river road, had pulled up his team, climbed the stone fence and come over to see what was up. He looked at the trout, at my naked friend whose hide had turned a shocking pink from too much ultra-violet, and then at me. His eyes made the rounds again. Seeing there was no harm done, except to the trout, he jetted a squirt of tobacco juice leeward, cleared his throat with a "gadfermighty!" and left.

That rainbow was the largest trout I had ever caught or even seen. It was the Granger catalog cover come to life, only bigger and with *all* the colors. When I made a bed of wet bracken in my wicker creel and laid the trout on the green bier it wouldn't fit. Its head stuck out one end and his tail the other. I spread more wet bracken on top so it wouldn't dry out and we set off for Hanover. On Main Street we stopped at the butcher shop where the fish weighed in at exactly 2½ pounds.

I couldn't bring myself to mutilate or otherwise disfigure the beautiful trout by cleaning it and relegating it to the pot, so I brought it to my erstwhile professor of natural history, Dr. Leland Griggs, who seemed worthy of such a gift. I presented it to him as one would make an offering to a high priest at the altar. He accepted the trout graciously and gave me the opportunity to

once again relate all the colorful details of its capture. I hoped the fish would be as toothsome as it was beautiful.

Twenty years passed before I finally got into *native* rainbow country, the Pacific Northwest. By that time I had acquired a new fly rod, and though not a Granger, it was a lineal descendant, a rod built by Bill Phillipson who had worked with Granger for twenty years before setting up his own business. Called a Paramount, it was an 8½-footer weighing 4½ ounces — a beautiful tool and still fully functional.

I knew nothing then of native rainbows or of rainbow-steelhead. When a friend in Portland asked me to open the season with him I readily accepted. We drove into the northwest tip of Oregon the day before the opening, found an old logging road and ended up on the Salmonberry, a tributary of the Nehalem, in a narrow valley nestled high in the Coast Range. This was new, altogether fascinating country to me, the homegrounds of the Roosevelt elk, blacktail deer and, of course, native rainbows. The forest had been logged and pretty well abused, but the second growth was luxuriant and there remained small clumps of timber that had been overlooked. We laid out our bedrolls under Douglas firs and western red cedars close by the stream. I was surrounded by species of plants new to me: big leaf maples, vine maples, tree-sized alders, prickly salmonberry and devil's club. The country smelled spicy and fragrant with all the pleasing scents of things growing and blooming.

Scraping away a patch of forest duff, I made a rude fireplace of rounded cobbles from the stream bank, got a fire going and the coffee pot on. The sun was low, and a chill settled over us as we hunkered close to the glowing coals and sipped steaming black coffee, reminiscing about earlier days in the swamps of Arkansas where a trout was a black bass and a ridge was a place where floodwaters didn't get quite so deep. Later, when the sun dipped below the rim of our valley, we pan-fried steaks, onions and potatoes. Finally, heavy with food and brimming with anticipation for the morrow, we crawled into our bedrolls, lulled by the murmur and muted gurgling of the Salmonberry.

Mercifully, it didn't rain, as it so often does in the Coast Range, and when dawn broke clear and bright we had a quick cup of coffee and set out, my friend electing to fish downstream while I moved up over water that looked ideal but sometimes difficult to work. Alders and vine maples frequently draped over fine-looking spots. In others I hooked a few small trout and put them back. They were native rainbows and, actually, probably were steelhead parr or smolts. At that time I didn't know the difference.

By mid-morning I hadn't turned a trout of decent size and so I began to explore, rather than merely flogging the water as if killing snakes. It was then I saw *the* fish — a monster — the damndest, biggest salmonid I had ever seen. I didn't know if it was a steelhead or salmon, only that it was big, a yard long, maybe. It just held in the current on the bottom, rhythmically pumping its gills. I watched until I regained enough composure to venture a cast. The fly drifted well above the fish and it took no notice. The fly sank deeper after I rubbed silt on my gut leader and I lengthened each succeeding cast. It was ignored until, when it seemed the fly would bump the fish's nose, it disappeared in a great, opening jaw. I tightened and felt an unyielding weight, as if I had snagged a log.

We started downstream, slowly, irresistibly. My reel held no backing and streamside brush blocked my path. I jumped in and floundered along, my boots full and bulging, until the monster held in a wide, deep pool. I clambered out briefly until I felt an ominous dead weight after the monster had surged around the pool. Groping shoulder deep I grasped an abandoned, rusty logging cable. The fish was gone. I stumbled back to the bank again, stunned. I was certain I had lost the biggest fish I would ever see.

That fish haunted my dreams for days and weeks until I finally learned enough about Pacific Coast salmonids to realize that my lost monster was a steelhead kelt, spawned out and spent, a fish to avoid hooking if possible. Had it been a bright, fresh-run fish it would have broken me off before I could have realized what was happening.

CHAPTER 16

Rainbow Trout - 2

THE SALMONBERRY EXPERIENCE helped me decide to get into the steelhead business seriously. I lived within easy striking distance of the Rogue River and its famed fighting native rainbow-steelhead.

And as I had yet to learn there are no ironclad rules, that the world of angling is wide open to experimentation and innovation, I believed "experts" who said my Phillipson was not enough rod for such fish. Still, though I was not undergunned, as they said, I do not regret my pilgrimage to R. L. Winston Rod Company in San Francisco, where Doug Merrick and Lew Stoner fitted me with a 9-foot powerhouse and a GAAF line to match. It has had its place over the years, and remains a beautiful and perfect hollow-fluted core stick.

All signs for good native fish that mid-September pointed to the Rogue River, so I drove homeward up the coast, bypassing such famous steelhead meccas as the Russian, Eel and Klamath rivers. In Gold Beach at the mouth of the Rogue I was directed to Frank Colvin's tackle shop, an unpretentious hole-in-the-wall opening on the main street. There Frank dispensed flies, other necessities and sage advice if requested.

My needs were simple: a few flies and much advice. Frank assured me the only flies I needed were Red Ants, Rogue River Specials and Bucktail Coachmens, all sparsely dressed by him on No. 8 and No. 10 hooks. I bought a half dozen each, about two dollars worth in those days.

Frank ducked his head a little, peering at me over the top of his spectacles.

"Go up to Gillespie Riffle," he said, "and when the sun is off the water, fish down through the broken stretch."

As he drew me a map on a wrinkled piece of brown wrapping paper, he stressed that I work through the riffle as many times as circumstances and inclinations allowed.

When I reached Gillespie Riffle, the river looked formidable to one accustomed to small streams. But I had my new Winston rod, Frank's flies and boundless enthusiasm to counter my ignorance and inexperience. There was another fly fisherman already on the riffle and I waded in a reasonable distance behind him to watch and learn. He threw a long line almost straight across, letting the fly swing in an arc. Once the line was directly below him he stripped in a few loops, made a false cast or two and shot the whole works out again. I noted how he stepped down after several casts, and I followed along behind once I found the rhythm of the big Winston.

We both stepped out once he reached the riffle's end, and I awaited his approach and any advice he might offer.

"Not much action," he said. "Water's too low and clear; need a good rain to bring some fish in."

I agreed then, but later learned at that time in September perhaps 85 percent of the summer fish were already in and "a good rain" would only move them further upriver.

"Got to get home," he concluded, "wife gets mad when I'm late for dinner."

Congratulating myself that I had no wife to get mad, for I most assuredly would be late for my dinner, I returned to the head of the riffle. My mentor had been fishing a Red Ant, a doublehook No. 8. I replaced my Bucktail Coachman with one of Frank's sparse Ants on a single hook.

A subtle change had come over the valley. The harsh glare of the sun was gone from the water and the spires of Douglas fir on the ridge tops stood out bold and black against the red sky. The river looked darker and deeper as it surged onward to the sea. A few gulls winged oceanward towards roosts on offshore islands. A water ouzel fluttered upriver to the bar just below me, bobbed and blinked its white eyelids and kept just ahead of me as if waiting for something to happen.

A violent, arm-jarring strike convinced me I had missed a big fish. The next hard strike and first run was simultaneous and when the fish burst into the air I was dumbfounded that it appeared to be no more than 15 inches in length. I was fast to my first "half-pounder," a grand, wild little fish, more torpedo-shaped than a non-migratory rainbow. Its back was blue-green shading to silver on the sides and belly; it did not have a red rainbow stripe — a silver dollar bright fish. Except for narrow, crescent-shaped black spots above the lateral line and spots on the dorsal and caudal fins, it was immaculate. I knelt, disengaged the Red Ant and held the half-pounder upright until it darted back into the flow. The water ouzel bobbed and blinked again as if in approval.

Before full darkness I hooked four more half-pounders which, I later learned, are unique to the Rogue and Klamath systems. After entering the sea as smolts they come back in a few months; why, no one seems to know, for they feed on little if anything while in the river and they are not capable of spawning. The next time they come back, probably the next autumn, they are 17 to 20 inches in length, sexually mature and on their first spawning run.

Shortly after that first memorable evening on Gillespie Riffle I came under the tutelage of Ray Gardner, conservation officer for the lower Rogue and surrounding area. Ray was an expert fly fisher with a keen insight into salmon and steelhead habits and an uncanny ability to read water. There was no road above Lobster Creek in those days and no jet boats. The only access into the upper river, between Lobster and Agness, was by conventional, propeller-driven craft. During the spring salmon season and high water there was no problem, but in August and September, when the summer steelhead were in and the water was at its lowest level, the upper river was practically deserted — a graveyard of sheared pins, broken shafts and propellers. Most fished below, but Ray knew the water and, in his small outboard skiff, introduced me to the mysteries of the upper riffles with their colorful names: Cold, Shallow, Boney Point, Hawkins, Quosatana Creek, Bacon Flat, Big Fish, Cole, Slide Creek, Nail Keg, Wakeup Riley and Rachel's Delight.

Very few folk lived there or visited. Fred Lowrey operated a fishing lodge opposte Bacon Flat, serviced by a shallow-draft launch fitted with a "jackass" to lift the shaft and propeller when the water got thin. Old John Adams had a hill farm below Copper Canyon, and Bob and Fid Owens, noted river guides, occasionally brought clients up from below in craft similar to Lowrey's. But for the most part, we could be on the upper river days at a time and never see another soul.

The country along the upper Rogue was steep, often precipitous, a great canyon cut by the river through the Klamath Mountains, and still cutting. The forest was virgin — old growth Douglas fir, Sitka spruce and cedar on the ridges, mixed with tan oak, myrtle, big leaf maple and madrona on the lower slopes. There were many blacktail deer, cougar, black bear and otter in a world far removed from mundane urban affairs and the constrictions of civilized existence.

The center and only artery into this paradise was, of course, the river, a magnificent river — strong, wild, uncompromising — and dangerous if you underestimated its power. A beautiful river it was with white-water cascades battering the rocks and ledges, dark swirling eddies, deep runs of broken water and dancing riffles plunging again into rough white-water chutes. And, at the right times, it was a river full of steelhead, chinook or coho salmon.

Fishing with Ray in that wild wonderland I learned much about steelhead and the river. By no means are all summer-run fish half-pounders, but they outnumber the larger spawners by far. Rogue summer fish are small by steelhead standards (a five-pounder is a good one and seven- or eight-pounders are rare, but they do grow even larger).

One evening I paddled my rubber boat across the river at Quosatana Creek and began hooking half-pounders at the very top of the riffle as fast as I could beach and release them. A guide saw the action and moved his big jet boat in just below me, holding his clients in the current to troll their lures. I kept hooking fish practically off his bow until the guide and his clients could stand no more and departed downriver. In the water where the boat had been was a dropoff and there I promptly hooked two four-pounders. I waded back in for one more try in that productive square yard, even though it was almost dusk. There was a great boil of water and I was fast to a huge, deep fish. Seven great jumps were only the exclamation points of a long exciting fight for both of us. When it felt the shoaling water, the battler made one last try for the heavy current but finally grounded in inches of water. The fly fell out of its mouth when I laid my conquest on the river bar. It was only 27½ inches long but weighed 9¼ pounds, the biggest summer fish I have ever taken out of the Rogue and the largest I have ever seen there.

At daybreak I was back on the riffle at Quosatana Creek and immediately hooked and beached a fish of above five pounds from the very same spot. I had no other strikes and saw no other fish. All but that one straggler I hooked had moved upstream during the night.

A family of otters would often join me in fishing a riffle on the section of the lower Rogue that I visit regularly. Though I like otters and enjoy watching them play, I feel out-competed when they move into the same riffle I am trying to fish and I leave the field to them. Old-timers had so advised and I believed them. One day, however, I had a remarkable and contradictory experience. By early November, most summer fish had already moved up, but I was still prospecting at Slide Creek in the gray dawn. I paused to savor the ephemeral, bewitching moment, the transition from night to day when the night creatures were just going to bed. A great horned owl had just sounded his last mournful note and two deer on the bar below were having a final snack of sweet clover before bedding down. The day creatures were just stirring. A water ouzel fluttered up the middle of the riffle, bursting with song more springlike than fall. A wedge of mergansers came driving upriver low, cutting the air like arrows. They veered slightly on sighting me, uttering startled, guttural squawks, but drove on through, wings whistling. A lone shag followed on his way to his own fishing hole. Soon the gulls would begin their patrols. It was time for me to start.

Near the riffle's lower end a lone merganser splashed off from the vicinity of a surging slosh that only a big steelhead or salmon could have made. Upstream I hooked five nice fish in a spot I could cover with my shirt; I had stumbled into a kegged up pod of steelhead.

My line was in the air again when something big boiled by my legs. I thought a mighty chinook had almost blundered into me, until the biggest otter I've ever seen raised halfway out of the water right where I had been hooking fish and looked me over. It was too late to stop my cast and as the fly swung across the spot still boiling from the otter's dive I was hooked to something powerful and fast.

"Holy cow! I've foul-hooked the otter!"

Just then, far down the riffle, a big steelhead jumped, and it was attached to me. That arrangement prevailed, despite the steelhead's strong objections, and when beached it weighed seven pounds, double the size of the others. I wondered if the old-timers would believe such a story.

Like so many other evolving steelheaders, I "discovered" the greased line method independently, long before reading A. E. H. Wood or Haig-Brown. Now, using a floater is an accepted practice for summer steelhead, although one generally thinks of sinking lines for unfavorable water conditions. I recall a recent September when Robin Thorp of British Columbia, an expert steelheader and an old friend from Arctic flying days, and I were rained off the lower Rogue. We drove upriver to Agness to check out the Illinois, the Rogue's largest tributary. The Illinois often clears sooner than the Rogue, providing a fishable mix just below the junction, but when we reached Hotel Riffle we couldn't see our toes in foot-deep water. We agreed this was one time we needed sinking lines. But we didn't change reel spools and we still caught fish all afternoon with floaters.

As one after another of the angling dogmas has become unhorsed, I discover that I write and talk of fishing in considerably more couched terms, with the qualifiers "sometimes" and "generally" popping up quite frequently. There are no ironclad rules in fishing. The angling world is wide open to experimentation and innovation and we are richer for it.

CHAPTER 17

Rainbow Trout - 3

THE CHALLENGING SPLENDOR OF its setting and the savageness of its native summer-run steelhead have attracted more journeyman fly casters to the North Umpqua than any other stream. The beautiful but fast heavy water challenges waders with slippery bedrock and ledges where water depth can vary from ankle deep to chest high within one wrong step. Good general water-reading ability doesn't take the place of local knowledge, for Umpqua fish favor certain lies and holds and, unless the river is full of fish, they seldom hold elsewhere.

The list of truly expert casters who shoot lines out over the North Umpqua is so long that any abbreviated version here would be unfair. They are attracted, as I first was, by native summer fish larger than those found in the Rogue. Anglers continue to come, in season, to hook native fish, not hatchery fish which now represent a serious flaw in the Umpqua fishery.

It took several trips to the Umpqua before I had accumulated enough local knowledge to find and hook native fish, but the apprenticeship paid off. In those days I often camped at Bogus Creek and haunted the nearby riffles of MacDonald, Rattlesnake and Wright creeks. One July morning, just at dawn, I paddled my rubber raft across to the head of MacDonald where I hooked one of those prized fish on the third drift with a No. 8 Skunk. This fish soon had me close to the end of my tether, literally. It ran the pool's lip and into a white-water chute. I watched the last of my fly line whip through the tip guide and the backing began to disappear. Whatever I had hooked — a steelhead or a chinook salmon — I was sure I had lost. To follow down was impossible. While I debated breaking off, the fish moved back into the current and started *up*, rather than down! My antagonist came slowly, from rock to rock and pocket to pocket. When I had it

almost opposite me I exerted side pressure, turning my load into easier water. The gratitude I had felt at its return magnified when I realized I hadn't deliberately broken off the biggest summer steelhead hooked to date! Eventually I snubbed its nose against rocks substituting for a beach, gilled it and hoisted it out. The Skunk had to be broken off in the rough cartilage at the corner of the trout's jaw. The perfectly formed male fish was silvery bright, the black spots above the lateral line like fine etchings. He measured exactly 30 inches and later, on scales at Frank Moore's Steamboat Inn, weighed in at ten pounds on the nose. The fish complied with the thumbnail formula: four pounds for the first 24 inches, plus one pound for each additional inch.

I have caught other North Umpqua steelhead that exceeded ten pounds and occasionally have heard of even bigger fish taken. But these are rare in comparison to the usual size range of from three and a half to seven pounds.

These natives are easily distinguished from what we dissidents refer to as *"Salmo pelleti."* I maintain I can determine within thirty seconds of hooking a fish whether it wriggled up through the gravel of a spawning bed and survived by developing all things inherent in wildness or whether it grew up in captivity, pampered and gorged on pellets in a concrete tank. It is not that I possess any unique qualities; I have heard the same story countless times from other experienced steelheaders.

"These factory fish sure are easy on the tackle!" one once told me.

The state compounds the *Salmo pelleti* insult by dumping in untold thousands of "rubber trout," apparently for tourists and others who have not developed the skill or do not have the perseverance to hook steelhead. Factory fish are also becoming more prevalent in the Rogue, and if this practice continues, future generations will never know what a really wild, cartwheeling steelhead feels like.

My largest summer steelhead, however, came from the Copper River, a Skeena River tributary in British Columbia. I had long known the reputations of such streams as the Morice, Bulkley, Babine and Kispiox, but the Copper was new to me. My chance to get acquainted came after I had been prospecting around the headwaters of the Peace River for Arctic grayling and bull trout and was en route to Prince Rupert. While looking for a camping spot near Terrace, I talked with a fisherman cleaning two steelhead of about 12 pounds each. They were taken, he said, in the nearby Copper as the tailend of the run moved through.

The private logging road was closed to public travel except on weekends, so I was on it the next Saturday. At first sight of the river I was disappointed, more at its color than its size. It was a small river and the water rolling over the freestone bed was milky from glacial melt. However, above a tributary, the source of the sediment, the main river was sparkling clear to the road's end at a long deep pool. Some of the fishermen there were just leaving — fishless — while others continued to pound the most likely water with hardware and bait.

"They all moved up," one fisherman told me.

He may have been right, but I wished to avoid the crowd at the pool and drove back to a promising stretch of broken water with deep, slick runs between large boulders. The heavy water was difficult to wade and I barely managed to reach a flat-topped rock for a precarious casting perch. I searched the best looking water, finally casting to the squeeze of the funnel at the run's lower end. As the No. 6 Thor swam through, the water welled in a great boil and I was fast to something akin to a runaway logging truck.

Water shipped over the top of my hippers as we played a game of give and take with the backing on my reel's spool. Once the fish was back on my fly line I worried less about the wild whitewater chute below us. Steady side pressure then won out over the beautiful hen steelhead. She was beginning to show a slight blush along the lateral line but was still bright from the sea. She was exactly a yard long and weighed 16 pounds even.

I met a car full of hardware fishermen in returning to my Beetle. They looked unbelievingly from the great fish to the Thor in my rod's keeper ring, then drove on muttering.

Left to my own devices, I decided to try the Kispiox, even though I was assured that mid-September was too early in the season. Still, I wanted to see this famous stream and to fish it. I found it quite a small stream considering its big reputation. I spent the first day exploring, returning the next morning encouraged by a report of an 18-pounder having been taken at the mouth. At a riffle and run of broken water I had located the day before, I met an angler just leaving the stream.

"No fish," he said, "too early in the season."

Two beautiful riffles later I had hooked only steelhead parr and it was lunchtime. Washing down bread and cheese with a can of good Canadian beer I reflected that steelheading *is* a matter of timing. I had lucked out on the Copper, despite being "too late," but here on the Kispiox I was, indeed, "too early." The fish, after all, were just excuses for being on beautiful water in beautiful surroundings and I had one more place I wanted to try.

The river trail led through an overgrown pasture with signs and smells of cattle about, though none were visible. Astream, a few more parr and small cutthroats took hold. Humpies finned in the shallows and, finally satisfied, I reeled in and walked back toward the pasture. As I circled a patch of blackberry brambles, a great black back was visible on the opposite side.

"A cow," I thought, "a black Angus, but with luxuriant long hair."

The "cow," now rising on its hind legs, was the biggest black bear I had ever seen, so close I could have poked it with my fly rod. The bear, sensing something amiss, was looking the other way. I couldn't run in chest waders so I let out a great bellow — "Hey, Oso!"

The bear didn't understand Spanish and never looked around — it just fled, blazing a new trail as it roared away. As the sounds of poles popping a quarter mile away faded, I gave a nervous laugh and felt my hackles settle back down. I will always remember the Kispiox more for the bear than the fish.

But there are other rainbows besides steelhead — non-migratory residents of coastal streams and lakes. These trout show great diversity throughout their range and it is small wonder since they have the most extensive scope of all North American salmonids. This vast territory spans the Pacific coastal drainages from within a half a degree of the Tropic of Cancer to four and one half degrees of the Arctic Circle; specifically, from Alaska's Aniak River to the Rio del Presidio in Mexico. South of California, however, rainbows occur only in isolated pockets — relic populations. This great spread was probably accomplished by marine dispersion during and shortly after intervals of glaciation when Pacific waters were cooler than they are now.

Being the last of the genus to invade this area, rainbows probably introgressed to some extent with those trout already present — cutthroats and redbands — so some of the diversity may be due to ancient hybridization. Almost one hundred years ago, David Starr Jordan recognized sixteen different species or subspecies of the rainbow tribe but now only three (having coarser scales than redbands) are considered as coastal rainbows.

Other than the common coastal rainbow, *irideus*, two races are still "carried on the books." One of these, the Eagle Lake rainbow, *Salmo gairdneri aquilarum*, is native only to Eagle Lake, California, a beautiful clear lake tucked away among the western ranges of the Great Basin. Lying within the edge of Lahontan drainage, the lake probably contained Lahontan cutthroats originally and it is thought that the rainbows gained access later on through a headwater transfer from the nearby Pit River. If so, they may be of redband origin plus some admixture of Lahontan cutthroat genetic influence. Whatever their origin, they are beautiful trout and some exceeding five pounds are taken occasionally. I have fished for these trout in years past and I took one of 4½ pounds on a trolled lure so it didn't really count, even though the lure was attached to my fly rod. After all, each of us makes his own ground rules but in times of desperation those of us of weak moral fiber are apt to fudge, using the time-worn excuse that the end justifies the means. Having made this confession, I must add that I'm glad I did it; otherwise I might not have seen these noble fish that resemble rainbows, redbands and to some degree Lahontan cutthroats.

The other described race of rainbow is a relict found only in headwater tributaries of west flowing streams draining the slopes of the Sierra San Pedro Martir, a mountain mass towering above the desert ranges of Northern Baja, California. This trout was named *Salmo nelsoni* by Evermann in 1908 but is now thought to be a coastal rainbow. If it does merit subspecific status, it would, of course, become *Salmo gairdneri nelsoni*.

During the course of my waterfowl surveys I have often flown over or near this imposing mountain, its upper slopes dark with pine and fir, and wondered about the trout there. Once I drove into a ranch at its base to arrange for horses to reach its clear streams, but the Aztec curse struck me down and so I had to give it up. But next year, perhaps, or the year after, Montezuma permitting, quien sabe!

The rainbows of the Mexican mainland occur as isolated populations at the extreme southern limits of the range, almost within the tropics. They are known only from two river systems, western drainages of the Sierra Madre Occidental, the Rio San Lorenzo and Rio del Presidio, although they may occur in other nearby streams. These trout have been little studied and though they are considered to be coastal rainbows they do exhibit many redband characteristics, thus their taxonomic relationship is not clear.

At the other end of North America the rainbows north of the Alaska Peninsula share with their Mexican relatives in redband characteristics, superficially at least. They have white tips on their anal, pelvic and dorsal fins, yellow orange tints on their lower sides and in many cases prominent orange slash marks. They are classic redbands at a glance, but are coarse-scaled fish and this makes them coastal rainbows. According to Bob Behnke they are identical to the rainbows across the Bering Strait in adjacent Asiatic streams which were named *Salmo mykiss* by Walbaum in 1792. Most ichthyologists believe they came to Asia from Alaska by way of the Bering land bridge and that their origin began here, in North America.

Those Alaskan rainbows of Bristol Bay and Kuskokwim River drainages are remarkable fish. All are resident stream fish with some occurring in lakes. None are anadromous but despite this they grow to great size. They are slow growing as would be expected of fish of high latitudes and do not mature until age seven or eight with a maximum life span of twelve; due to this life history pattern, they are vulnerable to overfishing. Fortunately, the Alaskans are aware of this threat and limit the bag on rainbows while many of the fishing lodges and guides encourage their clients to release rainbows unharmed.

I do not know how big these northern rainbows get, but those of Lake Iliamna probably exceed 15 pounds. The rainbows we caught in the Togiak, the Goodnews and the Kanektok were much smaller and a good fish was a five-pounder, but I did take one from the Goodnews that was a noble fish and the largest rainbow I ever caught.

Jack and I had been floating the Goodnews on a most inauspicious day. A gale of wind drove a steady rain flat across the water, picking up spume from the whitecaps. In the twistings and turnings of the river it came at us from all quarters and at times we were hard-pressed to pull the raft clear of the sweepers jutting out from the cutbanks. I didn't know two men could get so cold in July, even in Alaska. Our hands and noses were blue and we took turns rowing in an attempt to get warm. We had stopped to fish a few times, standing in the riffles humped up like disconsolate herons but the wind was too much. We had caught enough charr for supper and were looking for a sheltered place to camp. On an island just below we saw it. I bumped the raft against the shore but the current was so swift we were being swept by until Jack jumped out and hung on. Finally secured, we unloaded our gear and raised the tent, then took a long deep pull at the bottle.

With the burning in my gut I didn't feel any warmer, but the spark had kindled a small remnant of hope and courage, enough so that I picked up my rod and trudged through the dripping willows to a long narrow bar below that separated a deep blue backwater from the main flow of the current. Just where a thin trickle spilled across the bar into the quiet water, I cast an orange-bodied bucktail. Almost immediately I felt a slight pluck, raised the rod and hooked a humpback salmon of about three pounds. After a short but determined struggle I led it in, twitched out the hook and sent the fish back. Walking down a few steps I tossed the fly back and all hell broke loose. As the bamboo arced, a magnificent rainbow burst out in a shower of spray, leaped again, then tore out of the backwater into the heavy current. Fortunately, my leader was armed with a stout tippet, for in those waters one never knew whether the next fish hooked would weigh two pounds or 20.

The fish held in the current awhile and then, after a few more leaps, I forced it into the tail of the backwater. By then it was pretty well spent and after a few short rushes I led it to the bar. As the fish rolled on its side I drew in until it was grounded, then reached down and spread my stretched thumb and fingers along its broad sides, nose to tail. I measured three and a half spans — 28 inches, more or less, thick and deep. I estimated eight pounds but the rainbow would probably go more for it was heavier than a steelhead of the same length. After twitching the hook from its lip I held the gleaming beauty upright for a second before releasing it, now a wiser fish hopefully.

CHAPTER 18

Trout of the Sierra Madre Occidental

MOST OF US THINK OF TROUT AS northern fish, cold water adapted and therefore of necessity northern forms or at least fish of high altitudes. The interior of Mexico, of course, consists mostly of highlands where native trout occur along the backbone of the western Sierra from near the U. S. border to within a half a degree of the Tropic of Cancer, the most southerly locale of any native trout in the Northern Hemisphere. Even so, trout once occurred 250 miles farther south than known populations do today as revealed by a fossil form named *Salmo australis* which was recently found in the Lake Chapala basin.

These Mexican trout are relics of the Pleistocene Epoch and may be very ancient — not necessarily products of the last push of the ice. There are probably four separate races, but only one has been formally described, *Salmo chrysogaster*, the Mexican golden trout. The others remain an enigma, different from each other and separated by physiographic and thermal barriers. Due to the low latitudes of their range, they are restricted to the highest, coldest headwaters, all in Pacific drainages except in the extreme north where Rio Yaqui-like trout are found in the Casas Grandes, a one-time tributary of the Rio Grande. If there was a headwater transfer here it was probably accomplished in a bucket by early Anglo settlers.

There has been a shadow of doubt as to the origin of the Mexican trout due to a shipment of 33,000 McCloud River rainbow trout eggs to a hatchery in the Lerma basin in the 1880s; suspicion particularly exists regarding the rainbow-like trout of the Rio San Lorenzo and Rio del Presidio. However, the logistical problems of planting trout in the remote headwaters of the Sierra Madre Occidental in an early day argue against this as do the characteristics of the trout found there. In no way do they resemble the rainbows of the McCloud or any other rainbow stock commonly propagated in hatcheries, either in outward appearance or in meristic characteristics. Furthermore, the recent discovery of the fossil trout *Salmo australis* in the Lake Chapala basin clearly indicates that trout were much more widespread in Mexico during the Pleistocene Epoch than they are today. Consequently, the weight of actual evidence is overwhelmingly in favor of native trout.

It was the early '50s when I first heard rumors of the existence of these Mexican trout. Starker Leopold and I had packed into the Sierra with horses to the headwaters of the Yaqui on a turkey hunt and Floyd Johnson, our guide and packer, had told us there were trout in the watershed where we hunted. But we had neither the time nor the means to investigate the streams for trout — there were too many feisty gobblers about and they claimed our full attention.

Over thirty years later Jack James and I got back to have a look at those trout of the Sierra Madre Occidental and then we went on south in the Sierra to find some others that had been reported, among them the Mexican golden trout and the redband or rainbow-like trout of Durango.

Vast changes had taken place in the terrain since Starker and I had packed in with horses to hunt through virgin forests and open glades with grass reaching to our stirrups. Jack and I with guide Bill Martineau drove in by pickup over some of the worst roads I have ever seen, but still they were roads where no roads had been before. The Sierra had been logged over and the grass and forage were gone . . . eaten down to the roots. And there were people about where all had been wilderness. Ranchitos had sprung up wherever there was water and a flat place big enough for a patch of corn or beans.

Even so, the mountain slopes were still covered by a forest, for the Mexicans log selectively and they log with horses. They do not tear up the countryside with heavy equipment and they do not poison everything that won't produce a pine board. This in contrast to our own eroded clearcuts and ravaged watersheds makes us look like villains.

The streams, even the headwaters, are now probably all polluted to some extent, not only from human wastes, but from the leaching of sawdust dumped in or near the creeks by the numerous small sawmills. Wherever a stream flowed through a village it became the village sewer. Below a village one could judge its proximity by the amount of trash along the banks and draped in the streamside brush. Hardly water one would care to drink.

With all of these undesirable impacts on the land and the water there were still trout in the streams, not in abundance surely, but we did catch trout in every stream we fished except the Rio Mayo where the local people told us the trout were "muy poco." Fishing pressure is constant, year-round activity, mostly by the small fry of the ranchitos and villages. Everything caught is kept, regardless of size. Chubs, trout, minnows or suckers — everything goes into the pot. As this has always been the practice, it would seem that the trout are in no imminent danger of being wiped out.

When planning our trouting foray into Mexico it had been our thought to start at the north end of the Sierra and work our way south to Durango. Upon arriving at Colonia Juarez in northwestern Chihuahua, however, we learned that there had been a recent record breaking snow and we were fearful the nearby mountain streams would be high and muddy. Farther south there had been less snow so it seemed prudent to begin there and return to the upper Yaqui watershed on our way back north.

Colonia Juarez had been settled in the 1880s by Anglo-Americans, Mormons, and their descendants are still there, friendly and hospitable. It was through their efforts and especially the help of John Hatch, himself a trout fisher, that we secured the services of our bilingual guide and arranged for other contacts in Durango. Finally, all in readiness, we set off for the falls of the Basaseachic on the headwaters of the Rio Mayo, the first watershed south of the Yaqui.

We were prepared to camp out and had picked up a few necessities in the nearby town of Nuevo Casas Grandes — some canned foods, tortillas and, of course, beer and tequila.

The first leg of our journey was easy across rolling grasslands, through wide valleys and over a few low passes, all on a good blacktop road. There were a few isolated ranges across our path and climbing these we came into scattered trees — junipers and pinons first, then oaks and pines, dipping down again into more valleys and grassland. Finally, we climbed the east slope of the Sierra Madre Occidental and once on top it was like a great plateau dissected by deep barrancas where the streams had cut canyons, awesome gashes through the heart of the Sierra.

To a northerner the pine-oak forest presented a strange appearance. Here we were in springtime, April, and in low latitudes, yet the oaks were either completely bare or in varying shades of brown, yellow or russet, looking for all the world like October, and the grass, what little was left of it, was sere and tan. This was nature's response to the wet and dry cycle rather than hot and cold and this was the dry time. Later on, the thunder storms would come, soaking the land, bringing out new leaves and greening up the countryside.

Not that it didn't get cold. Even though the days were warm and bright, as soon as the sun dropped behind a ridge a chill set in leaving ice in the camp water bucket by morning. Though we were close to the tropics, the thin, clear air at 8,000 to 10,000 feet let the heat leak out in a hurry.

We ran out of blacktop just beyond the village of Tomochic and then bumped and thumped along in a cloud of dust, meeting innumerable logging trucks whose progress was even slower than ours. Finally, about dusk, we arrived at a campsite near the falls of the Basaseachic on a headwater of the Rio Mayo, spread our bedrolls under the pines, warmed up some canned food and turned in.

It wasn't a quiet night. The village dogs came snuffing around and gave us a thorough barking at and a burro with her fuzzy foal seemed determined to share our camp. And it was freezing cold!

In the gray light of dawn I poked my head out of my sack, turtle-like, and surveyed the world. In some mysterious manner I had parted company with my air mattress and was now lodged against some rocks, sharp rocks, which were poking me in the backside. Bill had a fire going and I scrambled out to get some heat.

Breakfast was a fast food operation — instant coffee and instant oatmeal — and then we were ready to see what the day might bring and possibly even find a fish.

Our camp was on a point between two small streams that merged a short way below, their combined flow forming a fair-sized creek. Below the junction this stream had carved a gorge through bedrock for a few hundred yards and then plunged over the brink of an awesome rent in the mountain, a sheer drop of about a thousand feet. Bill and I walked down to look and after peeking over the edge I was convinced that the upper water was the place to fish even though there were supposed to be trout at the bottom. Bill assured me there was a way down and I'm sure there was — just one small step over the edge!

Fishing back up the stream we worked some beautiful water — deep pools, dancing riffles, slow runs and foaming pockets. We tried both branches of the stream, Bill soaking worms while I tried many patterns of flies but we couldn't find a trout or see a sign of one, not even a chub. Finally, after several hours, we gave up. Back at camp Jack told us the same sad story. He had fished farther up the canyon and covered more water than we had. Yet a ranchero that we talked with confirmed the presence of trout in the waters we had fished but said they were "muy poco." Very few indeed! As far as I know only one trout of the Mayo watershed exists as a museum specimen. But I still believe that had we stayed with it longer and fished higher up we would have caught some.

The Rio Mayo trout were said to be similar to those of the Rio Yaqui so we backtracked over the divide and dropped down to the Yaqui watershed, an east flowing branch of the Tomochic paralleling the road. The farther down we went, the better the water looked and when we found a place to turn off we bumped down through a pasture to the water's edge. Here the stream had become a fair-sized creek winding sedately through a pastoral valley. The water was low but slightly milky, probably from snow we could see on the higher ridges. There were two other fishermen present, small boys who took off on a dead run when Bill approached to see what they had caught.

Even though the sun was still shedding warmth the water was too cold for me to wade wet so I pulled on waders and started up the stream, searching all the water with a natural drift — riffles deep runs, pools and pockets. Not a fish stirred at my offerings and no insect life was visible. Finally, at the head of a deep pool, I saw a fish show but not for my free floating nymph. Skirting around the pool I fished it from the top — down and across — and had a strike. Another cast and another bump and that was all.

But I had, at least, touched a fish and thus encouraged I changed my tactics, detouring around the good water and fishing down and across, letting the fly hang in the current and retrieving with slow twitches. And I caught two trout, hooked two that came loose and several others took a whack at it. The best one of all came up to take just as I lifted the fly from the water and I snatched it right out of its open maw.

These trout were beautiful. They were light-greenish on the back with a faint rainbow stripe, bright lemon yellow on the lower sides and having an immaculate white belly. The black spots were small and "X"-shaped, occurring mostly above the lateral line. The parr marks were long and narrow, almost rectangular, and the lower fins were bright orange; the pelvic, anal and dorsal fins were white-tipped. Said to resemble the Gila trout of New Mexico and Arizona, these fish were more colorful and the black spots smaller, altogether unlike any trout I had ever seen.

If these Rio Yaqui trout are actually related to the Gila trout, they could have reached Yaqui waters by a headwater transfer during the unstable drainage of the Pleistocene Epoch from a Gila River tributary, possibly the San Simon. Or maybe the sequence was reversed — the Yaqui trout populated the Gila by the same route. A headwater transfer from the Rio Grande by way of the Casas Grandes is more unlikely for the Yaqui trout are more rainbow or redband-like than cutthroat. Another alternative, of course, would be a marine invasion from the Pacific.

The next Pacific drainage to the south was the Rio Fuerte — Mexican golden trout water. To get there we had to go out and come in again, out through Chihuahua City, down to Hidalgo del Parral and then back west into the mountains. A good blacktop road took us to El Vergel, a village on top of the Sierra, but from there on the road was worse, if that were possible, than the one to Basaseachic. But the vision of the Mexican golden trout kept us going and finally after interminable jouncing along in clouds of dust we dropped down into a deep barranca and pulled off the road at the crossing of the Rio Verde, a tributary of the Fuerte.

We camped right there. There was no other place. Almost vertical rock cliffs hemmed in the stream which threaded among wide gravel bars. It was a small stream at this low water time but judging from the scoured canyon bottom it could get pretty wild during the summer rainy season.

There was a small tienda, a kind of Mexican "Mom and Pop" store, clinging precariously to the side of the cliff directly across the creek from our camp and the people there told us the best fishing was upstream so up we went, scrambling through brush along the cliff base or splashing from gravel bar to gravel bar in the creek bed. There were a few deep holes around the base of some of the boulders and we soon left Bill crouched by one of these soaking a worm. Jack and I continued on making a few tenative casts to the better looking spots and then came to where the creek forked, Jack taking the right hand branch and I the left.

My fork, like the creek below the junction, was pinched between steep canyon walls with the stream bouncing from one side to the other, working its way between huge boulders. There were many little cascades plunging into deep pools, and in one of these, fishing down and across, I caught a trout, a gorgeous Mexican golden trout, *Salmo chrysogaster*. It was only a small fish, about eight or nine inches, but a lovely thing to behold.

Like the trout of the Tomochic, the back was light-greenish with fine black specklings above the lateral line and the lower fins were bright orange with white tips on the dorsal, anal and pelvic fins. There was also a faint rainbow stripe extending about halfway back from the gillcover but there the resemblance ended. This golden trout was a chunky fish; the bluish parr marks were large and oval-shaped and there were many small round auxiliary parr marks on the lower sides which were a very light yellow. The belly was bright orange from vent to chin and there were two black spots of pigment in the iris on either side of the pupil giving the eye a masked effect, like that of the Apache trout of Arizona.

The meristic characters of the Mexican golden trout are also distinctive. It has the fewest number of vertebrae and pyloric caeca of any North American member of the genus *Salmo*.

Paul Needham and Dick Gard, in their original description of *Salmo chrysogaster*, postulated an ancient hybrid origin — rainbow X cutthroat, rainbow by marine invasion from the Pacific and cutthroat by headwater transfer from the Rio Grande, probably by way of the Rio Conchos whose headwaters interdigitate with those of the Fuerte. This theory appears logical as *chrysogaster* has many characteristics of both supposed ancestors as well as some distinctively its own. In any event, the Mexican golden trout is known from only three river systems — the Rio Fuerte, Rio Sinaloa and Rio Culiacan, all neighboring Pacific drainages.

I caught two more of those beautiful trout in that rocky gorge before a lowering sun warned me to turn back where, by pre-arrangement, I met Jack at the fork of the creek. We didn't tarry long on the way back to camp as the sun had slipped behind the canyon wall and the night chill had already begun.

In the morning, acting on a rumor heard from the patron of the tienda, we packed up our gear and ground up the long grade out of the barranca to another tributary of the Verde called the Loera, reputed to contain more and bigger trout than the stream we had just fished.

The Loera was a much larger stream, flowing through a wide pastoral valley with a village along the flats by the bridge crossing. There was a road, or more precisely a one-lane track, leading up the valley which we found after a number of false starts. Following this track we eventaully ended up at a rancho, our arrival coinciding with that of a cowboy riding in. The charro, who turned out to be the ranchero's son, informed us that we could camp anywhere and were welcome to fish on the property provided we used no dynamite or poison. This stipulation was agreed to, since we had neglected to bring any with us, but it did lend substance to some of the wild stories we had heard about the fishing techniques of some of the loggers.

On the way up from the village most of the water had looked flat and thin but just below the rancho a series of bedrock ledges across the water created a chain of deep pools while about a half mile above another similar formation could be seen. We therefore parked the truck halfway between and, remembering the charro's admonition, started out with our flies. Even Bill had become pure and had tied a fly to his five feet of nylon.

Dividing our attack, Jack and Bill went down to the lower ledges while I walked up the creek to see what I could find. Arriving at the ledges, I found good trout water — deep runs and pools, pockets and little cascades, all gouged out of solid rock. At the lower end I tried a few casts up, letting the fly drift naturally and, as I suspected, to no avail. I then tried a pool from the top, casting down and across, and hooked a trout. Strange beasts, these Mexican trout. Obviously they haven't read the books.

Clambering around the ledge water I went to the top, where the water flattened out again, then fished down through, letting the fly hang in the current and retrieving with slow twitches. And I hooked trout, lots of trout — no big ones but all beautiful Mexican golden trout and mirror images of those we had caught in the other branch of the Verde.

Finally, having exercised enough small trout, I sat on a ledge and listened to the water. The rock felt warm on my backside and I hoped I could soak up enough heat to last the night. An occasional raven circled over, keeping me under surveillance while a sickle-billed thrasher kept a stern yellow eye on me from under a bush. Fleet lizards darted about, unmindful of my presence. It was peaceful here and quiet, the only sounds the chuckle of the water or a distant burro sounding off. The low sun, though, told me it was time to go and I trudged back to camp along the creek. There Jack and Bill were preparing supper and they, too, had found trout plentiful down below.

Having sampled the golden trout of the Rio Fuerte, we backtracked to Hidalgo del Parral, found a motel and washed the accumulated dust of Mexico from our hides. In the morning, refreshed and clean again, we headed south for Durango, passing through interesting desert country that flaunted a pink-flowered ocotillo in contrast to the usual orange ones.

Arriving in Durango we found ourselves in a big city with the usual noise and traffic. Taking refuge in a motel we got in touch with Pedro and Jaimie Gerard, one-time residents of Colonia Juarez, and Bill's friends. The following day they paid us a call and we learned much about the trout of the area and how to find them, for the Gerards, father and son, were both trout fishermen.

Armed with the information and directions of the Gerards, we started out for the Rio del Presidio, driving about 100 kilometers down the highway towards Mazatlan. At the town of El Salto we turned north a few more kilometers over the usual miserable side road to a village of slab shacks adjacent to a sawmill. A small stream ran through the village, a tributary of the Rio del Presidio, and we followed it down on a track along the bank. The water was thin and flat, anything but good trout water, and then abruptly it took a dive — a sheer drop of forty or fifty feet into the head of a canyon. The canyon floor fell away rapidly, transforming the gorge into a steep-sided barranca crowned by rimrocks. Following down along the rim about a half a mile we found a semblance of a trail that could only lead to the bottom, so with fishing gear and cameras we took the plunge, slipping and sliding to the canyon floor.

It was beautiful and rugged there in the canyon. Car-sized boulders toppled from the rim were scattered about helter skelter, and the creek made its way around and between them in a series of plunge pools and cascades. Pines, oaks and madronas grew where they could find a foothold and overlooking all were the high, dark lines of the rimrocks etched along the skyline.

There was just one flaw to mar this beauty. The village, only a couple of miles upstream, obviously used the creek for trash disposal and gravity and running water had done the rest. Trying to ignore the occasional bottles, tin cans and assorted bits of plastic, I cast my flies to beautiful bubbly pools and deep runs, places where a trout just had to be, but no trout showed. Scrambling over and around the boulders, I worked on down the creek, fishing many different flies in every conceivable way but still no trout. I knew there were trout in the creek for Bill, fishing a fly as one would fish a worm, had managed to hoist two 11-inchers from under the cascades and I had snapped their pictures. But the only signs of life I saw besides Jack and Bill were three teenaged boys armed with slingshots, a beautiful blue-backed trogon flying through the trees and one startled frog. Jack hadn't done much better, but had managed to hook one trout of almost three inches.

Having worked down to the point where climbing out might be a problem, we started back, huffing and puffing our way to the top. Thanks to Bill we had two trout for specimens and I had their pictures.

These trout of the Rio del Presidio resembled neither the Mexican golden trout nor the trout of the Yaqui. The background color was more bluish or grayish and the black spots were large, oval in shape, with the long axis in a vertical plane. The lower fins were dark gray rather than bright orange and though the parr marks were very faint, they appeared to be round. Shared characteristics were the rainbow stripe and white-tipped dorsal, anal and pelvic fins. In many respects they resembled redband trout.

One feature not apparent to the eye is their large number of vertebrae. The Rio del Presidio trout have the greatest number of vertebrae of any North American *Salmo* in contrast to the Mexican golden trout which has the least.

If the Rio del Presidio trout are actually native, and since they appear to be a type of redband or rainbow, a marine origin dating from some time during the Pleistocene Epoch is most likely, and they were probably much more widespread then than they are today, as evidenced by the fossil trout found recently 250 miles farther south. However, Pedro and Jaimie Gerard told us they knew of no native trout south of the Rio del Presidio watershed even though there are three adjacent drainages just to the south with headwaters probably as cold as those we fished.

Another opinion as to the origin of these trout is that held by Dr. R. R. Miller, Curator of Fishes at the University of Michigan's Museum of Zoology. Dr. Miller believes they are rainbows of hatchery ancestry stocked by American lumbermen from El Salto during the early 1900s. This, of course, is a distinct possibility, since the Rio del Presidio is readily accessible from El Salto.

The Rio Truchas, a headwater tributary of the Rio San Lorenzo, was our next objective and as the access road was just back down the highway from El Salto we started out, hoping to put as many rough miles behind us before dark as possible. At first we were lulled into complacency; the road was well graded and relatively smooth, and we sailed along at a good clip. But not for long. At a bridge construction site the good road abruptly ended and from there on we were back to the usual rough and dusty track and when dusk overtook us we made a dry camp under the pines.

At dawn we headed out again, bumping along at a snail's pace. But there were compensations. Our slow progress gave us time to look around and we were passing through beautiful country — across the top of the Sierra plateau. Being unglaciated, there was no spectacular alpine scenery such as we find in our own Sierra Nevada, but a gentler, softer aspect as ridge after forested ridge undulated away to the horizon. Although close to the tropics, our altitude of 8,000 to 10,000 feet made for a temperate climate and there were temperate zone birds about: robins, bluebirds and band-tailed pigeons, Steller's jays and ravens, as well as many Mexican types unknown to me. Glossy-leaved madronas were in bloom, pink-flowered here while in Oregon they are creamy white; in the shaded canyons lupines thrust blue spikes toward the light.

In the little valleys between ridges there were a few ranchitos and we crossed two or three tiny streams — headwaters of the Rio Piaxtla. Finally, in the afternoon, we dropped down into a canyon and came upon the Rio Truchas, our long sought San Lorenzo tributary.

The Truchas was quite a stream, flowing from the base of a dam that backed up the water for several kilometers, storing water for a hydroelectric plant furnishing power to a mine back in the Sierra. Furthermore, the name itself held promise, truchas being the Spanish word for trout.

We forded the stream and drove a short distance to a small settlement where the people who looked after the hydro facilities resided. They were friendly folks who helped repair a flat tire and gave freely of their knowledge of the trout fishing, to wit: the best fishing was at the other end of the impoundment where the stream came in, but there was no road; a few big trout were to be found cruising around the reservoir, but they were hard to come by and lastly, there were many small trout in the stream below the ford.

We chose the last option, since it was the easiest and besides, we would rather fish running water anyway. So we drove back to the ford and set up camp on a long flat bar by the water's edge. Here the water was thin and flat with much filamentous green algae waving in the current — not very promising — but down a ways the creek entered a box canyon where there were many fine pools and cascades. Another good omen: an old friend in the shape of a water ouzel blinked and bobbed on a rock in midstream, the first one I had seen in Mexico.

The villagers were right about the trout being small. All we caught were about five to seven inches long although I did move one built on a grander scale. They were beautiful little things, though, smaller spotted than the Rio del Presidio fish but the spots did tend to be oblong with the long axis aligned vertically. They also had the white-tipped dorsal, ventral and pelvic fins and a faint rainbow stripe. Parr marks were round and numerous with many small auxiliary parr marks. Their coloration was more vivid than the trout of the Rio del Presidio, more yellow and orange on the lower sides and the eyes appeared to be exceptionally large and placed well forward on the snout. Altogether it was a very handsome member of the trout family.

There was only about a half mile of stream to fish before it was gathered into the intake pipe of the power plant and dropped into a deep gorge. There were probably trout below the generator but one look down into that awesome chasm was enough; we didn't go down to see.

If the trout of the Truchas are actually native, then a marine origin during the Pleistocene Epoch is probably likely. There is the possibility, of course, that rainbows were stocked in the reservoir but if the name Rio Truchas predates the early 1880s when the first rainbow eggs were sent to Mexico, then these trout are undoubtedly native for it would be unlikely to name a stream "Trout River" unless there were actually trout there.

On the way back out we fished another small stream that probably was the upper drainage of the Rio Truchas but our maps were so inaccurate and lacking in detail that we couldn't tell exactly where we were. In any event, we caught a few small trout identical to those we had found below the dam.

Unfortunately, it was just as far and rough going back out as it was coming in and we made another dry camp at a glade in the forest, sharing our campsite with a few undernourished cows. On the main road again, we headed back north to Colonia Juarez and to Rio Yaqui waters we had bypassed on the way down.

Back in Colonia Juarez we counseled with John Hatch again as to exactly how to get to where we were going next and it was a good thing we did for there were numerous forks in the road, all unmarked. Our destination was the Rio Gavilan, an upper Yaqui tributary roughly 120 miles north of where we had fished the Tomochic, the Yaqui's most southerly tributary.

Going out of Colonia Juarez we followed the valley of the Casas Grandes a ways, then headed for the east-facing fault scarp of the first of the Sierra's many parallel ranges. The track was narrow and steep, angling across the face of the scarp to a pass at the summit, then down the other side to another Casas Grandes tributary. Topping out on the next ridge we were astride the Continental Divide and from there on all water flowed to the Yaqui.

The Gavilan was down there somewhere, and eventually we found it, meandering along the bottom of a wide pastoral valley. It was a beautiful trout stream with white-boled sycamores growing along its banks.

Our track led us down to the stream which proved to be a good-sized creek and splashing across at a ford we drove to a group of ranch buildings, the headquarters of the Alvin Whetten ranch. Mr. Whetten was away but his son-in-law assured us that we were welcome to camp and fish and we wasted no time in getting started.

The best water appeared to be above us so we started up the stream, Jack fishing one side and I the other. We fished our free drifting flies in deep pools, pockets and slick glides but never moved a fish or saw one rise. After a decent interval of this classic method of presentation, and mumbling an apology to Skues, I reversed the procedure and fished a run from the top and almost immediately hooked a lively, jumping trout which we took time out to examine and photograph.

As expected of fish from the same watershed, it was very similar to the trout of the Tomochic but lacked the brilliant lemon yellow on the lower sides and was therefore not so strikingly colored. This variation may be due to the fact that only the extreme upper tributaries of the numerous branches of the Yaqui are cold enough to sustain trout; lower down they become too warm and so act as thermal barriers, preventing a common flow of genes throughout the system.

Working on up the stream I continued fishing from the top, casting down and across, catching several trout and losing several more. Why they showed no interest in a natural drift but would take a fly hanging in the current or on a slow retrieve is a mystery but that is what they did on all the rivers we fished in Mexico. Another peculiar thing about the Mexican streams: we turned over many rocks in all the waters we fished but never found any

insect larvae nor did we ever see a hatch of any kind; yet the trout we caught were all in good condition, fat and sassy.

We fished a very minuscule section of the Gavilan, as we did on the other streams of the Sierra Madre Occidental, a mere sampling of its diverse trout populations. Much remains to be learned about these trout and about other streams that might possibly contain trout such as the Piaxtla, Baluarte, Acaponeta and San Pedro. So there are still frontiers to explore in the world of Mexican trout and this is a challenge to ichthyologists and trout fishers alike. Possibly our collections and experiences with these trout and their streams contributed a little bit to the sum total of knowledge but I regard it more as laying the groundwork for future explorations.

CHAPTER 19

Atlantic Salmon

PROBABLY THE MOST ANCIENT of the genus *Salmo* and certainly the most exalted is *Salmo salar*, the "leaper." It is included within the scope of this book on trout for technically that is what it is. It is as much a trout as a steelhead and, though oceans apart, the two are almost identical in structure, life history and habits. The two also share honors among flyfishers as being the greatest of freshwater gamefish.

Salmo salar is a wide-ranging anadromous fish found on both sides of the North Atlantic and in Iceland. In North America the original range probably extended from the Delaware River in the south to Ungava Bay in Northern Quebec where all suitable rivers were ascended for spawning. In colonial days they were exceedingly abundant but unfortunately dams and pollution wiped them out in the southern rivers except for a few small runs persisting in Maine.

The Canadian fish have fared much better over the years but even these runs were greatly reduced by a commercial fishery that developed off the coast of Greenland a few years ago. Now, of course, the Maritime Provinces as well as the New England states are faced with the problem of acid rain which promises to get worse before it gets better.

In spite of these adverse impacts, however, the Atlantic Salmon Recovery Program is making some headway and small runs have been re-established in a few of the rivers of Maine and in the Connecticut.

The size of salmon varies considerably from river to river and is dependent on genetic programming as to age at maturity and how long they remain in the ocean before returning to their home stream as maiden fish. The largest fish run to the rivers of Norway which produced the record rod-caught fish of just under 80 pounds. On the other hand, some North American rivers produce only small fish of about three to six pounds, called grilse. Many rivers in the North American range, however, regularly yield salmon of 20 pounds or more.

Regardless of size, Atlantic salmon fresh from the sea are beautiful fish. They are bluish-black, with mint bright silvery sides and speckled with irregular-shaped black spots above the lateral line. The longer they remain in freshwater, the darker they become, and at spawning time have colored up considerably. Finally, kelts returning to the sea in the spring are locally called "black salmon."

Angling for Atlantic salmon is steeped in tradition for it dates back to at least the Fifteenth Century. In the British Isles, where the sport largely evolved, one fishes for Atlantic salmon properly attired, with the proper equipment and with traditional flies. The flies themselves are things of beauty, intricately dressed and having intriguing names, such as the Jock Scott, Black Dose, Durham Ranger, Silver Doctor and Blue Charm, among others. Consequently, when I stepped into my first salmon river I did so with hat in hand, you might say, showing the proper amount of humility and respect. I flailed away mightily, striving to achieve the approved delivery and pickup for I wanted to appear as though I knew what I was doing, but I hooked no fish, nor did I even see one. Of course, I was improperly dressed — no tie, tweed jacket or deerslayer's cap and very probably I was fishing in the wrong place. Salmon do have their special places where they hold and sometimes take a fly, and one should find out where these lies are rather than randomly flogging any likely looking water.

All this took place in Nova Scotia's St. Mary's River a number of years ago. I spent a month or more in Nova Scotia that summer, fishing the West River Sheet Harbour, the Moser, Ecum

Secum, as well as the St. Mary's and I did find where the fish were. It was easy. Just find a group of fishermen working a run and line up with those waiting their turn at the water. And I did catch some salmon, small ones to be sure — grilse — but beautiful, active fish and bright as new silver dollars.

Many interesting tales and probably some lies were told by the anglers waiting their turn on the river banks, mostly about salmon caught and salmon lost and about the merits of various flies. The consensus of opinion seemed to be that any old fly would take fish as long as it was a Cosseboom. I had no Cossebooms to begin with until a local fly tier furnished a supply, and thereafter that was what I took my fish on, probably because one was usually tied to my leader.

The best salmon I hooked, probably the largest and certainly the wildest, came loose right at the net in the Ecum Secum. It came from behind a rock in a tide pool, took my Cosseboom with a hard pull and proceeded to shatter the quiet serenity of a beautiful morning. It was all over the pool and in the air — I've forgotten how many jumps — but it really lived up to its name of leaper. According to the onlooking anglers, I had "ruined" that fish. They said it wouldn't strike again and I hope they were right, for a fish such as that deserves to be wild and free in the river to produce more of its own.

While all anadromous salmon are considered to be but one race, *Salmo salar salar*, there are two landlocked forms in North America classified by some ichthyologists as separate subspecies: *Salmo salar sebago* and *Salmo salar ouananiche*. Between these and the sea-run salmon, there are no structural or anatomical differences of taxonomic significance, but they are entirely different in habits as well as showing minor variations in coloration and spotting pattern.

At the time Maine began fish culture operations in 1875 the Sebago salmon was known only from four drainage systems in the state: the St. Croix, Union River, Presumpscot and the Piscataquis branch of the Penobscot. There is some evidence to suggest, however, that before being impacted by civilization it was much more widespread than that. Being such a popular gamefish, it was soon widely introduced into other Maine waters and into some of the neighboring states as well.

Near the turn of the century and before the days of heavy fishing pressure, large landlocked salmon were common, the record rod-caught fish from Sebago Lake weighing in at 22½ pounds while one reported netted in spawn taking operations weighed

36 pounds. Today fish of 10 pounds are occasionally taken with the average weight between two and three pounds, but even a two-pounder taken on appropriate tackle is a gamefish of the first order.

The cold, deep lakes are the landlocked salmon's "ocean" and there they spend most of their adult lives feeding on baitfish, primarily smelt. When the smelt enter the streams on their spawning runs, the salmon follow them, dropping back to the lake when the smelt return. Because of their predilection for smelt, a number of streamer flies resembling this baitfish have been developed by Maine tiers, notably the Black Ghost and the Gray Ghost, and many salmon are taken on these and other streamers trolled in the spring after ice-out when both predator and prey are in shallow water. When the salmon enter the rivers on their spawning runs in autumn or early fall, they can be taken on more conventional fly patterns.

I have never fished for Sebago salmon. The only ones I ever saw were reposing in an icebox at a resort near Rangeley Lake and they were beautiful fish indeed. Now this is the only member of the North American *Salmo* clan I have not put a hook into and something needs to be done about this and soon for I am close to the end of my backing. Perhaps next summer *Salmo salar sebago* will take my fly on a Maine river — one of its ancestral waters.

The *ouananiche* I *have* taken and what a fish it is! It is reported to have larger and more profuse black spots (St. Andrews crosses) than its Maine or anadromous cousins and to have larger eyes and fins. That part about the fins must be true for it would take powerful appendages to drive it so fast in the water and so high above it. This one I *know* is a leaper!

Salmo salar ouananiche is found north of the St. Lawrence River in Quebec and Labrador with its center of distribution in the Lake St. John area. Like its counterpart in Maine, it is primarily a lake dweller, entering the streams on spawning runs and though over most of its range it has access to the sea, it is programmed to remain in freshwater.

Primarily lake dwellers and fish eaters, *ouananiche* are usually angled for by trolling and considering the fact that they must do their fighting in stillwater without the rush of a stream to help, they put on a remarkable show. The fish I caught from Lake St. John were hooked on a trolled fly and I have never been attached to better fish for speed and action right up to the net. They were beautiful, trim, streamlined fish, silvery with a brassy tinge, having numerous black hash marks or St. Andrews crosses standing out in bold relief. They were well conditioned fish and would weigh between two and a half and five pounds, although some exceptional individuals reach eight pounds or more. When in the streams on their spawning runs in late summer or early fall, they are available to the flyfisher and I can well imagine what these fish could do in a heavy flow. I hope to find them there one day.

CHAPTER 20

Lake Trout

THE GROUP OF SALMONIDS known as charr are Holarctic, extending around the fringe of the Arctic Ocean and south into temperate zones. They are primitive type fishes and particularly adapted to cold water, some occurring further north than any other freshwater fish. Many species of charr are commonly called trout, such as the eastern brook trout, Dolly Varden trout, bull trout and lake trout. According to the definition given in Webster's Dictionary, a charr is a trout of the genus *Salvelinus*. They differ from our other native trout of the genus *Salmo* in having a different arrangement of teeth on the roof of the mouth and in having light-colored body spots rather than black spots. Some native charr are among the most beautiful of fishes.

The lake trout, the largest of North American charr, was first described as *Salmo namaycush* from Hudson Bay specimens by Walbaum in 1792. Later it was placed in the genus *Cristivomer* but to emphasize its close affinities to other North American charr, most authorities now recognize it as *Salvelinus namaycush*. Though the lake trout is indigenous to North America, it has close similarities to the Huchen, a Eurasian salmonid of the genus *Hucho* and to the Kundsha charr, *Salvelinus leucomaenis*, of Eastern Siberia and Japan. These apparent similarities, however, may be due to convergent evolution rather than close relatedness.

The common names of the lake trout are even more varied, depending upon the region. It is known as Mackinaw, Togue, gray trout, lake charr, and among French Canadians as Touladi. Only one species is generally recognized, although two deep-water forms were named as subspecies from the Great Lakes — *siscowet* and *huronicus.*

The natural range of lake trout is enormous, covering nearly all of Northern North America. It extends from Bering Sea drainages in the west to Labrador on the east and north to the Arctic Ocean, including some of the islands of the Arctic Archipelago. The southern limits, where relict populations were isolated following the withdrawal of the last ice sheet, are less precise. Thus, lake trout are still present in a few deep, cold lakes in New England, New York, the Great Lakes, Wisconsin, Minnesota and the headwaters of the Missouri and Fraser river systems. It is noteworthy that this entire area was covered by Pleistocene glaciation so that lake trout and other fishes had to re-invade the area following the labyrinth of waterways and proglacial lakes as the ice receded. Obviously there were refuges south of the ice edge where the lake trout survived the glacial onslaught and from whence they dispersed northward as the ice melted back. These refuges were probably in the mid-Atlantic states, the upper Mississippi watershed and the extreme headwaters of the Missouri River. As the last residual ice disappeared from Keewatin and Labrador only about 6,000 years ago, lake trout may still be extending their range to new waters.

Even though lake trout successfully spread across Northern North America from coast to coast, they never negotiated the Bering land bridge to Asia, nor did they cross the Strait of Belle Isle to Newfoundland. In the former, ecological conditions may not have been favorable. The land bridge was probably low lying tundra with shallow, marshy lakes, while in the latter case the predations of the sea lamprey, to which the lake trout is very vulnerable, may have prevented a crossing to Newfoundland. Throughout boreal and Arctic America, however, lake trout are one of the most abundant and widespread of fishes.

My early experiences with lake trout were typical, I suppose, of the time and place. I fished them more than fifty years ago at the very southern edge of their range, relict lakers, in the Quetico-Superior boundary waters of Minnesota and adjoining Ontario. There on the fringe of the ancient Laurentian Shield, the oldest land mass in North America, they occurred in a few of the very deepest and coldest lakes, nestled among outcrops of glacial polished granite and virgin forests of white and red pine, canoe birch, balsam and spruce. The country is strikingly beautiful and in early days witnessed the passage of fur traders and voyageurs in bark canoes laden with trade goods, bound from Lachine on the St. Lawrence to the rich fur country of the Saskatchewan and the Northwest. Later, during the first half of this century, Francis Lee Jaques left us a rich legacy in his beautiful paintings and sketches of the area and Sigurd Olson described its rugged beauty in his writings. In present times, as the "Canoe Country" became popular with recreationists, it has been almost overwhelmed by crowds of canoeists, vying with each other for campsites, but when I knew it my companions and I were there alone, with only the moose, the deer and the loons.

Fishing for lake trout in those waters consists of trolling with enough lead to get the lure close to the bottom, for it was always late summer when I was there and the trout were as deep as they could get. Any wobbling spoon seemed to work, but our favorite was a "Finlander" spoon resembling a shoe horn. Upon hooking a trout, the contest became a tugging match and eventually the laker emerged from the depths burping clouds of bubbles in a futile attempt to adjust to the lessened pressure. They were beautiful torpedo-shaped fish, gray-green on back and sides and profusely spattered with large, irregular-shaped whitish spots and with a markedly forked tail. The method of taking them, though, left much to be desired and served primarily to fill the pot with delicious orange meat. Even so, successful boating of a lake trout always highlighted a day of fishing for walleyes, pike and bass.

I had heard rumors that lake trout could be taken at or near the surface just after ice-out in the spring and just before freeze-up in the fall when surface water was sufficiently cold to bring them into the shoals. Furthermore, since lakers are primarily fish eaters, at least after they grow large enough, it seemed logical that at such times they could be induced to take a streamer fly or bucktail resembling a baitfish. At least such were my dreams.

Many years after my "canoe country" experiences I found lakers in the shoals, where the water was always frigid — even in summer, and I found that they would indeed take a fly. With

Bob Allen I had been flying aerial surveys searching for the nesting grounds of the whooping crane and by mid-summer had reached Aklavik and the Arctic Coast. Working out of Aklavik, we searched as far as the range of the Widgeon would allow, covering the Barren Lands, "Arctic Prairies," and the sub-Arctic taiga that merged with it on the south. Lakes and lakelets were everywhere and, as I was to find, so were the lake trout. Almost any lake that didn't freeze to the bottom had a good supply as did the numerous clear streams draining the area. They were even in brackish estuaries along the Arctic Coast, consorting with Arctic charr at the rivermouths.

One night, returning to Aklavik from a survey of the Anderson River country, we crossed a large Barren Land lake lying on the uplands just east of the broad delta of the MacKenzie. Seeing lake trout cruising along the shoals, there was only one logical course of action, and I put the Widgeon down to make my bid. It was still broad daylight, and though close to midnight, the sun had merely swung around in an arc to about a foot above the northern horizon. In fact, it wouldn't set for another month for we were close to seventy degrees north, well above the Arctic Circle. I taxied the aircraft to a sand beach, secured it and put my rod up while Bob, an inveterate bird watcher, draped his binoculars around his neck and struck off across the tundra.

Out from the beach a few yards was a dropoff to deeper water and I began working my bucktail along its edge. Soon, about a half-dozen trout showed up, cruising slowly along the edge of the break and I laid the fly well ahead of them and twitched it back. The fly and the trout were on a collision course but it showed no interest until the fly was about to pass. Then one turned, made a slashing strike and I hooked it. The ensuing struggle was a strong one, if not spectacular, and I finally steered the trout to the beach and up on the sand. It was a plump, full-bodied fish of about three pounds, a typical gray-green laker liberally spattered with large, cream-colored spots. I took two more that night of about the same size before Bob returned from his tour of the tundra completely enveloped in a gray cloud of mosquitoes. The Barren Lands were not barren of mosquitoes in summer.

Throughout many following summers I fished lake trout with the long rod on innumerable lakes and rivers, many of which had probably never been seen by man, including Eskimos and Indians, for our waterfowl surveys took us far from travel routes and settlements where no one had occasion to go. Most of the fish we caught were small by lake trout standards — from three to seven pounds — although the really big lakes, like Great Slave and Great Bear, produce a few pot-bellied monsters in the 50- to 60-pound range. The all-time record came from Lake Athabaska, a net-caught trout of 102 pounds! Such leviathans, of course, are very old. Studies have shown that it takes 17 years to produce a lake trout of 20 pounds in Great Slave Lake and that the growth rate in Great Bear is much slower.

Even though these far northern lakers were completely un-sophisticated, never having been exposed to artificial lures and flies, they were not always that easy to catch. Early one June during the mid-'50s, with Dr. Gus Swanson and Everett Sutton aboard as observers, I was flying a survey out of Ft. Smith, Northwest Territory, east across the Slave River Parklands and adjacent Pre-Cambrian Shield just north of the Alberta boundary. As the area was unmapped, I was navigating by time and bearing and after penetrating this wilderness for a couple of hundred miles I offset to the north fifty miles to return on a reciprocal heading. Part way back we crossed a lake where a great mass of trout were seen milling around the outlet. Under the circumstances there was but one thing to do; I circled the lake to check for reefs or other hazards, put the aircraft on the water and taxied to a shelving slab of granite near the school of fish, all the while watched intently by a white wolf standing on the shore.

It didn't take us long to put our rods up, Gus and I with fly outfits and Everett with his bait casting rig and Daredevil. As we picked our way over ledges and around boulders to the outlet, we could see the school of trout in a milling throng, close in within easy casting range. As soon as our flies and the lure were on the water, we each hooked a fish and as we worked them in, others swirled around and followed them in. This happened several times and then we hooked fish only occasionally which tapered off to a strike or a followup now and then and finally, nothing. The fish were still there, we could see them, but they wouldn't have any more.

That experience was repeated in different places many times over many years. It seemed to be a pattern: great activity at first which gradually subsides to nothing. Possibly if one rested the fish an hour or two, they might start all over again, but we were always many wilderness miles from our base and never had the time to try.

I never found that lake again. The white wolf, my only land-mark, had moved on, and without him the lake looked exactly like the hundreds of others in the area.

Stillwater fishing for lake trout requires some knowledge of where the trout might be; you can't just cast anywhere along the shore and expect to find fish, although you never know when one or more might come cruising along. We found that inlets and outlets generally held fish and sometimes a rocky point culminating in a submerged reef was productive. The most enjoyable fishing, however, was in the rivers, especially those that connected deep lakes. The Lockhart River was one of these, draining out of the lower end of Artillery Lake into the east arm of Great Slave, a big rushing river, clear and cold as ice for usually when we fished it both of the big lakes were still frozen. On the edge of the Barren Lands, it shared the best of two worlds — the limitless horizons of the Arctic prairies to the east and north and the more sheltered Hudsonian spruce forest to the south and west.

The Lockhart is not without its legends, for at its mouth is the site of Old Ft. Reliance where Capt. George Back, a veteran of two Franklin expeditions to the Arctic, spent the winters of 1833-34 during his explorations of the river that now bears his name. I tried to find this old fort once, in company with a local Indian rejoicing in the name of Drybones, but all we found was a crumbling stone chimney. No doubt lake trout were frequent items in Capt. Back's diet during those long cold winters.

Ernie Boffa, the veteran bush pilot of Yellowknife, had told me of the Lockhart and its trout — a different trout, he said, more like eastern brook trout. It just so happened that the head of the Lockhart was between two of my survey routes or transects and when we had finished with the first, we passed right over the Lockhart on the way to the second, so it seemed logical to stop and fish awhile. As Artillery Lake came into view, it was white with ice, with but a small open patch in a bay from which the Lockhart began its wild plunge to Great Slave Lake. Below the first rapids was a tranquil stretch of water, perhaps a mile long and big enough to get the Goose on and off again. Checking for submerged rocks and reefs, I put the bird down and taxied to a shallow cove just short of the fast water.

We rigged up our rods and went separate ways, Everett going below to a rocky point where he could fling his Daredevil into a deep eddy while I walked up the Chute about halfway where the water inshore was slower and shallower. Working the little eddies and pockets with a streamer, I was soon into a fish and with the current to help the fish, I had to follow it down. Finally beached, it was, as Ernie had said, "Different." Chunkier and fatter than a standard lake trout, it had more color. The lower fins were orange with white leading edges and there were salmon-colored tints on the lower sides and belly. It was, however, unquestionably a lake trout and whether the difference is due to sexual dimorphism, individual variation or genetic influence is not known. As lake trout are fall spawners, it was definitely not a breeding characteristic. In any event, most of the trout I caught that day were of this type, although some were the regular gray charr.

In later years I found other highly colored lake trout in both lakes and rivers, but they never occurred in pure populations. I have hooked both types standing on the same rock. While most of the bright fish I have caught have been smallish, three to seven pounds, I have seen some really large ones, so the difference is not due to size alone.

I was entertained that day on the Lockhart by more than the trout and the harsh, raw beauty of the land, vacated only recently by the Keewatin ice sheet. The open patch of water in Artillery Lake just above the Chute had attracted a large flock of old squaw ducks that continually drifted over the brink and went sailing down the rapids. When they hit the surging white water, they would dive and when opposite my fishing territory burst out of the rapids in full flight, fly back up and do it all over again. They were boisterous ducks, calling continuously in a high-pitched, yodeling clamor and it was obvious that they were enjoying their sport as much as I was mine. We were also visited by a flock of Ross's geese, those miniature editions of the common snow goose, beating their way across the barrens to their nesting grounds near Perry River on the Arctic Coast.

A few years later, I found other aberrant lake trout in Great Bear Lake. I had landed at Ft. Franklin, near where the Bear River begins its passage to the MacKenzie and having a few hours to spare, I obtained a canoe with an Indian pilot to prospect for big lakers. I had expected that we would work along the shore of the big lake, where the bottom shelves off steeply to the depths, but instead my guide took me into a wide, shallow bay where the water appeared to be no more than ten feet deep over a white sand bottom. This appeared to me the most unlikely place I had ever seen to find lake trout and my exasperation was about to boil over when a pod of trout appeared cruising along at mid-depth. There were six or eight of them, all about the same size — 14 to 16 pounds. As my guide maneuvered the canoe closer, I slapped a big streamer directly ahead of them, whereupon one surged forward and took it. The struggle lasted quite a while and in the in-terim the school disappeared. Continuing our prospecting, we found two other schools of about the same number and size and I took a fish from each one.

The strange part of this, aside from the type of water the trout frequented, was their fatness and shape. They were short, chunky fish, with relatively small heads and small mouths and the fattest lake trout I have ever seen. When they were dressed, they literally dripped with oil. All of these features correspond with the description of the *siscowet* subspecies named from Lake Superior and I have often wondered if these fish were the Great Bear counterpart of that race. The fact that *siscowet* was a deep water form in Lake Superior would not apply to Great Bear if water temperature was the controlling factor, for Great Bear's surface water in the summer is probably as cold as Superior's depths at the same season.

The largest lake trout I have ever caught on any tackle I took with the long rod on a red and white streamer at the outlet of Tsu Lake, where the Talston River makes a stopover on its tortuous route to Great Slave Lake. Working down from the lip of the outlet, where the river plunged in a steep rapid to a large eddy, I drifted the fly by a pocket formed by a partially submerged boulder. Immediately a huge trout rolled up but missed the bucktail. On the next drift, it took and started down, an uncontrollable force as I followed along on the spray-washed, slippery ledges. Once in the eddy it stayed there, making several complete circuits of the swirling gyre. Finally, with all the side pressure the Winston could muster, I steered it out of the flow into the shallows where its great bulk promptly grounded.

Dave Munro, my fishing partner, straddled the fish, slipped a hand under each gillcover and dragged it to the beach. The fish was completely done in, never moving or flopping. I was nearly as bad off. When we got back to Ft. Smith that night the only scales we could find were in the nursing station where they weighed in the Indian babies. The only trouble was that 25 pounds was the limit and when we draped the fish over the basket the needle flew around and hit the peg. I thought it might have made 30 or maybe 35, but even at 25 pounds plus it was and still is the biggest trout I have ever caught.

CHAPTER 21

Arctic Charr

ARCTIC CHARR, THE MOST NORTHERLY of the world's salmonids, are circumpolar in distribution. They occur across the top of North America and Eurasia, in Iceland and Greenland, and there are relict landlocked populations in the more southerly parts of its range, left stranded when the last ice sheet melted back.

Within this vast region, much of which lies above the Arctic Circle, Arctic charr have evolved into a complexity of somewhat diverse forms and there is much confusion and disagreement concerning their relationship and classification. The first to be described, a charr from Swedish Lapland, was named *Salmo alpinus* by Linnaeus in 1758 and since then a host of names have been proposed for other forms across its range. About the only thing most ichthyologists agree on is the change in the generic form to *Salvelinus* and even here some European authorities still use *Salmo*. Consequently, the names now in use should be considered provisional and subject to change as further research may resolve the nomenclatural problems within the complex.

In North America, seven species or subspecies of Arctic charr were recognized, plus one or two more undescribed races in Alaska and Northwestern Canada. The seven named races, all from Northeastern North America, are now considered to comprise but two subspecies, the eastern Arctic form, *Salvelinus alpinus stagnalis*, and a relict landlocked charr, *Salvelinus alpinus oquassa*, which includes the Sunapee golden trout, the Quebec red trout and the blueback trout. The races from Alaska and Northwestern Canada, also relict lake dwelling charr, have yet to be officially named, although Behnke has proposed *andriashevi* as the subspecific designation for the Alaskan form.

All of the relict landlocked Arctic charr of the Northeast, New England, Quebec and the Maritime Provinces are adapted to extremely cold water, hence are found only in the cool depths of certain deep lakes. Because of this they are, for the most part, unavailable to the fly fisher except immediately after ice-out in the spring and during late fall before freeze-up when they move into shallow water.

I caught some of these charr years ago, some smallish fish just above the outlet of a beautiful little lake tucked in between the worn-down stumps of the oldest mountains in North America — in the center of Quebec's Gaspe Peninsula. These were blue-backed, silvery little fish showing typical Arctic charr spotting, but too small to show adult characteristics. At that time this race was called the Quebec red charr, subspecies *marstoni* since lumped with the blueback trout, *Salvelinus alpinus oquassa.*

I found Alaskan Arctic charr only once — at the inlet to lower Goodnews Lake. There the channel shallowed and then spilled over a gravel sill into the deeper lake waters and in the eddies and riffles thus formed we hooked a number of these hard, fast fighters. Though they were not overly large — up to about two and one-half pounds — they gave a good account of themselves. They took our orange-bodied flies readily, even though their stomachs were crammed with dark, bean-sized periwinkles.

When I slipped the first one through the flooded sedges onto the shore I knew I had something different . . . no ordinary, run-of-the-mill Dolly. This was a much lighter colored fish with a sea-green back, silvery sides and a faint tan streak just above its pure white belly. The pink spots were fewer, paler and somewhat larger than are found on most Dollies, but the most striking feature was the form — long, lean and streamlined with a markedly forked tail. Dollies, at least mature fish, have square tails, but this one was definitely forked, almost as much as on a lake trout.

I have often puzzled over the problem of separating the northern Dolly from Arctic charr of the same waters based on external characteristics and here at my feet was the answer, plain as the nose on my face. The size of the spots (larger than the pupil of the eye in the Arctic charr, smaller in the Dolly) is according to the literature, the diagnostic feature, but here there is considerable overlap in both species and so it is not infallible. The shape of the fish, however, the long, narrow caudal peduncle ending in the forked tail, definitely places the Arctic charr apart. Other diagnostic features require dissection, for the Arctic charr has about twice as many pyloric caeca and significantly more gillrakers than the northern Dolly.

Sea-run Arctic charr occurring in the Eastern Arctic west to the Mackenzie have a distinctive seasonal distribution pattern. Most populations run into the rivers in the late summer or early fall, and after spawning overwinter in headwater lakes which remain slightly warmer than the sea water under the polar ice pack. During and shortly after spring breakup they return to the rich feeding grounds in the sea but probably seldom wander far from their home estuary. They ascend all suitable rivers having headwater lakes not too far inland and while larger streams are preferred, I have seen six-pound charr in a tiny Ungava brook not two feet wide.

In the harsh, forbidding environment of the high Arctic, Arctic charr are slow growers, requiring ten to fifteen years to attain a size of five pounds. Some do not become sexually mature until eight or ten years old and even then a female spawns only every other year. Consequently, any population homing to a particular river could be easily overfished.

The Eastern Arctic race of Arctic charr, occurring in Arctic drainages from Northern Labrador west to the Mackenzie River, has earned a considerable reputation as a gamefish in recent years. Prior to the 1950s, it was known only to the few people that lives along the Arctic Coast, Eskimos and a handful of Hudson Bay post managers, "Mounties" and missionaries. Primarily an anadromous fish, it was netted during spawning runs, dried and used as a winter food supply for both men and dogs. More recently it has been "discovered" by anglers and there are now a number of "fly in" camps where Arctic charr fishing is the primary attraction. Although these fish are most vulnerable to hardware and lures, they will take a streamer fly or bucktail resembling baitfish.

When I first heard about Arctic charr during the late '40s, they were described to me as "salmon." I had landed at Coppermine

on the Canadian Arctic Coast for fuel and there the "Mounties" told me of their yearly expedition to Tree River to net these fish for their annual supply of dog food. They said they went each September during the spawning run, that the fish were bright red and would strike at a cigarette butt flipped in the water. I was invited to accompany them but unfortunately it was then mid-July and by September I would be thousands of miles from Coppermine.

The next summer, however, found me close to Coppermine. I had flown to Cambridge Bay on Victoria Island where there was a radio and loran station operated by the Canadian Air Force and also a Hudson Bay post. Around this metropolis a group of Eskimos spent the summer, fishing and sealing in the adjacent waters of Queen Maude Gulf and Dease Strait.

The dubious benefits of civilization had yet to rub off on these Eskimos. Their culture was primitive and they lived off the land and sea as they always had, dressed in traditional caribou skin clothing with sealskin mukluks for footgear. Most of the older women were tattooed with short radiating lines on the chin and cheekbones. To be among these remarkable people was like taking a big step backward in time — almost to the Stone Age.

After flying waterfowl surveys all day over Victoria Island's bleak and barren expanse, we would return to Cambridge Bay and, as the sun didn't set, fish most of the night. At the head of the bay, a mile or two above the post, two small creeks came in, forming an estuary, and there in the brackish water were Arctic charr and lake trout. On my first night at Cambridge I walked up to the creek mouths and found that by wading out to a small rocky islet I could just cast to a fishy looking spot where the current lost itself in the estuary. I tried conventional wet flies first that produced swirls but when I tied on a gaudy streamer I hooked a fish.

The strike and the run were simultaneous, as with summer steelhead, and the run was long and fast. With the backing well out the fish paused and sloshed on the surface and, as I applied more pressure, changed directions in another mad dash, repeating this sequence until spent. Finally, I worked it back to the shallows by my rocky perch, its mint bright sides flashing in the low rays of the midnight sun.

Although Arctic charr develop high coloration during the spawning runs, bright red on sides and belly, this one was typical of those found in saltwater. A male of about four pounds, it was bluish-green on the back, silvery on the sides and snow white on the belly. There were numerous large, round pinkish spots both above and below the lateral line, and the leading edge of the lower fins was white. When I lifted it from the water it was cold as ice and almost as hard — the epitome of the high Arctic . . . clean, cold and primordial, looking every inch the fast, strong fighter than it was.

I hooked several fish that night, some of which were lake trout. It was easy to tell which I was fast to for the lakers just chugged around, strong and powerful, but not really doing much, whereas the Arctic charr repeatedly ripped off line in long, fast runs and spent themselves quickly. While most of the Arctic charr I caught were smallish fish, from a foot long to about four pounds, one weighed seven and a half and another nine pounds. They were beautiful, sleek, silvery fish in contrast to the lakers, which seemed quite dark and paunchy by comparison.

One always hopes, of course, to catch a really big fish. I had inquired about the possibilities of doing this at the Hudson Bay post and was told that they didn't bother much with fishing in Cambridge Bay, for the fish were few and small, but went to Wellington Bay about fifty miles west along the coast to net their winter supply of dog food. "How big are they in Wellington Bay?" I inquired. "Don't know for sure," was the reply, "can only get a couple of big ones in a coal sack — maybe 20 or 30 pounds."

Now 20- or 30-pound Arctic charr are mighty big fish in my book but when I pursued the subject further I got another jolt. Peter, one of the local Eskimos, told me that when netting seals under the ice in Dease Strait they sometimes would catch an Ika-lukpic (Arctic charr). "How big?" I asked. "Big as a man," came the reply. There is the possibility, of course, that Eskimos draw a long bow when describing the size of fish, like some others I know, but it must be admitted it would take a mighty big fish to get fouled up in the wide meshes of a seal net. Also, men, like fish, come in assorted sizes with Eskimos being on the short end of the range. But an Arctic charr the size of, say, even a small Eskimo, would be quite a fish and I would like to hook one.

I did encounter one, a brief meeting though and while it was not man-sized, it would certainly fall in the "coal sack" category. We had returned to our base at Cambridge from a flight to the north coast of Victoria, still slightly numb from flying over hundreds of miles of the bleakest, most barren country I have ever seen, just as raw and unaltered as when the last glacial ice melted. I sought solace with rod and fly and wandered along the shore of the inlet to its head. Here, at least, was the softening touch of vegetation, sedges and grasses and diminutive willows all of four inches high, forming dense mats in the swales through which ran a maze of lemming trails. Snow buntings flitted along ahead of me and a great white snowy owl regarded me solemnly from its perch on a lichen-splotched boulder.

When I reached the head of the inlet I waded out to my perch on the rocky islet between the mouths of the two creeks and cast my streamer into the slackened current. I hooked a smallish fish that soon spent itself in wild runs. As I continued to cast and retrieve I saw a wake such as a seal would make, the bow wave terminating in a great bulge at the fly and I was fast to an irresistible force. I had no control, could only hang on and let it run. And run it did, in alternate bursts of speed and slower cruising. Fortunately, it changed directions frequently or I would have been cleaned out as it had most of the backing. On one big circuit it swung around and came by me close and in that ice cold clear water I saw the fish plainly — a huge, silvery bulk that I guessed would go 30 pounds. Finally, after some surface sloshing, it was gone and I reeled in a forlorn looking streamer, the hook bend straightened. No need to describe my feelings for we have all experienced it; the Arctic charr of a lifetime free at last, heading out under the pack ice in Dease Strait.

That charr had to be an old-timer, maybe as old as I was, for Arctic charr, like lake trout in the high Arctic, are slow growers. Having lived that long maybe it is still there, poking its snout into the clear cold streams of Victoria's South Coast.

CHAPTER 22

Dolly Varden Charr and the Bull Trout

THE REPUTATION OF THE DOLLY VARDEN as a gamefish has been under a cloud as long as men have been writing about western trout. In fact, at one time a bounty was offered for Dolly tails in Alaskan waters under the guise of protecting salmon stocks. There is no doubt that big Dollies are predators, as are several other species of trout, such as the Kamloops, Lahontan and brown trout, when they attain sufficient size. There is also no question that they eat salmon eggs, as do other species of trout, but these are usually free eggs that escape from the redds during spawning and would never hatch anyway. It has also been affirmed that Dollies are ugly, somehow unattractive, and that their flesh is inferior to that of other trout. To this I can only say again that beauty does indeed rest in the eye of the beholder and individual tastes in food are equally varied.

What of the sporting qualities of the Dolly Varden? It has been said that it is a sluggish fish and will seldom take a fly, altogether an undesirable quarry. Obviously, those making such accusations have never been exposed to the sea-run Dollies of Alaskan Bering Sea drainages, for those fish not only take a fly readily, but are wild as steelhead and just as acrobatic.

Ichthyologists agree to disagree about the taxonomic status of the Dolly Varden. It was named *Salmo malma* by Walbaum in 1792 from Kamchatkan specimens but since has been placed in the genus *Salvelinus*. Behnke has recently shown that the Kamchatkan charr is identical to the one found in Alaskan drainages from the Alaska Peninsula north and east around the coast. Therefore, this Alaskan charr, formerly called the western form of the Arctic charr, *Salvelinus alpinus*, is now considered to be the northern race of the Dolly Varden, *Salvelinus malma malma*.

The origin of the popular name, Dolly Varden, is also of interest.

According to the most prevalent version, about 1880 David Starr Jordan and Spencer Baird, the eminent ichthyologists, were staying at Soda Springs Resort on the McCloud River in Northern California and upon showing their landlady a charr they had caught she exclaimed, "It's a regular Dolly Varden," a print dress material named for a colorful Dickens character. And so they christened the charr Dolly Varden. Actually, however, the name was in common usage, locally, at least, eight years before, as Livingston Stone used this name for the McCloud River charr in 1872 and so published in the report of the U. S. Fish Commission for 1873-74.

Anyway, the name stuck although the McCloud River charr is actually a bull trout, an entirely different species from the Dolly, but the name has been used indiscriminately for all charr of the Pacific slope excepting the lake trout — a case of mistaken identity. I have recently heard the Dollies referred to as Dolly Parton, but the resemblance escapes me.

The range of the northern Dolly is extensive, and so far, its habitat has not been much affected by man's meddling with the environment. It occurs from the north slope of the Alaska Peninsula, north around the top of Alaska and east across the Northern Yukon to, but not including, the Mackenzie River. It is primarily anadromous, running up all suitable rivers except the Yukon where there are resident Dollies in some of the headwater tributaries. These landlocked Dollies are also found in some of the headwater lakes throughout Northern Alaska where they live in harmony with lake dwelling Arctic charr without interbreeding.

In adjacent Siberia, the northern Dolly ranges from the northern drainages of the Okhotsk Sea around Kamchatka and the Chukotsk Peninsula and west along the Arctic Coast to the Kolyma River. Since Siberia and Alaska were connected by the

Bering Land Bridge at various times during the last glacial epoch, and as parts of these areas escaped glaciation, the northern Dolly probably survived the onslaught of the ice there and after it was over was free to spread in all directions. As mentioned earlier, Behnke considers the populations on either side of Bering Strait identical.

The resident Dollies in headwater streams and in lakes are apt to be dwarfed but the sea-run Dollies are noble fish, sometimes in excess of 12 pounds. Some of those we caught in the Togiak and the Goodnews rivers, short drainages to Bristol and Kuskokwim bays on the Bering Sea, would weigh half that amount, while most would weigh between a pound and a half to three pounds.

Jack James and I, with guide John Kibbons, had chartered a Widgeon out of Dillingham, Alaska, and had flown into Togiak Lake, our starting point for the river float that would take us fifty miles down the Togiak. There Tom Tucker, our pilot, picked us up and flew us into Goodnews Lake to begin a similar float on the Goodnews River.

We almost didn't make it in to Togiak Lake that first day. The weather was marginal, typical Alaskan coastal weather, low clouds and rain with fog along the mountain bases. Tom poked the nose of the Widgeon into the approach of several passes before he found a way through to the river. As we cruised low up the winding channel, we could see schools of fish, mostly salmon, moving up en route to their natal spawning gravels in various headwater tributaries, their first and only spawning run. The charr were there, too, as we found out later, but being lighter colored, were less visible. Upon reaching the lake landing conditions were ideal, just a slight ripple on the water surface and Tom put the Widgeon down with only a swish, lowered the gear and taxied onto the beach. After unloading our gear, Tom said, "Pick out a bar next to a long deep run anyplace below the Pungokepuk and I'll pick you up in six days," then taxied back into the water and took off.

Five full days of fishing new water and several new species of fish, surrounded by a wilderness of tundra and mountains . . . I felt like I was flying again! We inflated the rubber boat posthaste, loaded in our gear and rowed to the river outlet where we set up camp on an island.

While John got the camp organized, Jack and I put up our rods, tied on orange-bodied No. 8 flies with white wings and began casting just under the first riffle below the lake. Jack hooked a fish almost immediately, but I had trouble hooking one, although I felt numerous strikes, if one could call them that. Slight, almost imperceptible ticks were all I felt, and that, I found, was the way a Dolly takes. No savage strike as with steelhead, just light plucks. Finally, I hooked one, a strong wild fish that burst from the surface in mad leaps between fast runs. It never really gave up, fighting all the way to my feet. When I slid it onto the gravel bar, it really came to life, flopping and jumping. Who was it that said a Dolly is sluggish?

This was a beautiful charr of about two pounds, a typical northern Dolly. The back was bronze in color with a bluish tinge along the sides; the white belly was just beginning to show a pink blush. Small, irregular-shaped yellow spots dotted the back while the sides were speckled with round, fairly large pink spots, each surrounded by a faint blue halo. The pinkish-orange paired fins and the anal fin were bordered with white on their leading edges and the snout was yellow-tipped and had a pronounced kype. The lower half of the head and under the lower mandible was quite black. Altogether, the subtle blending of colors seemed quite suited to this torpedo of icy oceans and cold, clear streams.

The above description would fit all of the Dollies we caught, varying only in the amount of pink or reddish tints on the belly, these colors becoming more intense as the fish approach their spawning period.

We had grilled Dolly fillets for dinner that night; they were red-fleshed and as delicious as any salmon or steelhead I'd sampled.

The next morning the clouds lifted and became broken. The sun appeared and we could see where Tom had left us. Togiak Lake stretched away to the northeast with the slopes of the Ahklun and Wood River mountains crowding down close, barren except for thickets of low bushes in the draws. At the lower end of the lake, where we were camped, the valley broadened into a tundra-covered plain that rose gradually towards the mountains. The only trees visible were those on the immediate banks of the river, cottonwoods and willows, not over twenty feet high. As we drifted down the river, new vistas opened up, different ranges came into sight and wherever we looked all was virgin wilderness, barren but beautiful.

The Togiak is a fair-sized river, broad and fairly deep — too deep to wade in most places. While there is no white water, the current moves swiftly, three or four miles an hour. The only hazards to navigation are occasional low "sweepers," downed trees that have tipped over across the channel, especially where the river sometimes separates into multiple narrow channels around islands.

Fish were everywhere, most moving upstream, some to spawn and others following the spawners. There was a continual procession of sockeyes around the islands at the head of the river into the lake and many of the eddies lower down contained large schools of milling sockeyes, as well as dog salmon, kings and humpbacks. Rainbow trout and Arctic grayling were scattered throughout the river, nowhere particularly abundant, but the Dollies were in every riffle, from head to tail water. As we floated down we passed thousands of fish moving in large or small schools that merely parted ranks to let us by and we saw some really big kings, sockeyes, dogs and charrs.

While we caught all of the species present in the river, the Dollies were our standby. We hooked literally hundreds, releasing all but one or two for our dinner each night. Though not as heavy and strong as the big salmon, they were the wildest, best fighting fish in the river, except possibly for the sockeyes which at times are quite spectacular. The Dollies were stronger, faster and held out longer than rainbows of comparable size. Though their leaps were not as clean as a rainbow's, many were spectacular jumpers. The flies we used seemed to make little difference, from big coho flies to No. 8 standard type wet flies, but our standby was an orange-bodied fly, with or without wings, and these took every species of fish in the river. All flies were fished wet on a sink tip line although our guide, John Kibbons, took a few Dollies on dry flies, just to prove it could be done.

We floated and fished the Togiak for five days to a point just below the mouth of the Pungokepuk, about half way to the sea. There Tom picked us up on schedule and moved us over to Goodnews Lake, the headwater of the Goodnews River. The Goodnews is the next major drainage north of the Togiak, draining the same type of country and except for its smaller size is very similar. All of the fish species found in the Togiak were also in the Goodnews and in addition we caught lake trout and Arctic charr a short distance below the outlet of the lake. Thus, on flies, we took nine species of fish and had we waited another two weeks, we could have added cohos. Certainly, there are few river systems in the world where this could be duplicated.

We found the salmon in the Goodnews not quite as abundant as in the Togiak and they were closer to maturity — more highly colored. In fact, dead dog salmon were beginning to show up on the bars and we saw dogs digging redds in the gravel. The charr however, were present in almost unbelievable numbers. We drifted through riffles where the Dollies were lying as close as they could tolerate — about a foot or two apart, from bank to bank.

The Goodnews, being smaller, was easier to wade and fish than the Togiak and the riffles were spaced closer together and were more extensive. Almost any riffle we chose to fish held charr in good numbers and the hooking and releasing of fish was a constant process. Many charr were lying in very shallow water and when coming to the fly we could see the bow wake. When the wave stopped we struck and many times hooked the fish even though there was no other indication of a take. When to strike was determined more by intuition than anything else; a slight pluck at most was all that was felt.

We floated the Goodnews for six days and then Tom picked us off a bar and flew us back to Dillingham. We had drifted the two rivers for eleven days and had seen and hooked more fish of more species than one is likely to find in several years of fishing outside of the Bristol and Kuskokwim bay drainages.

There is another race of the Dolly Varden occurring in the Pacific Northwest from the southern drainages of the Alaska Peninsula and Aleutian Islands to the Columbia River, although it is not common south of Puget Sound. This is the southern Dolly Varden, *Salvelinus malma subsp*. Possibly it will be graced with the name *lordii* when its taxonomic status is straightened out. It differs from the northern race in having significantly fewer vertebrae and fewer gillrakers. Where the two ranges abut on the Alaska Peninsula, intermediate forms are found.

Undoubtedly, the southern Dolly has been isolated from the northern race for a long time — at least since the last glacial invasion during the Wisconsin period. It probably survived the glacial crunch in Pacific drainages south of the Cordilleran ice sheet which stalled just south of Puget Sound and re-invaded its present range as the ice melted back. It may have also survived on the unglaciated parts of Kodiak and the Queen Charlotte Islands. The northern race, on the other hand, probably survived glaciation in the Bering Refuge, the land bridge, eastern Siberia and adjacent parts of Alaska.

The southern form is the common Dolly found throughout coastal Alaska south of the Aleutian Islands and the Alaska Peninsual, in coastal British Columbia and coastal Washington. During glacial periods, it must have been common in Oregon coastal streams, but now it occurs there but rarely, if at all. It is found in headwater streams and lakes as a resident fish and also as anadromous populations.

My encounters with southern Dollies have been limited to a few small streams of Alaska's Kenai Peninsula, all draining to Turnagain Arm on Cook Inlet. I was fortunate to visit the Kenai with Dave Spencer who had lived there as manager of the Kenai Moose Range for many years and knew the country thoroughly. Larger than many New England states, it is a vast area of remarkable contrasts, the northern half low and flat while the southern half rises abruptly to the peaks and glaciers of the Kenai Range. It gives one pause to view these massive ice fields and if indeed we are living in an interglacial period, the heights of the Kenai haven't yet heard about it. Dying glaciers they may be, but they die hard and slowly.

As might be expected in a land of such topographical diversity, the vegetation varies accordingly — meadows of alpine tundra bright with blues and yellows of spring flowers, somber rain forests of hemlock and Sitka spruce, extensive muskegs and low brushy plains.

I learned much about the land, its vegetative zones and its wildlife from Dave, but we didn't find many Dollies. Our timing was wrong for sea-run fish — in between runs, for they follow the salmon and the cohos had yet to appear. We did, however, find some dwarf resident Dollies in a beaver pond and in the small outlet stream draining Summit Lake on the divide separating the Kenai River drainage from water flowing to Turnagain Arm. One from the beaver pond, dredged up by twitching a small nymph through the deeper holes, proved to be quite dark with numerous small orange-yellow spots and yellow fins while those from the outlet stream were rising avidly to some minutiae invisible to us but readily took small dry flies or nymphs fished in the surface film. The stream fish were much more silvery than that from the beaver pond with spots of creamy white to pinkish. They, too, had yellow fins which accounts for the local name of "yellow-finned charr" or "golden trout." Several of these were preserved in a jug of formalin for Bob Behnke's analysis. He later reported that they were indeed typical southern Dollies.

Sometime, perhaps I will be on the Kenai when the "run is on" and find anadromous Dollies of greater dimensions ascending the streams in force.

The bull trout, *Salvelinus confluentis*, is a charr that has caused much confusion in the group broadly called Dolly Varden. For years it has been lumped with *malma* and thus it is difficult to separate the two species from the early records. It has since been shown, mainly through the work of T. M. Cavender, that the bull trout is a species unto itself and not merely a subspecies of *malma*. It differs from the southern Dolly in having a more rounded body in cross section, a longer, wider and more flattened head, a fleshy knob at the tip of the lower jaw with a corresponding notch at the tip of the upper jaw, and more robust and heavily denticulated gillrakers. In coloration is strikingly different from the Dollies. The ground color is dark — brown or greenish-brown to deep bronze, profusely spotted with small, round, yellow or orange spots; the belly is usually grayish and the dull orange-paired fins and anal fin are white-bordered on the leading edges. Altogether it is a very distinctive looking fish and there is little excuse to confuse the two species.

The bull trout was one of the first of the trout to invade the range now occupied following the withdrawal of the ice sheet, for they, along with the cutthroats, got into drainages that were later blocked by barriers. Probably the mid-Columbia Basin was where the bull trout survived glaciation and, from there, upon the arrival of suitable conditions, they spread in all directions. They crossed the Continental Divide at several places and got into the Peace, Athabaska, some of the western tributaries of the Mackenzie and the North and South Saskatchewan. They also found their way, probably by other headwater transfers, to the headwaters of the Yukon, but their presence in the interior basins of British Columbia may have been by a marine dispersal from the Columbia. Southward they penetrated to the Upper Klamath watershed and to the headwaters of the Sacramento River.

Bull trout in large lakes and rivers grow to huge size, the largest recorded being a fish from Kootenay Lake, British Columbia, that weighed slightly over 40 pounds. In early days bull trout of 20 pounds and more were not uncommon in Flathead Lake and made spawning runs into the Flathead River and its tributaries. Such large fish, of course, are voracious predators, living principally on other fish, but they will take just about anything that comes their way, provided it is big enough. While most susceptible to hardware and bait, these big trout will take a large streamer type fly fished deep enough. The smaller fish — up to two or three pounds — are apt to take any kind of a wet fly. Though not spectacular fighters like the nothern Dolly, they are strong and tough and give a good account of themselves.

While I have never taken a big bull trout, none over three pounds, I have enjoyed many rewarding encounters with the small ones — 10- or 11-inchers — taken in tiny mountain streams tumbling down through forests of lodgepole and spruce on the high slopes of the Blue Mountains — extreme headwaters, for bull trout are cold water fish. Many have been caught inadvertently while fishing for cutthroats, but the higher one goes, the more likely it is that bull trout will be found. On some streams, if you go high enough, eventually you find a pure culture of bull trout, and I know of a few ice cold brooks where there are no other trout. They will take a free drifting wet fly or nymph readily and there is something satisfying in lifting these little charr from a tiny pool or pocket onto the streamside moss and duff.

Some of these little fellows taken from dark-shaded pools are almost black with the brilliant yellow orange spots shining through like pinpoints of light, seeming to blend in perfect harmony with the half-light of their somber world. Perhaps this is part of the charm of finding these symbols of wilderness, true natives, far from the clutter of men and their doings. These fish are the real thing, the end point of long evolutionary responses to a pure, cold environment — the way it always was.

CHAPTER 23

Eastern Brook Trout

THE EASTERN BROOK TROUT, or squaretail, was the trout of our forefathers as far back as our very beginnings on this continent. In fact, it was the only trout present in the settled parts of the country until the late 1800s and so has assumed an almost legendary character, a *sans pareil* among trouts. If we can believe the prints of the early illustrators, it was angled for by gentleman in impeccable attire — top hats and all — gracefully wielding long rods of greenhart and lancewood. It was the trout upon which our fly fishing heritage was established and so, to most of us, it occupies a special place.

So much has been written about the eastern brook trout, in fact, that I hesitate to add more to the pile. I have read so many different versions of how Daniel Webster subdued the big squaretail of Carman's Pond on Long Island that I almost believe the tale. Not that I doubt "Black Dan's" competence as a fisherman nor do I doubt that there was such a great trout and that somebody caught it. It would seem, however, that such a momentous event would have been duly recorded and chronicled with Webster's many accomplishments, but no mention is made of the trout. I would like to believe the tale because Webster and I attended the same college. In fact, I caught my first trout in Mink Brook, a small stream that wanders over the Hanover Plain almost at the edge of the Dartmouth campus, a stream that in all probability Daniel fished when he was an undergraduate, albeit some 130 years before my time. That trout was a squaretail, a native, and started me on the road to being a fly fisher. It was barely legal without stretching — far short of the Carman's Pond monster but a beautiful fish with worm-like vermiculations and brilliant red spots enclosed in blue halos. It was the first trout I ever held in my hand and I'll never forget it.

The eastern brook trout is a charr and as the name implies, a native of Eastern North America, but it did occur naturally west of the Mississippi River — just barely; a relict population in a glacial refuge covering a small area in Northeastern Iowa and Southeastern Minnesota. Why the ice sheet split and avoided this broken, hilly tract of spring-fed creeks is not clear, but in the process it left a pocket of brookies intact. This happened during each glacial advance of the Pleistocene Epoch, spanning roughly a million years, so the trout that survived there may have been of very ancient lineage. Finally, as the last ice receded, there was for a time a direct water connection to Lake Superior and thus those trout may have been one of the sources from which the Great Lakes were repopulated. It is ironic that this remnant of the brook trout clan, having withstood all of the vicissitudes of nature over the millenia, was undone in a few short years by man's meddling — the introduction of non-native trout. It is doubtful that any of the original genotype persists today.

The natural range of the brook trout spans a tremendous area in Eastern North America, throughout the Appalachians from Northern Georgia to Northern Labrador and Quebec. West of Hudson Bay, it extends north to the Seal River in Manitoba and south to the Great Lakes drainages of Northern Wisconsin, Michigan and as mentioned previously, the disjunct relict in the corner of Iowa and Minnesota. It was the common trout of New England, New York and Pennsylvania and probably provided the stimulus that prompted Samuel Phillippe, a gunsmith of Easton, Pennsylvania, to build the first split six-strip, all-bamboo fly rod during the 1850s.

In coastal drainages from Northern New England north through the Maritime Provinces of Canada, Labrador and In Hudson Bay, there are sea-run populations of brook trout — bright, silvery fish when they are fresh in from the salt, but otherwise most brook trout are remarkably look-alike and comprise but two subspecies — the common brook trout, *Salvelinus fontinalis fontinalis*, and the Aurora trout, *Salvelinus fontinalis timagamiensis*.

This Aurora trout is the odd ball of the brook trout clan, a unique char native only to three headwater lakes of the Montreal River, a tributary of the Ottawa. It differs from the common brook trout in lacking vermiculations on the back and having fewer spots or none at all. It is also of a decidedly different temperament, high strung and excitable, requiring careful handling in a hatchery. I have never fished these Aurora charr, but I saw some held as brood stock at a hatchery near Cochrane, Ontario. There I was told they were being propagated for introduction to new waters as the stock in their native lake had become hybridized with planted domesticated brookies, a sad story I had become all too familiar with.

There was one other brook-trout-like charr present in New England. This was called the silver trout and described as a separate species, *Salvelinus aggassiz*. It was a deep water form known only from Dublin Pond, New Hampshire, and possibly a few other deep lakes of the area. This charr, a relict of an earlier evolutionary strain, is now presumed extinct, at least none have been found since 1930. The cause of their extinction, as you might guess, was the planting of "non-native" hatchery brook trout in their native waters.

Within the type subspecies of the brook trout, *fontinalis*, are two distinct life history strains. The brookies south of Northern New England and the Great Lakes are short-lived, early-maturing fish and consequently never attain a large size. Those north of there, particularly beyond the St. Lawrence, live longer, mature later and grow to lunker size. These big, northern fish are known as the "Assinica" strain and within their range lie all of the famous brook trout streams: the Nipigon, Albany, God's River, Broadback, Minipi and others less well known but harboring large trout. It was from the Nipigon that the world record brookie was taken in 1916 and while this grand fish weighed 14½ pounds, E. R. Hewitt wrote of a Nipigon squaretail of 19 pounds recorded by an early survey party of which a friend of his was a member. It is probable then that some Nipigon trout must have exceeded the 20-pound mark in those great days before a hydroelectric development ruined the fishery forever.

I have fished these Assinica strain brookies in Hudson Bay drainages but never caught a lunker. One summer I was flying a "Beaver" aircraft out of Povungnituk, an Eskimo village on the northeast coast of Hudson Bay. We were leg banding Canada geese and their young while the adults were flightless during the summer molt. As the young grew large enough to band, the family groups joined together in larger flocks and were readily herded into hastily-built corrals of netting, banded and then released. Each drive usually took a full day for first we had to locate a flock by aerial search near a lake where a landing was possible, build the trap and then corral the geese.

One day everything went well, the geese were cooperative and we finished up shortly after noon. On the way back to camp, from a lake about 50 miles north of Povungnituk, I searched our flight path for a place to fish — a lake to land on with a stream nearby. We were over forbidding country — rock-ribbed barrens stripped bare by the last ice sheet. Every depression was filled with water — shallow, boulder-strewn lakes and ponds connected by a labyrinth of creeks and drains seeking a way to larger streams and the sea. The country looked new and raw, the time so short since the last glacial ice melted that water flowed from depression to depression in poorly defined channels. There was not a tree within hundreds of miles and precious little other vegetation to soften the bleak landscape. Yet geese nested here as well as a few swans and in suitable waters there were fish . . . lake trout, brook trout and Arctic charr in season.

We hadn't gone far until I saw a proper stream with a lake connecting, large enough and with sufficient depth to put the "Beaver" on and it didn't take us long to put down and get secured. From the looks of the weather, we hadn't much time — a bank of low clouds was moving in from the northwest and the wind was building up. Quickly we rigged up our rods, hurried to the stream and began to cast; there was no time to look the water over or explore. In less than an hour I hooked and beached three brookies of about three pounds each, beautiful plump fish, the blue-haloed red spots glowing like gems. I didn't realize at the time that I had caught these north of their known range but they were there and in numbers. While squaretails are not renowned as flashy fighters, these trout were strong and tough and even made a few leaps. But what impressed me most was the fact that these trout were absolutely pure strain from a wilderness stream that in all probability had never had a fly cast on it before that stormy afternoon.

I would have liked to spend the rest of the day there with those beautiful trout in their brawling habitat but the weather had caught up with us and we had to get out while we could. By the time we had scrambled back into the airplane and cast it off, the wind was gale force, too strong to taxi down wind. I couldn't even turn it around and just let the gale take us down wind far enough for takeoff. When I opened the throttle we were airborne before you could say "Parmachene Bell."

CHAPTER 24

Mending the Cast

BACK IN THE LATE '40s WHEN I was involved in the search for nesting grounds of the then near-extinct whooping crane, I found myself stumped by the question:

"What good are they?"

I could never give a satisfactory answer to those who could frame such a question in the first place. Our values and philosophies were too far apart. I could only counter with more questions:

"What good is a rose? An eagle? An orchid blooming, unseen, in a woodland glade?"

The same question can be asked concerning native trout, I suppose:

"Why all the fuss? Why worry about them?"

We are able, after all, to raise "factory trout" by the ton, and there are many people who don't know the difference. But there are many who seek quality experiences, and this is a matter of quality.

Why else do many trout fishermen prefer beautiful, wild trout to drab, flabby hatchery products? Why do so many of them fish with flies, preferably in beautiful wild streams as the backdrop for their recreation?

Were this not so, all of us might be content to fish for carp with a doughball in a muddy ditch or sewer outlet.

The devil's advocate can say of our native western trout that, since there are only a half-dozen full species now recognized, and although some do exhibit great variability throughout their ranges, why be concerned with subspecies or geographical races?

"A cutthroat is a cutthroat, and that's that. Right?"

Well, that's *not* quite that — far from it. The various subspecies of trout *are* different. Even I, a layman, can tell the difference.

Trout differ not only in appearance but also physiologically, molded by diverse environments to different adaptations, different feeding habits, different tolerances to temperature. Some have become predators, growing to great size, and some can tolerate temperatures or salinities lethal to other trout. These differences are of potentially great significance in fisheries management, as Bob Behnke has so ably pointed out in his recent *Monograph of the Native Trouts of the Genus Salmo of Western North America*.

As a group, native trout, with the exception of charr, are in a precarious position as pure strain populations. Some survive only as merest remnants in a few tiny headwaters after one-hundred years of stocking non-native trout and mixing of races by federal and state agencies and by private individuals. Even the best stocks of some races may be hybridized to a greater or lesser degree.

Ironically, it has been the very people we entrusted to protect and enhance our natural resources who have brought us to this deplorable state. True, there are many villains in the degradation of the environment for all living things including wild trout. They are manifest in water pollution, damming and diversion of streams, faulty forest practices and livestock overgrazing. All have had their negative impact in significantly reducing the amount of suitable habitat available. But in the final analysis it was the introduction of non-native trout by state and federal conservation agencies that delivered the coup de grace.

The record speaks for itself. Of the fourteen races of cutthroats that are currently recognized two are probably extinct and eight others have been brought to the brink of oblivion as pure strains — all victims of hybridization and/or displacement by non-native trout. Four races still occur throughout most of their original range or sizeable portions of it.

Rainbows and redbands have fared little better. Indiscriminate stocking has so hopelessly mixed local races that no one is sure what the original stocks were. Special adaptations to specific conditions over the millenia have been lost. Wild steelhead races have been and still are being diluted and replaced with inferior hatchery fish. To those interested only in big bags or pounds of meat this makes little difference, I suppose, but in the process we have lost quality, an innate wildness and unique gene pools evolved to cope with specialized conditions. The Gila trout and the Apache trout are in similar straits and hang on precariously.

The two most serious threats to trout habitat in our western states are the clear cutting of the forests and the overgrazing by livestock, with resultant trampling and denuding of stream banks. The Forest Service and Bureau of Land Management seem determined to convert our forests into stump lands, and though they tell us that clear cutting is the best and most economical way to harvest timber, it is significant that many of the big timber companies do *not* clear cut their *own* lands but harvest them selectively.

Little can be said in favor of great barren tracts of raw earth left on mountain sides to erode and silt in the streams, and one wonders whatever became of the multiple-use concept, one of the objectives being the protection of watersheds. We, the people, have to live here on our little planet in space, along with the trout, and it behooves us to take better care of it.

An increasing awareness of the values of our wild places and of the creatures that live there offers some light at the end of the tunnel. We have added to our wilderness areas — not enough, perhaps, but better than nothing. We have an Endangered Species Act that gives more rare forms special protection and restricts land use or abuse that might affect them adversely.

The concept of wild trout management *is* gaining momentum, as well it should, for this is a cost-free fishery, maintained and controlled by regulation rather than by costly hatchery input. Hatcheries will probably always play a part, insofar as we can afford them, in providing trout fishing in waters that cannot produce trout naturally. It makes little sense, however, to allow a fisherman with a ten dollar license to take, in a week, fish that cost a hundred dollars to produce. That kind of mentality, subsidizing artificial fisheries and financing hoggishness, must be replaced.

I was in a forest camp on Muir Creek, a tributary of the upper Rogue, for awhile one summer, where the hatchery truck came once a week to dump in a load of "catchables." The fish were hardly in the water before the camp turned out en masse and dragged them out. Those that took their limits of ten promptly stashed them in a cooler and came back for another limit, and in a few hours had caught them all. They then sat back and waited for the next regular delivery . . . like waiting for the milkman. The saddest part was that Muir Creek, a beautiful little mountain stream, was capable of producing its own trout and, under proper regulation, could be a quality wild trout fishery.

I am realist enough to know that we can never again have native trout established throughout their original range. Once non-native trout become firmly entrenched in any big river system they are there for good and could not be eradicated even if it were desirable to do so. There are, however, numerous small tributaries where it would be possible to re-establish the natives — not just as museum specimens but as fishable populations. Several states are doing it now: California, with the Paiutes; New Mexico, with their Gila trout; and Nevada, with their Bonneville cutthroats. Both Wyoming and Montana now favor their native trout in their stocking programs and Idaho has established a notable native cutthroat fishery on the St. Joe River. There probably are other similar projects in other states, so progress is being made.

Time and money are needed to accomplish even a little, and money is not always forthcoming. Diversion of a portion of the funds committed to hatchery production to stream habitat improvement and the establishment of wild and native trout fisheries would enhance the cause of self-sustaining, high-quality trout fishing. Most states are heavily committed to hatchery production, however, and, having a large capital investment, will resist change.

It is up to us, then. We can either sit back and moan to ourselves about the situation or we can let our voices be heard in the right places. If enough of us choose to be heard, future generations will have the opportunity to fish for beautiful, wild native trout in their ancestral streams, high in the alpine meadows amidst the grandeur of the mountains and among the rimrocks of the high desert.

About the Author

The author, a Dartmouth graduate trained in biology and geology, had been a wildlife biologist for all of his working career. As such, he has seen all the wild areas of North America by foot, horseback, canoe and airplane from ocean to ocean and Arctic to Tropics. He made the original aerial surveys in the Arctic on breeding waterfowl, found the first whooping cranes on their northern breeding grounds and has written numerous scientific papers on wildlife conservation as well as being a contributing author on books about waterfowl. Since retirement he has focused his interest on native trout and has caught, photographed and documented all of the recognized species and subspecies on the continent as well as some yet to be described. In this book he writes of these trout, their home waters and his experiences in seeking them out. The color photographs are definitive; each race speaks for itself.

Native Trout of North America was recently selected by Trout Unlimited as one of the "Best trout fishing books of the last 30 years."

Frank Amato Publications
P.O. Box 82112, Portland, Oregon 97282
ISBN 0-936608-14-5